EQUAL SUFFRAGE

EQUAL SUFFRAGE

THE RESULTS OF AN INVESTIGATION IN
COLORADO MADE FOR THE COLLEGIATE EQUAL
SUFFRAGE LEAGUE OF NEW YORK STATE

BY
HELEN L. SUMNER, PH.D.

HARPER & BROTHERS PUBLISHERS
NEW YORK AND LONDON
MCMIX

Copyright, 1909, by HARPER & BROTHERS.

All rights reserved.

Published November, 1909.

CONTENTS

CHAP.		PAGE
INTRODUCTION		xiii
I.	THE PROBLEM AND LOCAL CONDITIONS	1
	1. Purpose and Scope of the Investigation	1
	2. Methods	5
	3. History of Equal Suffrage in Colorado	15
	4. Social, Economic, and Political Conditions in Colorado	18
II.	PARTY MACHINERY	23
	1. Caucuses and Primaries	24
	2. Conventions	31
	A. Women Delegates	31
	B. Effect on Outward Appearance	34
	C. Activity of Women	38
	D. Attitude of Men toward Women Politicians	40
	E. Effect on Choice of Candidates	44
	F. Effect on the "Slate"	48
	G. Women Candidates	50
	H. Effect on the Platform	54
	3. Political Committees	57
	4. Women's Political Clubs	66
	5. Campaign Meetings	71
	6. Elections	77
	7. Corruption in Politics	83
	8. Conclusion	92
III.	STATISTICS OF ELECTIONS	97
	1. Registration and Vote	101
	2. Ownership and Tenancy	111
	3. Naturalization and Race	114
	4. Conjugal Condition	118
	5. Occupations of Women Voters	120
	6. School Elections	122
	7. Vote Cast for Women Candidates	123

CONTENTS

CHAP.		PAGE
IV.	WOMEN IN PUBLIC OFFICE	128
	1. State Legislators	130
	2. State Superintendents of Public Instruction	131
	3. County Superintendents of Schools	137
	4. Women in Other County Offices	140
	5. Women in City Offices	141
	6. Women on School Boards	143
	7. Women on State Boards	145
	8. Conclusion	147
V.	ECONOMIC ASPECTS OF EQUAL SUFFRAGE	150
	1. Public Employment	151
	2. Private Employment	160
	3. Women in Trade Unions	170
	4. Conclusion	178
VI.	INFLUENCE OF EQUAL SUFFRAGE ON LEGISLATION	180
	1. Legislation in the Interest of Women and Children	181
	2. General Reform Legislation	197
	3. Municipal Regulations	204
	4. Conclusion	211
VII.	EFFECT OF EQUAL SUFFRAGE ON THE WOMEN OF COLORADO	214
	1. Belief in Equal Suffrage	216
	2. Interest of Women in Politics	221
	3. Influence of Women in Politics	227
	4. Political Independence	231
	5. Effect on the Moral Character of Women	235
	6. Effect on the Intelligence and Public Spirit of Women	239
	7. Effect on the Home and the Children	244
	8. Conclusion	258

CONTENTS

APPENDIXES

APPENDIX		PAGE
A.	Text of Equal Suffrage Bill and Equal Suffrage Proclamation	261
B.	Documents—Woman's Republican League of Colorado, 1900	262
C.	Vote and Registration in Pueblo County, 1904–05	267
D.	Tables Showing Tenancy, Naturalization, and Conjugal Condition of Denver Persons Registered in 1906, by Wards	268
E.	Proportion of Teachers to Persons of School Age in Seventeen States and the United States	271
F.	Women in Office	272
G.	Teachers in Colorado by Counties, Sex, and Salaries in 1906	275
H.	Wages of Men and Women in Manufacturing Industries in Denver and Pueblo, 1905	276
I.	Population and Number of Retail Liquor Saloons in Denver and Pueblo, and in the Five Cities Ranging Next Above and the Five Cities Ranging Next Below Each in Population, 1903	278
J.	Number of Divorces Granted in Denver and Pueblo, the Five Cities Ranging Next Above and the Five Cities Ranging Next Below Each in Population, 1903	279
K.	Equal Suffrage Testimonials	280

PREFACE

THIS investigation is a serious attempt to disentangle from other political factors the influence of equal suffrage upon political and social life. It is not pretended, of course, that such a study can affect in any way the right of women to the ballot. It has been made for the purpose of assisting toward a rational conclusion those fair-minded, impartial men and women who, without possessing a political theory as a touchstone, wish to determine, in the light of evidence rather than of assertion, whether equal suffrage is a sound and helpful measure under our present political system.

One of the stipulations in my contract with the Collegiate Equal Suffrage League was that the investigation should be conducted "in an impartial and scientific manner." Having at the beginning no formulated conclusions on the question, I endeavored to the best of my ability to live up to the spirit and the letter of this clause. Neither the League nor any member has shown the slightest disposition to interfere with my liberty in the matter. I could not possibly have had a greater degree of freedom in studying conditions and formulating conclusions.

The work was begun in September, 1906, and the

PREFACE

actual field-study was not concluded until December, 1907, after which another half-year was needed to sift results, prepare summaries, and formulate conclusions. In all I have spent nearly two years upon the subject of equal suffrage, with special reference to its actual results and achievements in Colorado. Half a dozen or more assistants, too, have given, under direction, valuable aid, for which I am deeply grateful.

Though the present study does not pretend to perfection, either in methods or conclusions, it is hoped that it may point the way toward a sane, rational study and discussion of the question of the political position of women under a democratic form of government.

I wish cordially and gratefully to acknowledge the co-operation of the advisory committee of the Collegiate Equal Suffrage League of New York State, and also the valuable assistance rendered by Prof. John R. Commons and Prof. T. S. Adams, of the University of Wisconsin, and by Dr. John B. Andrews, of the American Association for Labor Legislation. To Professor Commons' insight into political questions are primarily due the conclusions in regard to machine methods in politics. Professor Adams' assistance was especially valuable in the preparation and discussion of the statistical tables and in the arrangement of data. Doctor Andrews has given, from the beginning to the end of the investigation, but especially in the arduous task of sifting and weighing evidence, invaluable advice, assistance, and encouragement. From my father also, who for twenty-seven years practiced law or occupied a judicial position in

PREFACE

Colorado, I have received important help in the preparation of the chapter on legislation, and from my mother continuous and unwearied aid and sympathy throughout my task.

HELEN L. SUMNER.

MADISON, Wisconsin.

INTRODUCTION

THE Collegiate Equal Suffrage League of New York State, in submitting to the public the following report of conditions in Colorado in 1906, after twelve years of complete woman's suffrage, made by Miss Helen L. Sumner for the League, wishes to draw the attention of the reader to certain salient points in it. As Miss Sumner states, the investigation was conducted by her with absolute impartiality and with no preconceived ideas. The purpose of this Introduction is to comment briefly on the facts presented, and to direct the reader's attention to what appear to be the most significant of them.

The report is divided into two parts, one concerned with public opinion in Colorado, and the other with actual political and social facts. While the first division is no doubt of less absolute value than the second, it is still of interest and significance. Complex and difficult to interpret as public opinion is, varying, too, in a manner that often seems quite irrational, it yet follows certain logical tendencies, and in spite of the uncertainty inherent in any investigation of it, the answers to Miss Sumner's questions, given by twelve hundred and one different persons of both sexes and all conditions, show a number

INTRODUCTION

of things of interest to the student of social psychology.

Before considering these lessons in detail, it is proper to examine the peculiar influences to which public opinion in Colorado is subjected. On the north, Colorado is bounded by Wyoming, where women have been citizens on the same terms as men since 1869, and on the west by Utah, where women voted in territorial days from 1870 until, in 1887, Congress deprived them of the right, and where now they have enjoyed full citizenship since the state was admitted to the Union in 1896, while near by, to the northwest, is Idaho, a woman's-suffrage state since 1896. The fact that the states which have given full citizenship to their women are all grouped together about Wyoming seems to show that, in the eyes of near-by observers at least, Wyoming's experiment has been a success, and that it has fostered a growing belief in woman's suffrage. Thus public opinion within Colorado is subjected on the north and on the west to influences decidedly favorable to universal enfranchisement. But the outside influences which are unfavorable are clearly far greater in point of quantity than the favorable influences; for to the east and south and beyond Colorado's immediate neighbors in all directions lie states where women are not yet enfranchised. Moreover, from these states the ranks of Colorado's citizens are constantly being recruited; for in addition to the usual migration of population from one state to the other, and especially from the East to the West, Colorado, because of its climate, receives each year a certain number of out-

INTRODUCTION

siders who come to her in the search for health, and all these people bring with them the beliefs that have been fostered in them by their native surroundings. It is, I think, fair to suppose that the majority are not believers in woman's suffrage, and that, coming from communities where publicly to advocate it has until quite recently constituted, in the eyes of many people, a kind of social and intellectual disgrace, a fairly large proportion of them are strongly prepossessed against woman's suffrage. Intrenched, moreover, many of them, behind the prestige, fancied or real, of their Eastern origin, these individuals will open their minds slowly to the influences about them, and thus they will tend to form little circles of fixed opinion, influencing probably their neighbors to a certain extent, and counting always as part of the public of the state which forms its public opinion. Foreign-born citizens naturalized in Colorado are also, of course, an element to be considered, but probably in this relation a less important one, since they are, for the most part, strange to all American customs, and for that reason presumably less likely to react in a decided manner to any one especial custom than are citizens from other American states where it does not obtain. The Mexican population in the south forms still another confusing element, but as Miss Sumner has discounted it in her report, there is no need of emphasizing it here. As there was nothing in Miss Sumner's questions to show from what part of the world the person answering them originally came, we cannot, in each case, take this element into consideration; but in drawing conclusions from the an-

INTRODUCTION

swers as a whole, we must not fail to remember the complexity of the phenomenon we are attempting to study.

Analyzing her results with a view to discovering what they show in regard to general sentiment about woman's suffrage, Miss Sumner tells us that of the 616 men who answered the question-blank sent them, 94, or 15.3 per cent., did not definitely state whether or not they are in favor of it, and are therefore presumably indifferent or still undecided about it; and of the 585 women answering, 73, or 12.5 per cent., are still undecided; while 340 men, or 55.2 per cent., and 422 women, or 72.1 per cent., are favorable, and 182 men, or 29.5 per cent., and 90 women, or 15.4 per cent., are unfavorable. Although the figures concerned are very small, the way in which the question-blanks were sent out and answered makes it seem probable, Miss Sumner assures us, that they are fairly representative. It is clear from them that there still exists among certain men and women of Colorado a disbelief in the wisdom of woman's voting, and that this disbelief is more prevalent among the men of Colorado answering Miss Sumner's questions than among the women. When, in 1893, woman's suffrage was voted for at the polls, 35,798 men cast their ballots in favor of the amendment, and 29,451 against it—that is, of the men expressing themselves on the question, only 54.9 per cent. were believers in woman's suffrage. Those who were undecided or indifferent refrained, it is to be presumed, from voting at all on the question, this fact accounting probably for the small vote cast. Now, of the 522 men expressing themselves definitely in answering Miss Sumner's question, we find that 340, or 65.1 per cent., were in favor, so that if the figures here submitted show anything, they show a notable gain in sentiment favorable to women's voting among the men of Colorado. Some men are still unconvinced by its twelve years of trial that it is a good thing, some are still doubtful, and some have been converted to it, since the proportion of men favorable has grown larger by more than 10 per cent.

Unsatisfactory as this gain may seem to people who are looking for rapid results, when the circumstances of the case are taken into consideration it is seen to be really most satisfactory; for the reasons that, as a rule, prevent people from believing in woman's suffrage are of a very fundamental nature, involving, on the one hand, a deep-seated conviction as to the essential nature of women as women, and, on the other hand, one of the most sacred human ideals, namely, the ideal of what a woman should be, and they thus partake, in a measure, of the quality of scientific and religious opinions which are modified only with great difficulty and slowness. This double opposition has been offered all over the world to all changes in the condition of women that have been consciously sanctioned by the community, and not unconsciously submitted to, as have the great industrial changes growing out of our modern factory system, for instance, and revolutionizing the conditions of their lives for the great mass of women. Pseudo-scientists have never hesitated to proclaim the outcome of each experiment before the experiment has been made, and idealists have never failed to deplore any change in the future type of woman. We have learned, it is true, by experience that the educated woman who may, if she wishes, attend colleges and universities and practise professions, is a different creature from the illiterate or the uneducated woman, and that the woman whose right in her children is legally recognized, and who may control property or engage in business independently of her husband, is not quite the same person as the woman who is legally at every point dependent on her husband; thus, people are justified in foreseeing that the woman on whose shoulders rests her recognized share of responsibility for the government of the community will be, in some respects, different from the politically irresponsible woman. Therefore, some people, precisely because they cherish an idealizing admiration for woman as she now is, fear to sanction this change in the conditions that have produced her. It is obvious that the convictions of such *a priori* scientists and the fears of such idealists cannot be much affected by an experiment of only twelve years' duration.

On the other hand, it not infrequently happens that the idealizers of women are favorable to woman's suffrage, and it is unfortunately true that they also have proved, in some cases, a danger to the cause. Disillusionment only can result from the claim that women when enfranchised will at once right wrongs, however deep-seated they may be in the body politic, and abolish corruption, though it is intrenched in an established, complicated system, and practised by astute and experienced men in the interest of their own personal profit; for such a claim is, in its nature,

INTRODUCTION

unreasonable, and doomed to disappointment. We cannot expect from many people the combination of common sense and enthusiasm shown by the man from Weld County, quoted by Miss Sumner on page 220. He says: "I am entirely satisfied with the results that have been achieved. I voted for women's suffrage in 1893, at the time it was carried in Colorado, but I did not expect the maturity of 5 per cent. of the promises made, and felt that extravagant predictions and radical claims were not only unwarranted but a positive harm. It is not only right that women should have power of suffrage, but it is an almost incalculable benefit to humanity as a whole. True progress is slow. Woman suffrage will not be done away with in Colorado." The average person, not seeing the predictions of the propagandists immediately verified by experience, will pronounce against a reform. Thus, Miss Sumner finds that nineteen men declaring themselves unfavorable to the enfranchisement of women were once favorable. They form a trifle more than 10 per cent. of the whole number of unfavorable men. Every reform suffers from the fundamental psychological tendency of its advocates to claim too much for it, and from the consequent inevitable reaction against it after it has been carried through. The believers in the particular reform we are studying can congratulate themselves that the ranks of its supporters among men thus thinned have been recruited from the ranks of those before indifferent or hostile, so that their number, as indicated in Miss Sumner's investigation, has not only not diminished, but has increased to a notable degree.

INTRODUCTION

We have, unfortunately, no means of comparing the belief in equal suffrage among the women of Colorado in 1906 with that before the vote was actually given them, and we must, therefore, content ourselves with noting that while the proportion of women declaring themselves indifferent or undecided is nearly as large as the proportion of men, the proportion of women believers is much greater, being nearly three-fourths of the whole number. These figures, if they are considered representative at all, warrant the assumption that a large majority of the women of Colorado believe their enfranchisement to be a benefit.

Favorable, then, as are the answers to Miss Sumner's general question about a belief in woman's enfranchisement, the answers to her more detailed questions are even more favorable. First in importance, perhaps, comes the convincing testimony, given by answers to several different questions, that women more often than men vote split tickets. The practical outcome of this one fact is that, in Colorado, political bosses are less able to put the candidates most pleasing to them into office than are bosses in non-woman's-suffrage states, and that they have less power to dismiss from public life office-holders who have dared to displease them.

It is interesting to note that more than a year after this testimony was given Miss Sumner, Judge Lindsey, of the Children's Court of Denver, hateful to Denver politicians, and nominated, therefore, by neither party, was, after a short and inexpensive campaign, in which many women worked as volunteers, re-elected by the

INTRODUCTION

voters of Denver, and primarily, it is conceded, by the women voters. A few experiences of this sort are teaching the bosses some most salutary lessons, even while they keep in their grasp the power over the votes given them by the present primary laws. Already it has come about that saloon-keepers and men of notoriously immoral lives are rarely, if ever, nominated in Colorado, because the women of Colorado cannot be driven by party loyalty to vote for them. Since this is so, the failure of women to do their proportional share of party management and of voting at primaries, indicated by Miss Sumner, is not very significant. As long as they exercise the right of scratching their ballots, women are very useful voters under a form of government that lends itself, as experience has shown, to boss rule.

A considerable number of men and women who do not believe in equal suffrage were, as has already been said, among the people who answered the question-blank sent them, and Miss Sumner has faithfully reported all their opinions, suppressing nothing. By analyzing their answers, indeed, as well as the answers of the people favorable to woman's suffrage, she has, in many cases, thrown light on the psychological state at the basis of the particular opinion. Thus, in spite of dry statistics, much of her report is very amusing reading for the psychologically curious person. The very difficulty of finally deciding how far fixed ideas and beliefs have influenced observations and inferences from observations, and how far the ideas and beliefs themselves have been results rather than causes, adds to the fascination of the problem, and is, moreover, well adapted to teach the student a most salutary lesson in open-mindedness. It is of the very greatest interest to see what these unfavorable men and women have to say to justify their disbelief in equal suffrage.

Almost no support is given to the contention that women's influence on politics would be bad, and hardly a mention is made of the possibility of domestic discord arising from differences of political opinion between husband and wife. When it is considered how often both these contingencies have been referred to in arguments against woman's suffrage, this fact is most striking. We do, however, find some support of the argument that enfranchisement would tend to have a bad effect on women themselves. Almost none of Miss Sumner's informants go so far as to say that the mere consideration of political questions and casting of ballots has an evil influence upon women, but a certain small number do state that women who become active politicians deteriorate morally (page 235). This is offset by a larger number who think the effect of enfranchisement on woman's moral character good, besides the still larger number of both sexes who think no effect is observable, and it is in itself surprisingly small when, on the one hand, the sentiment adverse to woman's suffrage is remembered, and, on the other hand, the idealizing exaltation of women as women. To many people there is something unspeakably more painful in the contemplation of a corrupt or dishonorable woman than in the contemplation of a man of like character, so that a woman politician using methods

INTRODUCTION

long practised by many men and sanctioned, tacitly at least, it must be believed, by some women, makes an exaggerated impression. No person, however unreasonable, maintains that all women are honorable, and no reasonable person fails to realize that political power will uncover a certain amount of moral weakness in women now passing as honorable. But the vote is not withheld from men on the plea that politics gives dishonorable men a chance to profit by their crookedness; no reasonable person, then, can argue that it should be withheld from women for that cause.

The public attitude toward women pointed out above is well illustrated by the people who stated to Miss Sumner that women politicians are more corrupt than men politicians because "a bad woman is worse than a bad man." It is this kind of double standard that sanctions the marriage of dishonorable and impure men to honorable and pure women, and in so doing works disaster to the family and the state, since the laws of inheritance seem cruelly insensible to such distinctions.

It is this kind of double standard, also, that makes the possible or certain voting of prostitutes seem an unanswerable argument against woman's enfranchisement to many people who are well aware that men quite as infamous as the women in question vote and are politically powerful. The class of men known as "cadets," who live in idleness on the money earned by prostitutes and extorted from them by various means, vote, and no outcry is raised. The police grow rich on the tribute paid them by these women and

INTRODUCTION

their exploiters, and yet the police continue to hold their offices. In Denver, soon after the enfranchisement of women, they even carried their insolence so far as to force the prostitutes to vote for them to help keep them in office, and this fact raised a storm against woman's suffrage from many high-minded people. It was well known before that the police and the saloon-keepers and the low politicians had these women in their absolute power, but when the fact became a political fact it somehow suddenly took on much greater importance. If the story ended here it would be, in my opinion, highly favorable to woman's suffrage, since anything that uncovers the veiled evils of a community, and makes them appear clear and intolerable to the persons before ignorant or indifferent, is a gain, and a great gain. But the story does not end here; the most significant part is to come. The prostitutes of Denver, because of the peculiar conditions of their lives and the shame attached to them, hated to register and vote, as would all prostitutes everywhere; they therefore appealed to the Woman's Republican Club to protect them. The chief of police was threatened with dismissal, and forbidden by the Fire and Police Board to carry out his plans. The consequences of this first warning were not, however, wholly satisfactory. Miss Sumner has shown that the prostitutes had still, to a certain extent, to vote. But the news now comes from Denver that another chief of police, who attempted in his turn to deliver the vote of the prostitutes, was dismissed, in 1908, for this offence, and for brutality toward arrested men and suspects. Thus, the prosti-

INTRODUCTION

tutes of Denver no longer vote in large number, but the respectable women to whom they appealed do vote, and in time—for they must have time—they will help to save the prostitutes from other things more harmful to the community than their voting.

Quite a number of people unfavorable in principle to equal suffrage, answering Miss Sumner's questions, say that its effect on women's intelligence and public spirit has been good. So large a proportion, indeed, of all the men and women subscribe to this judgment that Miss Sumner tells us it is fairly well established if public opinion can establish it; and a strong confirmation of it is found in the statement often made that one firm in Denver sold a larger number of books on political economy during the first eight months after the equal-franchise victory than it had sold during the twenty years before.

To offset this, a very small per cent. of men and an even smaller per cent. of women say the effect of enfranchisement has been intellectually bad (page 240). Larger, but still not very impressive, is the proportion of persons who think the effect on the home has not been good (page 243), and on this point, again, we find a certain number of persons favorable to woman's suffrage joining with those unfavorable. The complaint, as before, is made chiefly against women politicians; and to ascertain, in so far as she could, the basis of these objections, Miss Sumner has given all the facts obtainable about the families of women in political life. These facts seem to indicate that a large number of women politicians are either unmarried and have no children or have

INTRODUCTION

grown-up children only, and that others with little children enter politics as a means of getting money for them, which cannot be called neglect of them, though it may seem such to superficial observers.

In the second part of her investigation, which has to do no longer with public opinion, but with ascertainable facts, Miss Sumner has shown that the women of Colorado, in 1906, exercised their power to vote in such numbers as to refute the statement that they are indifferent to the duties of citizenship. Her tables deserve careful study. The tendency of the women from better residence districts to go to the polls in greater numbers than the women from less prosperous and also from less respectable districts was established for Pueblo in the elections of 1904 and 1905 by Mr. Lewis in his article in the *Outlook*, though its significance was not emphasized by him. It is now confirmed by Miss Sumner's study of the vote cast in the different wards of Denver in 1906. This tendency should make the transition from manhood suffrage to universal suffrage less of a stumbling-block to people who fear the increased proportion of the so-called ignorant vote. Moreover, a smaller proportion of the foreign-born women than of the native women of Colorado are shown by Miss Sumner to have voted in 1906. Since there are fewer women than men immigrants in Colorado, as in the rest of the United States, the enfranchisement of women has thus tended in two ways to minimize the total influence of the foreign vote.

There has been no rush of women for office; for the most part they have held in Colorado, during the

INTRODUCTION

twelve years under consideration, posts for which their experience as non-enfranchised citizens has most obviously prepared them. It is both natural and fortunate that this should be so, for we must not forget that we are studying a period of transition. Women have always been the teachers of children; they form a large majority of the public-school teachers in the United States; they have served as county superintendents of public instruction even in non-woman's-suffrage states. As state superintendents of public instruction in Colorado they have now signally distinguished themselves. The tribute paid one incumbent, Mrs. Helen M. Grenfell, by an ex-governor of the state, is such, indeed, as to be an honor to all women (page 137). The present compulsory education laws of Colorado were passed since the enfranchisement of women, and have been administered with women in the chief positions of power. Even if we were to assume the extreme position, quite at variance, however, with the fact, that men have taken the whole initiative in educational affairs and that women's part has consisted chiefly in their being instruments for men, Colorado's school record must show something about the effect of equal suffrage on the educational problems of the community, and Colorado's school record is brilliant. The coming-in of the great mass of new electors, against whose ignorance and irresponsibility we are so often and so feelingly warned, has not lessened, to say the very least, the chances of the rising generation.

Again, the duty of caring for the sick and the unfortunate and the hungry of the community has

INTRODUCTION

always in large measure fallen upon women, and the sentiments of sympathy and pity to which women are usually more susceptible than men, and the greater leisure they often enjoy, have always made women, however powerless politically, concern themselves with the fate of unfortunate individuals about them, even when these individuals were not their direct charge. Godiva, of legendary days, using her influence with her lord in behalf of his oppressed subjects, is the very type of the benevolent unenfranchised woman. Women are everywhere active in charitable endeavors, and since the state took over the care of the orphaned young, the ill, the unfortunate, and the indigent, women have concerned themselves more and more with state institutions, serving often on state boards, but in non-woman's-suffrage states in a hopeless minority. If there were any force in the argument advanced by many good and sincere and benevolent women, that women would lose rather than gain in influence for benevolent activity in a community by having the power to vote, we should see the effect of this loss in Colorado. Reforms in state institutions and moral reforms of all sorts should have advanced in Colorado at a slower proportional rate than in states where the influence of the good women of the community is unhampered by their possession, and the possession by other women, of political power. No reader of Miss Sumner's investigation can, I think, honestly maintain this to be the fact. English observers of American public charitable institutions, moreover, are not accustomed to find them superior to like English institutions over which women's

INTRODUCTION

municipal and county vote gives them joint control with men. In fact, English philanthropists frequently point out that in America, as a rule, private charities in the management of which women take a large share are better run than public charities to which women contribute much less, while no such disparity exists in England. A study of English public charitable institutions is recommended to people especially interested in this aspect of the equal-suffrage problem.

One of the first effects of the victory in Colorado was to increase the number of women on the boards of control of state institutions, which are all appointed by the governor. In January, 1894, women held only 7 out of 140 such positions, Miss Sumner tells us (page 146), but by 1895 the number was increased to 17. On the boards of two of the institutions most interesting to women they have been in a majority, and they have been about one-third of the Board of Charities and Corrections, of which a woman, Mrs. Sarah Platt Decker, is at the moment president. Helpful as this increase of their proportional representaton and power on these boards is, it constitutes by no means the whole gain; for women form an important element of the electorate to whom the actual administrators of these institutions are in the final analysis responsible. As we in New York State have learned by experience, it is easily possible for a corrupt official to make large sums of money buying supplies for state institutions, furnishing bad eggs, to mention only one article, to the insane and other defenceless wards of the state, and putting in his pocket a satisfactory

INTRODUCTION

per cent. of the price charged the state. Now, in Colorado, a woman member of a controlling board, or it may be a woman housekeeper of an institution, has power to make the people responsible for such meanest of all thefts really afraid of dismissal, for she has behind her a great mass of silent women voters quite ready, when a moral issue is at stake, as they have shown, to scratch their tickets.

There is nothing in the facts given by Miss Sumner about women's employment in Colorado to show that the increased opportunity for government employment resulting from their possession of the franchise has induced the women of Colorado to leave their homes and become wage-earners. Many women, indeed, have been able to add to the family income by doing political work on election-day, but this occasional employment does not take them for sufficiently long a time away from home to be considered in this relation. Women are employed in greater numbers in Colorado than in non-suffrage states as public stenographers, clerks, etc, but there is no reason to suppose that for this cause a greater number of them become wage-earners than would otherwise do so. The question of women's employment and the wages paid to women seems to be still in Colorado a question of economic rather than political conditions. Every new form of employment open to women in any place becomes, of course, a factor in the economic market, but only a small factor, since the labor market is not confined within the boundaries of any one state or even of any one country. The working-men of America have hardly yet learned how to use the ballot

INTRODUCTION

effectively in their own interest, and it is, of course, idle to expect the small number of women now enfranchised in the United States to control so vast a problem. Therefore, it should surprise no one that Miss Sumner finds the wages of women in Colorado very little, if at all, affected by their possession of the vote. But, none the less, the conclusion that enfranchisement will not prove an advantage to wage-earning women is by no means warranted. Government more and more controls the conditions of manufacture and commerce, and all classes in the community are coming to understand the immense power of government in this particular. It is too much to ask the working-men of the community to carry the political burdens of the working-women as well as their own. Women require peculiar conditions for work which employers show themselves wholly reluctant to grant unless forced to do so, and the power to look after their own welfare, which is also the welfare of the state, should be given to women. The term "industrial democracy," describing our form of civilization, is now often on the lips of many people, but so long as the ever-increasing number of women being forced by economic pressure into gainful occupations have no political power it is the merest mockery.

A far smaller proportion of the women voters of Colorado than the men voters hold, it appears, government positions or run for office. Women in Colorado appear to constitute, in the main, a class of voters comparable to the politically inactive class of men voters made up of doctors and professors and clergymen and

INTRODUCTION

other men practising professions that prevent their active participation in politics. Bringing up children and managing a family are time-consuming occupations, especially when the mother must also help in supporting it, as too often happens; and precisely for this reason it would seem that women should be given an easy way, like the ballot, of making the qualities fostered in them by motherhood effective for the community. To argue that public responsibility should not be laid upon the already overburdened shoulders of mothers is idle. No form of government can possibly relieve right-thinking women of their share of responsibility for the conditions into which the children of the community are born, though it can and does make the fulfilling of this responsibility extremely difficult and time-consuming. Moreover, dirty streets, impure milk, the smoke from soft coal, heavy taxation, and other such things, are burdens they might like the power of helping to legislate off their own shoulders, but that is another question. As a civilized, educated human being, every American woman must bear a share of moral responsibility for the way in which the community in which she lives deals with the education and protection of the young, the care of the unfortunate, and other like social problems.

The question of the laws passed in Colorado since 1894 requires little comment. The fact is well known that the first equal-suffrage legislature made the fathers and mothers of children joint guardians of them with equal powers—a justice obtained in Massachusetts only after years of agitation, and not yet

INTRODUCTION

obtained in California; and the laws concerning homesteads, made in the interest of the family, have also often been cited. It should cause small wonder that little was left to do in putting women on a legal equality with men in regard to property and business opportunity, since the granting women the franchise is but the last logical step in their gradual emancipation. Of the greatest interest is the less generally known fact that although the men and women of Colorado did, upon the demand of the women for proper protection of girls, enact a law which proved in practice to work injustice to young boys, they have already recognized this injustice and obviated it by amending the law. One has only to remember the long years during which girls have been unjustly treated by the old laws concerning the age of consent, and the strenuous efforts of the good women and men of the community required everywhere to have these laws amended, where they are amended, to understand the difference in such matters, even in enlightened modern communities, between government by one sex and government by both sexes.

The need for special governmental bodies to look after the interest of children has been recently brought to the attention of the public by the effort made at Washington to have a federal children's bureau established by Congress. In 1901 the Humane Society in Colorado was made by law a State Bureau of Child and Animal Protection, and Colorado is one of the very small number of states to have a bureau expressly concerned with children. Of its seven hundred agents in all parts of the state, a large proportion

INTRODUCTION

are women, Miss Sumner tells us (page 191). The benevolent women of Colorado are doing their humane work, not as private individuals in private societies, but as citizens under the control of a government for which, as voters, they are responsible, a fact very salutary, in my opinion, both for them and the government. Thus, when in 1907 an effort was made to have the bureau in question turned into a political board, the politicians were not able to carry the measure, as it is all too probable that they would have done had not the sex most interested in the matter been able to go to the polls.

Miss Sumner's comparison of Colorado with other states in regard to legislation having reference to women and children and to questions of public morality demonstrates clearly that, allowing for conditions peculiar to the various states, Colorado makes a very good showing indeed. But such a comparison, though it is of very great interest, is, for purposes of weighing the effect of women on reform legislation, by no means as significant as appears. For the very legislation of other states that the women of Colorado might be reproached for not surpassing has often been brought about by the women of those states, many of them ardently desirous of enfranchisement. It seems an odd twisting of issues to use, as is sometimes done by anti-suffragists, the public work of such women as Mrs. Lowell, of New York, and Miss Jane Addams, of Chicago, as an argument against women's enfranchisement. In our rapidly growing manufacturing cities the conditions of the factories and the tenements are such as to excite horror in

INTRODUCTION

the minds of humane people who know about them, and I venture to submit that this horror is responsible for the emergence into public life of our women philanthropists against heavy odds. They have been goaded by overmastering pity to use their abilities for the good of the community against the will, as it were, of the community, since the community does not believe in the fitness of women for government. Colorado has enlisted the interest of all its women in the welfare of the state; the ambition to do something for the good of the state has become a normal ambition for its women, and already, without the pressure of such wrongs as exist in our more thickly settled industrial commonwealths, Colorado is producing an ever-increasing number of able publicspirited women citizens. Miss Sumner's statement of what these women have already helped to accomplish may well give one confidence to believe that industrial conditions in Colorado will never be allowed to grow as bad as they have grown in New York and Pittsburg and Chicago, for instance. I personally even venture to believe that in time the good women of Colorado will be able to do something really effective toward purifying the corruption of the machine, for which, as voters, they must now bear a share of the responsibility. In the period of transition we are studying they have been able to accomplish very little in this respect. True to their traditions in the past, they have devoted themselves largely to the educational and humane side of government.

Miss Sumner thinks the good effect on the intelligence and public spirit of the women of Colorado is

INTRODUCTION

the chief gain to the state from their enfranchisement, and it seems, indeed, as though very few things could be of more importance to a state than the intelligence and public spirit of nearly half of its members. But this improvement in the women of the community is by no means the whole of this gain, since women exert an immense influence over the rising generation, boys as well as girls, during their most impressionable years, and it is clear that they can effectively inculcate only those virtues they themselves possess. Intelligence and public spirit and a morality that can withstand temptation are what is chiefly needed in its citizens for the welfare of a community. If women are to be in the future in the United States as they have been in the past and now are, the teachers of the children of both sexes, it would seem the part of wisdom, merely in the interest of the boys, to foster in women the virtues useful to society; and to foster in the boys who are their pupils a belief that the particular code of morality imposed on them by their mothers and their teachers is valid outside the home and the school, for citizens as well as for teachers and mothers. The different standards maintained by society for the two sexes neutralize the influence of the training now given to boys, since where the example and precept of their teachers are most needed they fail to operate. Our present system thus works injustice alike to women and men.

HELEN THOMAS FLEXNER.

EQUAL SUFFRAGE

I

THE PROBLEM AND LOCAL CONDITIONS

1. Purpose and Scope of the Investigation

SHALL women vote? Upon this question nearly every one has an opinion—usually founded upon a more or less conscious and coherent philosophical theory of the relation of the sexes. The consistent advocates of the theory of natural rights usually favor equal suffrage, upon the ground that women have an inalienable right to the ballot. Many follow unconsciously this line of argument, because it is based on the theory embodied in the Declaration of Independence. If the doctrine of natural rights is accepted, the only question is: Have women, as well as men, "certain natural and inalienable rights"? But this is a philosophical question which should be left to the philosopher. This investigation of equal suffrage in Colorado has no direct bearing upon the abstract right of women to the ballot, but is concerned merely with the political, economic, and social expediency of allowing them to vote.

Eliminating without deciding, then, the question of right, the investigation proceeds on the assumption that the answer to the proposition, "Shall women vote?" is to be found in the good or evil results of equal suffrage in practice. "An ounce of fact is worth a ton of theory." Here, again, however, it must be kept distinctly in mind that there are at least three phases of the problem. Equal suffrage is a political question, but it is also an economic and a social question. The usual arguments in favor of suffrage for women are based upon the political reforms which it is said the woman vote would effect; and the usual arguments against it are based upon the social evils which it is said would result—divorce, neglect of home and children, and general loss in womanliness. It is also argued, on the one hand, that equal suffrage would lead to better wages and wider industrial opportunities for women; and, on the other hand, that, if it produced any economic effect whatever, it would mean merely the displacement of men by women— a weakening of the forces that hold human society together in families, and a strengthening of the forces that make bitter the competitive struggle. Three phases of the subject, then, must be considered—the effect of equal suffrage upon politics, its effect upon economic life, and its effect upon the moral, social, and intellectual character of the women voters.

Equal suffrage has been tried, in part or in full, in many regions. As early as 1839 Kentucky gave school suffrage to widows, and Kansas extended it to all women in 1859. Michigan and Minnesota granted school suffrage in 1875, and Colorado embodied

THE PROBLEM AND LOCAL CONDITIONS

this provision in the constitution under which the state was admitted into the Union in 1876. New Hampshire and Oregon followed in 1878, Massachusetts in 1879, New York and Vermont in 1880, Nebraska in 1883, Wisconsin in 1885, North and South Dakota, Montana, Arizona, and New Jersey in 1887, Illinois in 1891, Connecticut in 1893, and Ohio in 1894. At present there are twenty-four states in which women have school suffrage. In addition, four states—Montana, Iowa,[1] Louisiana, and New York[2] —allow women who are taxpayers to vote when some special question involving an appropriation for a given purpose or the borrowing of money for some public improvement is submitted to taxpayers.[3]

Women have had municipal suffrage for from fifteen to forty years in the various colonies of Australia, and for over twenty years in Kansas. England gave municipal suffrage to single women and widows in 1869, and Scotland to the same classes in 1881. To-day the women of England, Scotland, and Ireland have all except parliamentary suffrage. In 1883 Ontario granted women municipal suffrage, and soon afterward New Brunswick, Nova Scotia, Manitoba, British Columbia, the Northwest Territory, and Quebec followed this example. In Norway women who pay taxes on a certain small income, or whose husbands pay taxes on such an income, are allowed the municipal franchise, and Swedish women

[1] In Iowa all women, whether taxpayers or not, have this right.
[2] In New York only women in towns or villages have this right.
[3] *Nineteenth Century*, 56 : 833, Foxcroft, "The Check to Woman Suffrage in the United States."

vote on all questions except the membership of the national legislature. In Russia municipal officers are elected by the votes of real-estate owners regardless of sex.[1] It is said that women possess at the present time some form of suffrage in every European nation except Greece, Spain, Portugal, Holland, and some German states.

Only in Finland, New Zealand, and four of the United States, however, have women equal political rights with men under conditions that make possible a real test of the measure under a democratic form of government. The reform, moreover, is new in Finland, and New Zealand and Australia are noted for so many other unusual experiments that many persons do not regard them as paralleled in the United States. Wyoming, Colorado, Utah, and Idaho furnish, then, the best examples of equal suffrage under normal democratic conditions. In order, however, to obtain scientific detail and accuracy, it has been necessary to still further limit the field of investigation. The women of Wyoming have had full suffrage since 1869, but Wyoming is a sparsely populated state decidedly backward in industrial development and containing no large city. Idaho and Utah have had equal suffrage since 1896, but neither of these states seems as typical of normal industrial and social conditions as Colorado, where the women first voted in 1894. Colorado, then, has been

[1] Woman Suffrage Hearing before the Committee on the Judiciary, House of Representatives, February 18, 1902, and Hearing before the Select Committee on Woman Suffrage, United States Senate, February 18, 1902.

selected for an intensive study, in the belief that this state furnishes the best example of the practical working of equal suffrage and the best indication at present obtainable of its probable results if introduced into other communities.

2. METHODS

The principal methods employed in the investigation were four: First, the circulation of question-blanks, designed to cover points incapable of direct statistical measurement and to obtain certain details in regard to the women actively engaged in political work; second, the study of newspaper files to determine what women have done in past years, selecting for special study 1894 and 1900 to compare with 1906; third, the examination of registration-books to obtain statistics showing the proportion of women and the classes of women who register and vote; and, fourth, the study of state, county, and city reports and records to determine the number of women office-holders, their records and salaries, and other similar points. Another set of question-blanks was sent out to all the cities and towns of the state, asking about the women who have served in city offices. Further general sources of information, such as the Census, United States Labor Bureau Reports, etc., were used. In the fall of 1906 political conventions and other meetings were attended during the state campaign, and hundreds of persons actively engaged in politics were interviewed.

On some points, as in regard to women in office,

the investigation covers conditions in the whole state, but on certain other questions, such as the proportion of women voting, it was impossible to cover the entire state with the thoroughness desired, and, therefore, nine representative counties were selected for special investigation. Denver was, of course, chosen as the largest and most important industrial centre. The other counties chosen were Boulder, Delta, Huerfano, La Plata, Las Animas, San Miguel, Teller, and Weld.

Of these, Weld and Delta are almost wholly devoted respectively to agriculture and to horticulture. Weld County is distinguished as the location of the famous Union Colony, of which Horace Greeley acted as patron saint, and which has left a strong impress upon the people and the life of the section, while Delta County represents more typical Western life. Teller County contains Cripple Creek and Victor, metalliferous mining-camps, with American laborers, and, to the surprise of Easterners, it is said by many political workers to be the county in which women have more real influence in politics than anywhere else in the state. A woman delegate to the Democratic State Convention explained this by saying: "Our husbands are all deported, and we women have to defeat the Republican Party so they can come back again." San Miguel County is in the southwestern part of the state, and is a metalliferous mining-camp where foreign laborers predominate. Las Animas County is primarily a coal-mining region with Mexican and foreign laborers. Huerfano is almost purely foreign and Mexican. Boulder and La Plata counties,

THE PROBLEM AND LOCAL CONDITIONS

one on the eastern slope and one on the western, combine agriculture with mining and smelting, Boulder being the seat of the State University, and Durango the county-seat of La Plata County and the "Metropolis of the Southwest." The results obtained by a careful study of these communities should furnish a fair picture of conditions throughout the state.

The questions on the blank mentioned as the first method of investigation related to the following points: (1 and 2), the interest and the influence of women in politics, and whether it is increasing or decreasing; (3 and 4) the proportion of women, as compared with men, who attend caucuses and political meetings and vote at primaries; (5) whether women usually vote the same ticket as their husbands or fathers; (6) whether men show any disposition to keep women out of politics by discourtesy; (7) whether women can control their own candidates for offices conceded to them by the men; (8) whether women politicians derive strength from the support of men or of women; (9) whether women are more or less corrupt than men in politics; (10) how they compare with men in various phases of political work, such as canvassing of precincts, etc.; (11) what has been the effect of equal suffrage on political conventions and on various kinds of legislation; (12) what has been its effect on the intelligence and public spirit of women; (13) on their moral character and business and political honor; (14) on their wages; and (15) on the home and the children. There followed eight personal questions, such as whether the person answering believed in equal suffrage, what political work he or she had done or offices held, what was his or her occupation, whether married or single, and how many children. The replies to these last questions give interesting facts in regard to the women who are active in politics.

These question-blanks were sent to women and men delegates to conventions, members of political committees, state legislators, county and city officials, and other prominent persons. A special point was made of obtaining as many replies as possible from the nine counties above mentioned. In many cases, when persons failed to reply, the blank was sent to them a second time, and, if their answers were deemed especially important, even a third time. In all, about five thousand blanks were sent out, and twelve hundred and one were returned answered in whole or in part; that is, nearly one in four was answered, which is a fair proportion, considering that the list of questions was somewhat formidable, and that a large number of persons asked to fill out the blanks were possessed of very little book-learning—some of them, in fact, being almost illiterate.

In Denver a house-to-house canvass was made of the women delegates to conventions and precinct committee women who failed to reply after the blank had been sent to them a second time, and many additional answers were secured by this means. Out of 620 women delegates to conventions and precinct committee women in Denver during the fall campaign of 1906, 225 filled out the question-blank at least in part, 233 refused or neglected to fill out the blank, and 162 could not be located. Of those who refused to fill the blank, twenty-six said they were not interested in politics, a number of them denying that they had ever taken any part whatever, though their names and addresses had been published as delegates to conventions. Two said they had never even voted. Eight or ten more who refused gave enough information to answer a number of questions, and are consequently considered as replying. Only about thirty-five of those counted as refusing or neglecting to answer gave pointblank refusals, and the rest were persons who, on personal solicitation, promised to mail the blank to the office, and then failed to do so. Most of those refusing were evidently suspicious of the purpose of the investigation. The great majority of those who could not be located by the canvasser were not merely "away from home," but, on inquiry, were found to be absolutely unknown to other workers of their own party in the precinct where they were supposed to reside.

The replies are, naturally, of very different value, but the mere fact that they are many of them given by persons of slight education does not invalidate them. Many a shrewd and fair-minded person whose opinion is valuable upon subjects coming under his or her direct observation has little book-learning. The thing desired in these answers was that they should furnish a cross-section of the experience of persons of all classes who were familiar with practical politics, and it is probable that most of the answers received were from persons who had clearly formulated and more or less valuable opinions. Varying degrees of intelligence, however, were shown, from the woman who, asked the effect of equal suffrage upon the platform adopted by political parties, replied that she thought men looked better on the platform than women, to the state legislator who volunteered the following general observation: "The advocates of female suffrage make a great mistake in claiming wonderful advantages and improvements as sure to result therefrom. Women are not naturally more honest or more unselfish than men. Equal suffrage should be demanded as a matter of justice and right, and as such the result is sure to be for the best." Whether we agree with this man or not, he evidently expressed a reasoned conviction.

In all cases, however, in which other more trustworthy information is available the importance of these answers is minimized.

The classification of the replies to all questions on the blank is based primarily upon two different points: belief in equal suffrage and sex, and, secondarily, upon a rough division of the persons answering according to political experience, residence in Denver or some other part of the state, and general prominence and intelligence. The first division is into (1) those who were favorable to equal suffrage, (2) those who were unfavorable to equal suffrage, and (3) those who were indifferent to equal suffrage, *i.e.*, who did not answer or gave non-committal answers to the direct question as to whether they did or did not believe in the measure. It is natural to suppose that, while in some cases favorable or unfavorable answers to the other questions were dictated by the opinion formed in regard to equal suffrage in general, in other cases the belief in equal suffrage was based on the experience of its workings. In either case this division should be helpful in the effort to arrive at unbiased conclusions. The second point of division, that of sex, is obviously desirable not merely because of the probable influence on the average

THE PROBLEM AND LOCAL CONDITIONS

of sex prejudice on the one hand and sex pride on the other, but also because what the men think and what the women think is of separate interest and importance.

These two points of classification are carried out for all questions except the personal descriptions furnished by Questions 18, 19, 22, and 23, where the division according to belief or disbelief in equal suffrage is dropped. In Questions 18 and 19, relating respectively to whether the persons have any relatives active in politics in the same party, and whether they are or have been members of any political club, the sex division is retained, but the answers to Questions 22 and 23, relating to occupation and conjugal condition, are tabulated only for the women.

The other division of the replies is designed to bring out the actual knowledge of conditions possessed by the persons answering. First, are the replies from men members or ex-members of the State Legislature and women county superintendents or ex-county superintendents. Second, are replies from experienced political workers throughout the state, *i.e.*, outside of Denver. It is essential to understand, in considering this division, that the degree of experience of the men here classified is far greater than that of the women, for all of these men, at one time or another, have served as county chairmen of one of the political parties, while among the women are included any woman who has attended a convention as a delegate or has done ward or precinct work for her party. This observation in regard to the greater political experience of the men applies also to the first division into men state legislators and women county superintendents, for some of these women, in spite of having held political office, have never attended a convention, while the men have usually attended all the conventions of their party for years. In the third class, too, of those who are called merely "Other Citizens of the State," nearly three-fourths of the men have done more or less active political work or have held local offices, while none of the women in this

EQUAL SUFFRAGE

class have had any experience in politics. Most of these women are either in business, or are teachers, postmasters, or officers of local women's clubs.

With the exception of the answers from the few Denver people classified as members of the State Legislature or county superintendents, and from a dozen or so wholly inexperienced persons classified among the other citizens of the state, all of the Denver answers were divided into those from prominent citizens, whose wide experience and broad intelligence entitle their opinions to especial weight, and men and women delegates to conventions. Most of these were delegates to the county conventions of the Democratic and Republican parties in the fall campaigns of 1906. It will be observed that this division of the Denver people into delegates and prominent citizens corresponds roughly to the division of the people of the rest of the state into legsitators and county superintendents and experienced political workers.

There are, then, five main classes: (A) State Officers, including legislators and county superintendents, (B) Political Workers, State, (C) Other Citizens, State, (D) Delegates to Conventions, Denver, and (E) Prominent Citizens, Denver. These divisions are carried out for all Questions up to the sixteenth, with the single exception of Question 14 in regard to the effect of equal suffrage upon women's wages and conditions of employment. Here the state legislators and county chairmen were thrown together to form one class of experienced men, and the county superintendents and women workers to form one class of experienced women. Then a class was added of employers, socialists, and trade-unionists, whose answers to other questions were elsewhere distributed. The answers to the questions in regard to reasons for interest in politics, relatives in politics, membership in political clubs, occupation, and conjugal condition were not classified for the inexperienced women, and the question of prominence was also eliminated as of little or

THE PROBLEM AND LOCAL CONDITIONS

no importance by adding the prominent Denver women's answers to the answers of the Denver women delegates. The main divisions made for answers to these latter questions are, then, only three: (A) State Officers, (B) Political Workers, State, and (C) Delegates, Denver. The summary tables of the answers to each question will be found under the section in which that question is considered.

The other methods of investigation require no detailed description beyond explanations to be made in connection with the facts which they have brought to light. It should be here said, however, that under the state law it is necessary to preserve registration and poll books for only two years, and that, consequently, few counties have records covering anything but the last election. Statistics have been gathered showing the vote and registration of women and men at the fall election of 1906 for Boulder, Delta, Denver, Huerfano, La Plata, Las Animas, San Miguel, Teller, and Weld counties, and figures showing tenancy and naturalization for both sexes and conjugal condition and occupation for women at the same election for the cities of Boulder, Longmont, Denver, Durango, Trinidad, Telluride, Goldfield, Victor, and Cripple Creek. The latter facts are recorded only for city precincts, as the registration-books used in country precincts give only name and residence. There are also other scattered statistics given in Chapter III.

The results of the investigation fall naturally under six main subjects. In the first place, it is necessary to consider the participation of women in the political work which precedes elections, in caucuses, primaries, conventions, and political meetings. This includes a consideration of the corruption of women in politics, whether greater or less than that of men, and takes women through the partisan work of election day. Though several of the subjects considered do not relate exclusively to the two great political parties, they fall under the general heading, "party machinery." The next subject is naturally the statistics of elections, which include the number and proportion of women voting in different counties and at different elections, and the vote cast by both men and women for women candidates. This obviously introduces the subject of the number of women serving in public office and their records, which is followed by a consideration of the industrial opportunities offered by equal suffrage to women, both in public and in private employment, and the effect of equal suffrage on wages. This chapter on the economic aspects of equal suffrage again leads to the question: What has been done to advance the interests of women, of children, and of the public generally through legislation?

So far consideration will have been given to the effect of the woman vote upon political methods, elections, public office, the public and private employment of women, and legislation. Then comes the most difficult and at the same time perhaps the most important part of the subject—the effect of the possession of the ballot upon woman herself, her intellectual and moral character, and upon the home and the children, her special charge and her peculiar birthright.

THE PROBLEM AND LOCAL CONDITIONS

3. History of Equal Suffrage in Colorado

As early as 1868 an effort was made to introduce the equal-suffrage question in the Territorial Legislature of Colorado, and in 1870 Governor Edward McCook recommended the measure in his message to the legislature. This was followed by the introduction of a bill, which was defeated in the Council-Chamber by a majority of one, and in the House by a two-thirds vote.[1] Again, in 1876, when the Constitutional Convention was in session, the question was brought to the front, only to be defeated by a vote of 24 to 8. The way was paved for the future adoption of equal suffrage, however, by the insertion in the state constitution of the following clause:

"Section 2. Article 7. The General Assembly may at any time extend by law the right of suffrage to persons not herein enumerated, but no such law shall take effect or be in force until the same shall have been submitted to a vote of the people at a general election and approved by a majority of all the votes cast for or against such law."

The Constitutional Convention also adopted a resolution instructing the State Legislature to provide an equal-suffrage law and submit it to the vote of the people. This was done, but, after a hot campaign, the measure was defeated by a vote of about 20,000 to 10,000. The Mexican vote was supposed to have been largely responsible for this result.

In 1881 a bill giving municipal suffrage to women

[1] Brown, *History of Equal Suffrage in Colorado*, p. 7.

was defeated in the legislature, and in 1891 a bill asking for a constitutional amendment giving full suffrage went by default because of failure to introduce it within the required time.

It was not until the wave of Populist enthusiasm of 1892 that equal suffrage became again a live political issue. The Populists had an equal-suffrage plank in their state platform, and their victory was followed by the introduction of four suffrage bills in the State Legislature of 1893. The bill, which was endorsed by the Equal Suffrage Association, and which was finally passed, was drawn up by the late J. Warner Mills, generally recognized in Colorado as one of the stanchest friends of "equal rights to all, and special privileges to none," who has ever given the best energies of his life to reform.

The bill was passed by a vote of 34 to 27 in the House and 20 to 10 in the Senate. Of the total of 54 votes for the measure, 34 were Populist, 19 Republican, and 1 Democratic, but there were only 9 Democrats in both branches of the legislature, while there were 44 Republicans and 38 Populists. It is evident that the Populists, with the aid of a few Republicans, were responsible for equal suffrage. This appears also in the result of the popular vote on the measure in the fall of 1893. Although equal suffrage was endorsed at a called meeting of the Democratic State Central Committee, and at the Arapahoe County conventions of the Republican and Prohibition parties, the decisive support of the measure was given by the Populist Party. This is shown by the fact that the counties which went Republican and Democratic gave a majority of 471 against equal suffrage, while those that gave Populist pluralities rolled up a majority of 6818 in its favor.[1] The total vote was 35,798 for, and 29,451 against—a majority of 6347 votes. It is of interest to note that the equal-suffrage amendment was not submitted at the time of a state election, but at the county elections, which were then held in the odd years. The total vote on the proposition was only 65,249, while the total vote cast for governor in 1892 was 93,756.[2]

The women entered the political arena under conditions which were anything but typical of ordinary Colorado politics. The state, from the beginning normally Republican, with an occasional local Democratic victory of no wide significance, had been swept temporarily by the high tide of Populism. At the municipal election in the spring of 1894, when women first voted, it was clearly demonstrated that they intended to make use of their new power, and at the state election in the fall of the same year women are said to have been a powerful factor in defeating, with the cry, "Redeem the State from Populist misrule!" the party which had given them the ballot. Their great activity was due probably in part to the fact that both politicians and business men were thoroughly aroused and decidedly worried over the effect of the new political element, and consequently made a greater effort than has ever been made since to interest and organize women along strictly party lines. In part, too, it was due to the attitude of the women themselves, who were appealed to, not only by the

[1] Susan B. Anthony and Ida Husted Harper, *History of Woman Suffrage*, p. 518.
[2] For the text of the bill and the equal-suffrage proclamation, see Appendix A.

novelty of their position, but also by a strong sense of responsibility over a new political situation, not the least important factor of which was the split on the silver question which soon afterward divided into two factions both of the old political parties.

The Populist free-silver excitement of 1892 to 1896, combined with the industrial depression of those years, constituted a distinct epoch in Colorado political history, an epoch during which both personal concern over public affairs and party loyalty ran high. During these years there was a general tendency to appeal to government for relief from burdens that were well-nigh unendurable. This tendency is illustrated by the fact that nearly 32,000 more votes were cast for governor in 1894 than in 1898.[1]

Later, with the return of prosperity and the increased production of gold as compared with silver, the state resumed normal political conditions, which have been maintained, in spite of the labor excitements of later years.

4. SOCIAL, ECONOMIC, AND POLITICAL CONDITIONS IN COLORADO

In order that the workings of woman suffrage in Colorado may be fairly discussed, it is necessary to understand and make allowance for the influence of special and peculiar conditions in Colorado. Some of these conditions, such as the comparative absence of large industrial centres, would perhaps tend to make equal suffrage more successful, but other factors,

[1] *Legislative Manual*, Colorado, 1903, pp. 110, 130.

THE PROBLEM AND LOCAL CONDITIONS

such as the general roughness of mining-camps, would naturally have a contrary tendency.

Colorado had, according to the census of 1900, a total population of 539,700, scattered over an area more than twice as great as the state of New York. Its average density of population was 5.2 persons per square mile, while that of New York was 152.6 persons, and that of the entire United States 25.6 persons. The state is divided into fifty-nine counties, only six of which had, in 1900, a population of over 20,000. Of these six, three contained respectively the cities of Denver, Pueblo, and Colorado Springs. The other three were Boulder, Las Animas, and Teller counties, containing the cities of Boulder, Trinidad, and Cripple Creek. These six counties together contained 291,455 persons—considerably more than half of the total population of the state.

Colorado is famous for its mining industry, as it produces more gold than any other state in the Union. In 1900, however, only 13.7 per cent. of all the persons ten years of age and over engaged in gainful occupations were employed in mining and quarrying. Agriculture, which long ago surpassed mining as a state industry even in value of product, had a much larger proportion—20.6 per cent. of the persons engaged in gainful occupations.[1]

---

[1] Manufacturing and mechanical pursuits, including smelting, contained 18.7 per cent. of the gainfully employed population; trade and transportation, 21.6 per cent.; domestic and personal service, 19.1 per cent.; and professional service, 6.3 per cent.— *Twelfth Census*, vol. ii, pp. cxxxv—cxxxvii. It will be seen from these figures that, though there are certain places, notably Cripple Creek and Telluride, which are dominated by the mining industry, the state as a whole is not influenced nearly so much by this industry as is commonly thought. The smelting business,

It should also be pointed out that of the 20,519 wage-earners in Colorado employed in mines and quarries in 1902, 7955, or considerably more than a third, were engaged in the mining of coal[1] under conditions not strikingly dissimilar to those in Pennsylvania. Only about 9 per cent., then, of the gainfully employed persons of the state appear to be engaged in metalliferous mining. Of 43,747 persons in agricultural pursuits, too, only 4835, or about one-ninth, were stock-raisers, herders, and drovers.[2] Adding these to the metalliferous miners, we see that, roughly estimated, only something like 10 per cent. of the gainfully employed persons of the state of Colorado are engaged in occupations not common to such a state, for instance, as Pennsylvania. Industrially, then, Colorado does not differ as radically from an Eastern community as is popularly supposed.

Nor does it differ radically in political matters. Except for the Populist free-silver agitation which swept the state in the early nineties, Colorado has swung back and forth between the Democratic and Republican parties, with a slightly greater leaning toward the latter. Political corruption and charges of corruption are mainly confined to two classes of districts—the larger cities and the predominantly Mexican counties where the vote is "controlled." Nevertheless, Colorado is a typical corporation, machine-politician-ruled state, with the addition, per-

too, though an important one, does not constitute a peculiar condition in Colorado as distinguished, for instance, from the iron and steel manufacturing regions of the East.

[1] *Special Census Report, Mines and Quarries*, 1902, p. 183.
[2] *Special Census Report, Occupations*, p. 236.

THE PROBLEM AND LOCAL CONDITIONS

haps, of a degree of wild Western recklessness and contempt for law. If an election is to be stolen or an unpopular measure pushed through it may be done by cruder, more openly aggressive methods than would be employed in an Eastern community, but the result is the same in the end. The Smelter Trust, the Colorado Fuel and Iron Company, the railroads, and the public-service corporations of Denver, including the telephone company, are Colorado's dominant corporations.

On the whole, the most noteworthy feature of Colorado politics, and especially, perhaps, of Denver politics, is that there seems never to have been any real awakening to civic righteousness. In 1897, under the Civic Federation and the Taxpayers' Party, both non-partisan organizations, the first of women and the second of men, and again at the time of the adoption of the new Denver Charter in 1903, strong efforts were made to bring about reforms, but both movements were defeated at the polls. The people of Denver, as a whole, do not wish reform. They wish "safe" politics of the brand furnished by enterprising business men who have developed, among other things, the city's famous tramway system and a telephone service which has grown *pari passu* with the growth of the city, and now connects practically every part of the state with the capital city. Denver people are afraid of checking individualistic enterprise; their public-utility corporations have, upon the whole, given efficient service; no serious dearth of opportunities for energy and ability has as yet been felt; and the average citizen is content to "live and let live." The same may be said of the rest of the state. The shibboleth of rapid development of natural resources, regardless of future interests, has ruled the history of Colorado as completely as it has ruled the history of other Western commonwealths, and the dominant sentiment, in spite of grumblings, ominous for the future, is probably still honestly friendly to the great corporations which, by exploiting the natural resources, are making the state industrially a "going concern."

In spite, then, of the reputation for radicalism gained during the Populist movement of several years ago, Colorado is now probably little more "excitable" than an average Eastern community. Since 1893 the mining industry has swung over from silver to gold production, and the issue of "16 to 1" has quietly died and been buried. The state has been rent by labor conflicts which have had their reflection at every stage in political life, but, though these disturbances have been somewhat more severe and bitter than have recently occurred in Eastern communities, this constitutes a difference merely in degree and not in kind. The "labor wars" of Colorado prove in certain ways the precocity of its industrial development and not its backwardness—as, for instance, in the completeness of the organization of employers' associations and citizens' alliances.

The Colorado experiment in equal suffrage, therefore, except for the sparse population of the state, is a fair trial under nearly normal conditions in an approximately representative community.

II

PARTY MACHINERY

THE first question usually asked in regard to equal suffrage is: Do women vote? But there is another inquiry which comes logically and chronologically first: To what extent do women assume the political responsibilities which precede and lead up to the casting of the ballot? Under our plan of government, in which parties are recognized as the nominating power and political issues are presented in party platforms, the responsibility of the citizen begins when the first caucus is called to nominate delegates to the local convention. We should, then, first study party machinery to learn how effectively women have assumed the duties of citizens.

Women are, probably, more often than men, independent of party, as is shown by the larger proportion of split tickets since they voted, and by the generally acknowledged increase in the difficulty of forecasting the result. But effective political work is done by means of party machinery of one sort or another, which means caucuses, conventions, campaign meetings, clubs, canvassing, distribution of circulars, instructions to voters, and so forth. The women of Colorado have taken part in all of this work. The extent of their activity in each branch, and the question of their political corruption as compared with that of men, will be considered in this chapter.

1. CAUCUSES AND PRIMARIES [1]

A summary of the replies to the question, "How many women, as compared with men, attend caucuses and vote at primaries?" is given in Table I.[2] Analyzing these replies, it appears that of the total number of men and women answering the blank, including those who gave no definite reply to this ques-

[1] It is impossible, owing to an entire absence of records, to obtain accurate figures concerning the attendance of women as compared with that of men at caucuses and primaries. An attempt was made to induce the county chairmen of the Republican and Democratic parties in the counties selected for detailed study to obtain from ward and precinct workers the actual figures for the caucuses and primaries preceding the fall election of 1906. But only two of them made any reply to the request, and one of these gave merely the attendance in his own precinct, where, he said, ten men and no women were present. The other chairman, from Las Animas County, said: "In the country there seldom if ever any women attend the primaries either in the Mexican, mining, or farming precincts. In the town there is often one-third of the people women, and at other times you will not find any women there. They sometimes go when they have a friend as a candidate before the convention."

Naturally, as no exact information can be obtained for the present time upon this subject, the evidence to be derived from contemporary newspaper files for previous years is exceedingly meagre. However, in 1894 an effort was made through the newspapers to induce women to attend the primaries—an effort to which they appear to have responded in considerable numbers. As will be shown, women, when certain issues are at stake, are generally active, and in 1894 the issue was combined with interest in the novelty of the experience.

[2] Some confusion was caused by the inclusion in the question of two distinct points—caucuses and primaries. Most persons answered as if it was a single question, but many replied to each part of the inquiry separately.

tion, 48.4 per cent. of the men and 30.6 per cent. of the women said that women constitute less than one-fourth of the attendance, while 10.3 per cent. of the men and 4.1 per cent. of the women said that no women attend, and 14.8 per cent. of the men and 17.1 per cent. of the women said that from one-fourth to one-half are women. Of the women 15.6 per cent., but of the men only 7.6 per cent., said that the numbers of men and women are equal, while a few, 6.7 per cent. of the women and 2.4 per cent. of the men, said that more women than men attend caucuses and vote at primaries. No definite answer was given by 16.5 per cent. of the men and 25.9 per cent. of the women. Taking into consideration the element of belief or non-belief in equal suffrage, it is seen that the range of difference between the percentages for the answers of persons who were favorable, unfavorable, or indifferent to equal suffrage is not great. The general conclusion is, therefore, that, taking the state as a whole, less than one person in four attending causuces and primaries is a woman.

Locally there were far wider divergencies in total result and also far greater differences of opinion between men and women. The largest number of Denver women delegates is found in the table in the "Same" class and the next largest in the "From ¼ to ½" class. Among the men this order is reversed, and as many men answered "Less than ¼" as "Same." The opinions of "Prominent Denver Citizens" drag down the average for Denver, however, by concentrating slightly for both sexes in the class "Less than ¼." These answers, however, on this particular point, are probably of no greater weight than the same number of answers from "Denver Delegates."

EQUAL SUFFRAGE

TABLE I

Question—What proportion of women, as compared with men, attend caucuses and vote at primaries?

	More Men	More Women	Same Men	Same Women	From ¾ to ¾ Men	From ¾ to ¾ Women	Less than ¾ Men	Less than ¾ Women	None Men	None Women	No def. ans. Men	No def. ans. Women	Total Men	Total Women
I. Favorable to Equal Suffrage														
A. State officials	2	2	4	7	8	12	15	23	1		2	5	32	49
B. Political workers—state		4	3	18	8	20	15	40	5	2	5	20	36	104
C. Other citizens—state	9	1	26	9	45	16	102	39	20	4	40	26	242	95
D. Delegates—Denver	2	25	4	41	15	32	17	17			4	44	19	159
E. Prominent citizens—Denver	1		2	2	1	3	3	5			4	5	11	15
Total	14	32	39	77	67	83	139	124	26	6	55	100	340	422
Per cent	4.1	7.6	11.5	18.2	19.7	19.7	40.9	29.4	7.6	1.4	16.2	23.7	100	100
II. Unfavorable to Equal Suffrage														
A. State officials			1	1		2	6	2	5	1		1	12	4
B. Political workers—state			2	11	7	3	18	11	6	3	1		25	16
C. Other citizens—state	1		3		5	6	77	7	16	4	17	4	120	19
D. Delegates—Denver		3			2		10	10	1	2	3	18	22	50
E. Prominent citizens—Denver							2	1					3	1
Total	1	3	6	12	14	11	112	31	28	10	21	23	182	90
Per cent	.5	3.3	3.3	13.3	7.7	12.2	62.3	34.5	15.3	11.1	10.9	25.6	100	100
III. Indifferent to Equal Suffrage														
A. State officials					3		6	3	2	1	2	1	13	5
B. Political workers—state		1	1	1	6	5	4	9	2	1	1	1	7	16
C. Other citizens—state			1	1		1	33	10	5	4	18	8	63	24
D. Delegates—Denver		3					2	2		4	4	20	7	28
E. Prominent citizens—Denver					1		2			1	1		4	1
Total	1	4	2	2	10	6	47	24	9	8	26	29	94	73
Per cent	5.5	5.5	2.1	2.7	10.6	8.2	50	32.9	9.6	11	27.7	39.7	100	100
Grand total	15	39	47	91	91	100	208	179	63	24	102	152	616	585
Grand per cent	2.4	6.7	7.6	15.6	14.8	17.1	48.4	30.6	10.3	4.1	16.5	25.9	100	100

PARTY MACHINERY

But it is evident, on comparing these figures with those for the rest of the state, that a considerably larger proportion of women take part in caucuses and primaries in Denver than in other parts of Colorado. The answers from the other sections are concentrated in every case in the class "Less than ¼." Among the first three groups in the table a considerable proportion of both men and women declare that no women attend caucuses or vote at primaries. This is doubtless the case in some localities.

The conclusion, however, that in Denver nearly the same number of women as of men attend caucuses and vote at primaries, though in the rest of the state less than one-tenth of the persons performing this political duty are women, is probably substantially correct.

Many answers stated that the activity of women in caucuses and primaries depends upon the issue, and some said that if a moral issue is at stake, generally the saloon or some similar question, a great deal more interest is manifested. Both of these statements are probably true. It is also generally conceded, as several answers stated, that usually more women attend caucuses in good neighborhoods than in bad—in residence precincts than in lodging-house precincts. In residence precincts the caucuses are ordinarily held in private houses, and they often assume the nature of social functions. In many country districts little or no interest is taken by women, though in some localities women take an active part. There are great differences on this point, too, in small towns.

Considering separately the counties, exclusive of Denver, which were under special investigation, it is found that in every county, except Huerfano and San Miguel, the answers concentrate in the class "Less than ¼." In Huerfano County they concentrate in the "None" class, and in San Miguel County there are exactly the same number of both men and women who say that no women attend caucuses or vote at primaries as who say that women constitute less than one-fourth of the attendance.

Huerfano is a coal-mining community with a large foreign population. One man from that county said: "Never saw a woman attend a caucus or primary except once, and then they were relatives of candidates." Another fact tending to show that women in this section take little interest is that only one woman in the county could be induced to answer the question-blank, and she had no experience in any kind of political work, and was indifferent to equal suffrage. The principal industry of San Miguel County is gold-mining, though there is some agriculture in the western portion. Testimony from the agricultural part of the county, however, is to the effect that women take no part in political work, and what little interest they take in the other sections seems to be wholly in the town of Telluride, which is essentially a mining-camp. One man who believed in equal suffrage said, however, that no women take part in caucuses or primaries in Telluride because there are "too many saloon men and gamblers." The truth probably is, as another Telluride man indicated, that frequently, perhaps usually, there are no women, but that occasionally some special issue or the earnest solicitation of interested friends brings them out in considerable numbers.

In the other mining community, Teller County, women evidently take much more active part. Only one man said that women never attend caucuses and primaries, while twelve men and nine women said that they constitute from one-fourth to one-half the attendance. The result of the inquiry in the strictly agricultural counties, Delta and Weld, shows conditions very similar to those in Teller County, and no noticeable difference can be discovered in La Plata and Las Animas counties. A number of answers from these communities, however, show that the activity of women depends on the issues and the candidates, and, while usually dormant, can be aroused on occasion. This accounts for many contradictory opinions.

PARTY MACHINERY

The answers from Boulder County are decidedly contradictory, but probably this is due to the fluctuating interest of women and to the diversity of conditions in different parts of the county. In the small mining districts of the western part women take little or no interest. One man from this section said: "In this locality the proportion is probably less than in almost any other in the state. We think no women have attended the caucuses here for years, but women have generally responded on election day, and exercised their right of suffrage." On the other hand, in the cities of Boulder and Longmont women show more than average interest. One man said: "In Longmont during my six years' experience the women have been seldom if ever less than one-third of the total attendance at caucuses. In city elections they sometimes outnumber the men."

The conclusion to be drawn, therefore, is that, while women nowhere take quite their full share of responsibility over the preliminary political work represented by caucuses and primaries, their activity depends, first, upon the size of the community and the proportion of women, and, second, upon the issue and the candidates. The larger the community and the higher the proportion of women as compared with men,[1] the larger the proportion of women who attend caucuses and vote at primaries. This may be called a static condition. The dynamic factors are the issues and the candidates, and these make wide differences on special occasions.

Some interesting causes for the attendance or non-attendance of women at caucuses and primaries were

[1] See chap. iii, section 1, for the proportion of men and women in the total population by counties in 1900.

suggested. Of the Denver women delegates who answered that more women than men attend primaries, four said this is true of working-class precincts because primaries are held in the afternoons when men are at work. A county chairman said: "That is the trouble with both men and women; they don't attend and make their influence felt enough at the primaries." One of the prominent Denver women complained that there are not so many women as men because the meetings, evidently referring to caucuses, are generally held evenings, "and, furthermore, the politicians do not desire any one not in the 'ring,' so do not advertise the meeting." Another prominent Denver woman answered: "A very small proportion of women attend because the men cannot manipulate them, and hence they are not welcome." A member of the State Legislature said that one of the reasons why so few women attend is "because they are yet mystified by the wire pulling," and a politically experienced Pueblo woman complained that "men do not let women know the real inwardness of the caucus."

Several other persons testified that the ordinary citizen, whether man or woman, has no influence over caucuses or primaries, as these are run by professional politicians.

A politically inexperienced club-woman from outside of Denver finally touched the heart of the problem when she said: "Very few, the principal reason being our lack of primary laws, thus leaving the primaries to politicians." This suggests, perhaps, both the chief cause and the best remedy for the small part taken by women in primaries. If Colorado had a

PARTY MACHINERY

direct primary election law similar to that, for instance, of Wisconsin, it is probable that women would express their opinions at the primaries in nearly if not quite as large numbers as they now do at elections. But this suggestion involves the whole question of party machinery, and will be treated, therefore, in the final conclusion of the chapter.

2. CONVENTIONS

In regard to the part played by women in political conventions, somewhat more accurate information may be obtained, as lists of delegates are sometimes published in the newspapers. For their influence, however, on the outward appearance of conventions, drinking, smoking, etc., and for their influence on the selection of candidates, the making or breaking of the "slate" and the platform adopted, the answers to the question-blank furnish the only available information. From these answers, too, indications may be derived of the attitude of men toward women in politics, whether they are usually courteous or show a disposition to discourage their active participation. The answers also give opinions on the comparative strength of women politicians among men and among women. These latter questions have no direct bearing upon the expediency of equal suffrage, but they furnish an interesting side-light upon its practical workings in Colorado.

A. WOMEN DELEGATES

In some parts of Colorado it is customary to elect women delegates to county and even to state conventions, though in other places it is very unusual for women to serve in conventions. Of the counties under special investigation, Boulder has usually had from one to six women at its county conventions, and in 1894 sent three women and twenty-seven men to the Republican State Convention. But in 1902 it sent only one woman to the Republican State Convention, and in 1906 none. Delta County has never, so far as ascertained, had more than two or three women delegates to any convention, though in 1902 it sent a woman to the Republican State Convention. Huerfano County, which had two women delegates at the Republican Congressional Convention of 1894, seems never to have had a woman delegate to any convention since that date. La Plata County has occasionally had two or three women delegates from the country precincts at county conventions, but none recently. Las Animas sent four women and twenty-one men to the Republican State Convention of 1894, and one woman in 1902, but has not kept up this record. San Miguel County seems rarely or never to have had women delegates, but Teller County has usually a dozen or so women at all county conventions, and sends from two to six women delegates to state conventions. Weld County had one woman delegate at the Republican County Convention of 1906.

Denver is the only one of these counties which elects any considerable number of women delegates. The following summary shows the number of men and women delegates elected to conventions there in 1894, 1900, and 1906. The figures for 1894 and

1900 are for Arapahoe County, which at that time included Denver, and the figures for 1906 are for the city and county of Denver.

DELEGATES TO CONVENTIONS

Conventions	From Arapahoe County				From Denver	
	1894		1900		1906	
	Men	Women	Men	Women	Men	Women
COUNTY						
Republican.........	359	122	...	...	728	124
Democratic.........	273	21	679	88	623	87
White Wing Demo...	178	18	...	...	...	...
Speer Democratic...	...	...	...	...	590	84
STATE						
Republican.........	106	4	129	15	149	18
Democratic.........	81	9	142	7	194	21
Populist............	...	...	89	17	...	...
Silver Republican....	277	48	...	...	...	...
TOTAL...........	1274	222	1039	127	2284	334
Per cent.	85.2	14.8	89.1	10.9	87.3	12.7

A man from Pueblo testified of delegates to conventions that "when the law first passed about one-third were women. In the last Republican Convention in this county, with over 300 delegates, 22 were women, 7 of them colored; in the Democratic Convention, 12 were women, 1 colored."

In 1902, 35 women from 13 counties, and in 1906, 34 women from 8 counties were delegates to the Republican state conventions.

Adding together all the data obtainable for the entire state in regard to the proportion of men and women at conventions, it was found that in 1894 the ratio was about six to one, in 1900 about ten to one, and in 1906 about nine to one. Though this is a rough estimate, it seems to confirm the impression given by the more accurate figures for Arapahoe County, that there was a falling-off in the number of women delegates about 1900, but that since that date the loss has been in part recovered.

Here, again, as in the case of caucuses and primaries, it was found that, usually, the larger the city or town the greater the activity of the women. In regard to conventions, however, this rule is perhaps less uniform, for the accidental local factor of leadership among women plays a more important part. This leadership seems to have existed mainly in Denver, Pueblo, Colorado Springs, and Cripple Creek.

B. Effect on Outward Appearance

As for the influence which the presence of women has had on the outward appearance of conventions —drinking, smoking, etc.—the summary of the answers to this question is given in Table II. Half of the men and 62.7 per cent. of the women, inclusive of those giving no definite answer to this particular question, said that it has had a good effect; 30.7 per cent. of the men and 14.4 per cent. of the women that it has had no effect; and 19.3 per cent. of the men and 22.9 per cent. of the women gave no definite answer. Two factors should be taken into consideration, however, in studying this table. First, the testimony of the men on this point is naturally more valuable than that of the women, for the latter knew only by hearsay what political conventions were like before they were admitted. Second, there

PARTY MACHINERY

TABLE II

Question—What has been the effect of equal suffrage on the outward appearance of conventions—drinking, smoking, etc.?

	Good Men	Good Women	None[1] Men	None[1] Women	No definite answer Men	No definite answer Women
I. Favorable to Equal Suffrage						
A. State officials	24	39	6	2	2	8
B. Political workers—state	23	87	8	3	5	14
C. Other citizens—state	169	55	35	10	38	30
D. Delegates—Denver	11	120	4	14	4	25
E. Prominent citizens—Denver	8	9	2	5	1	1
Total	235	310	55	3	50	78
Per cent	69.1	73.4	16.2	8	14.7	18.6
II. Unfavorable to Equal Suffrage						
A. State officials	4	2	8	1		1
B. Political workers—state	8	7	14	8	3	1
C. Other citizens—state	23	4	67	4	30	11
D. Delegates—Denver	5	15	14	24	3	11
E. Prominent citizens—Denver	2	1			1	
Total	42	29	103	37	37	24
Per cent	23.1	32.2	56.6	41.1	20.3	26.7
III. Indifferent to Equal Suffrage						
A. State officials	8	2	2	1	3	2
B. Political workers—state	1	13	5	1	1	2
C. Other citizens—state	16	7	21	1	26	16
D. Delegates—Denver	2	6	3	10	2	12
E. Prominent citizens—Denver	4					
Total	31	28	31	13	32	32
Per cent	33	38.4	33	17.8	34	43.8
Grand total	308	367	189	84	119	134
Grand per cent	50	62.7	30.7	14.4	19.3	22.9

[1] Eleven persons classified as saying that equal suffrage has had no effect stated that the effect has been bad.

was evidently in the minds of many persons answering a close connection between this question and general belief or disbelief in equal suffrage—a connection which seems to indicate the probability that many answers were given from purely *a priori* considerations. Some local variations, too, are shown. In Denver, for instance, where women are always found at conventions, there is a somewhat greater tendency than in other counties, in a large number of which women seldom or never attend, to declare the results good. Equal suffrage has, naturally, little effect on conventions unless women are actually present.

Eleven persons classified in the table as saying that equal suffrage has had no effect on the outward appearance of conventions stated in essence that the effect has been bad. Of four Denver women who thought the effect bad, three believed in equal suffrage and one did not. One said that more women approve of drinking and smoking now than formerly, and another that though, when equal suffrage was new, it cleared the atmosphere a little, women "now go in for the equal plane." Two Denver men who did not believe in equal suffrage thought the effect bad. One answered: "Degrading, as it puts women in bad company, or company other than they are accustomed to." The other said: "The first few years drinking, smoking, etc., were looked down upon and almost discontinued, but the past few years it is about the same as before women voted, and the women now do not seem to mind it." In addition to these, two county chairmen who did not believe in equal suffrage, one Huerfano man who did not say whether or not he believed in it, one Pueblo man who was also indifferent to it, and one trade-unionist who favored equal suffrage, thought the effect upon conventions bad. The reasons

PARTY MACHINERY

for this belief, however, seem to relate wholly to the effect of conventions upon women and not at all to the effect of women upon conventions, and consequently these answers cannot be counted as showing even a minority opinion on the subject now under discussion.

The probability is that the presence of women had at first a slight tendency to prevent the choosing for political conventions of halls attached to saloons. Also, at first, the rule was made and enforced with some degree of consistency that there should be no smoking in convention-halls. The Republican Party, though its women are generally supposed to have less political power than the Democratic women, at least in Denver, still lives up fairly well to these rules, but a Democratic Convention in Denver is often conveniently attached to a saloon, and the request of the chairman that "gentlemen shall not smoke" is liberally interpreted to mean that they are asked not to smoke in the front of the room, where the women delegates are supposed to sit. The women do not usually seem to object to the smoke, but it is difficult to see why they should, as the majority of them are doubtless accustomed to it in their homes. It should not be forgotten that most of these women delegates to conventions are married and are accustomed to the ways of man. The testimony as to drinking is more conflicting, but naturally the tendency, when women are present, is toward less drinking and the use of less rough and profane language.

Extravagant statements of "vast improvement" in the general decorum of conventions should not, however, for two reasons, be credited. In the first place, the most trustworthy evidence goes to show that conventions in Colorado before women voted were not orgies of rowdyism, violence, and drunkenness, and consequently that no "vast improvement" was needed. Of course, men often became eager and excited and sometimes overstepped the bounds of dignity, but women who are interested enough to take an active part in conventions also become eager and excited. One woman said in answer to this question: "I have attended committee meetings which broke up in riot, but that only increased the delights of attendance. We are only human, you know."

This leads to the second reason why statements of "vast improvement" should not be credited, which is that any one who takes the trouble to attend a political convention, especially in the larger cities of Colorado, may see for himself that these gatherings are not "as quiet and orderly as church meetings." Moreover, the nearer this supposed ideal convention is approached, the more certain is it that the real spirit of representative, democratic government has been overridden by boss rule, and that, thrust everywhere between men and women delegates, is the insidious finger of political corruption.

C. Activity of Women

In the actual conduct of conventions the part played by women depends, of course, upon their numbers. If only one or two or three women delegates are present, they are usually mere figure-heads. But if,

PARTY MACHINERY

as in Denver, there are enough women to prevent them from being curiosities, they frequently assume more than their proportionate share of the work. Women, for instance, by their attitude in the two conventions in 1894, are said to have brought together and united the divided wings of the Democratic Party. In 1896, moreover, a woman served through a stormy session as the efficient chairman of the State Silver Republican Convention.

Women are usually appointed upon committees in the state conventions and in those of Denver, as formerly of Arapahoe County, which included Denver, but not often in other places. Taking the state and the Denver conventions together for the years 1894, 1900, and 1906, at least two-thirds of the large committees had from one to three women members. At the regular Democratic Convention of Denver County in the fall of 1906, one woman was appointed upon each of the four standing committees, and two women upon one—each committee being composed of sixteen members, one from each ward. In the Republican County Convention three of the four committees, each with the same membership as the Democratic, had one woman member. The Republican State Convention of that fall, however, did not have one woman on a committee, though there were thirty-four women members. But the Democratic State Convention had two women on the Resolutions Committee. Women sometimes act, too, as assistant secretaries of conventions.

Aside from their committee work and their duty of voting upon nominations and resolutions, women delegates usually confine their activity to questions directly concerning their sex. A woman rarely either nominates or seconds the nomination of a man, except in some cases where the man has shown himself unusually favorable to women in politics. The nominating speech, indeed, is usually made by a man even when a woman is nominated for an office, though women turn out in force to second the nomination of a woman, one after another making brief speeches in honor of the candidate. In the Democratic State Convention of 1906 the chairman declared it his rule to recognize the ladies first, and no man could gain recognition while a woman was on her feet.

D. Attitude of Men Toward Women Politicians

In regard to the attitude of men toward women politicians or women who are doing active political work, two points come up for consideration. First is the question as to whether men are courteous to women or, as has been sometimes asserted, endeavor to "snub them out of politics." Public opinion upon this point is summarized in Table III. Of those who said that men are courteous to women, 20 men and 42 women who believed in equal suffrage, 13 men and 11 women who did not believe in equal suffrage, and 6 men and 4 women who were indifferent on this point—in all 39 men and 57 women—testified that, though courteous, men do not wish women in politics. This was probably, also, the opinion of others, though they did not definitely so state. Many gave answers, however, similar to this: "Courteous. It would be

TABLE III

Question—Are men usually courteous to women, or do they show a disposition to snub women out of politics?

	Courteous Men	Courteous Women	Not courteous Men	Not courteous Women	No definite answer Men	No definite answer Women
I. Favorable to Equal Suffrage						
A. State officials	25	46			7	3
B. Political workers—state	35	100		2	1	2
C. Other citizens—state	218	83	1	2	23	10
D. Delegates—Denver	15	136	1	2	3	21
E. Prominent citizens—Denver	8	13	2	2	1	
Total	301	378	4	8	35	36
Per cent	88.5	89.6	1.2	1.9	10.3	8.5
II. Unfavorable to Equal Suffrage						
A. State officials	10	3	1		1	1
B. Political workers—state	24	13	1	1		2
C. Other citizens—state	73	12	9	5	38	2
D. Delegates—Denver	16	34	3	7	3	9
E. Prominent citizens—Denver	3	1				
Total	126	63	14	13	42	14
Per cent	69.2	70	7.7	14.4	23.1	15.6
III. Indifferent to Equal Suffrage						
A. State officials	10	1			3	4
B. Political workers—state	7	13			18	3
C. Other citizens—state	44	15	1	1	18	8
D. Delegates—Denver	2	20		3	5	5
E. Prominent citizens—Denver	4					
Total	67	49	1	4	26	20
Per cent	71.3	67.1	1.1	5.5	27.6	27.4
Grand total	494	490	19	25	103	70
Grand per cent	80.2	83.7	3.1	4.3	16.7	12

death to a man's political ambition to be otherwise."

The men and women agreed surprisingly well upon this subject, a very large majority declaring that men are courteous. Of course, all men in politics are not polished gentlemen, and women sometimes, by an aggressive attitude, invite an "equal plane" treatment which could be interpreted as discourtesy. But evidently Colorado men, upon the whole, have behaved very well under their new political problems, for only 3.1 per cent. of their own sex and 4.3 per cent. of the women found anything of which to complain. Moreover, less than 2 per cent. of the women who believed in equal suffrage made complaint on this score. It is safe, therefore, to say that direct discourtesy is rare.

Naturally, however, if a woman does not do what the "boss" wishes, he will endeavor to prevent her from exercising political power, just as he would if she were a man. Resentment of this fact probably accounts for the answers of some of the women who state that the men try to "snub" women out of politics. This, however, is not a sex question—even when, as was done in one town at the spring election of 1907, the "wet" party more or less openly declared that "women ought to stay at home and wash dishes." Another kind of contradictory, improbable statement of prejudice is illustrated by the following answer: "Since men have found they cannot count on women voting with their party unless a good and chivalrous candidate is put up, they snub them."

Though several persons asserted that men are not as courteous to women as formerly, using such expressions as "a veneer of courtesy, but not of the old, chivalric kind," it seems doubtful whether such a testimonial to man's treatment of woman as appears in the table could be obtained for the non-suffrage states or for other relationships of life. Are men courteous to their wives? Are they courteous to their stenographers? Ask practically any similar question concerning any class of women, except their sweethearts and women whom they meet at "parties"—ask it of all classes of society. Surely men may be highly congratulated if not five per cent. of the answers are unfavorable. One of the prominent women politicians said: "I find men just as courteous to women in the states where women vote as in other states, and they seem to value the opinion of the women in Colorado more than in New England."

The second question relates to the source of strength of women politicians, whether among men or among women. On this point the testimony, as shown in Table IV, was fairly evenly divided between, "Among Women," "Among Both," and "Among Men." About forty answers were to the effect that women politicians have little or no strength, and as many as fifty persons outside of Denver said that there were either no women politicians in their locality, or too few to justify generalization. The latter localities included Boulder, Delta, Huerfano, La Plata, Las Animas, San Miguel, and Weld counties. Women recognized as politicians are, apparently, little in evidence in any of the counties under special investigation except Denver and Teller.

The question is, of course, general, and does not distinguish between the different kinds of political work done by women. But whether their strength is among men or women obviously depends upon

EQUAL SUFFRAGE

TABLE IV

Question—Is the source of strength of women politicians usually among men or among women?

	Among women		Among both		Among men		No definite answer	
	Men	Women	Men	Women	Men	Women	Men	Women
I. Favorable to Equal Suffrage								
A. State officials	9	7	9	13	10	17	4	12
B. Political workers—state	13	30	3	24	9	16	11	34
C. Other citizens—state	70	25	54	18	56	15	62	37
D. Delegates—Denver	6	37	2	41	4	38	7	43
E. Prominent citizens—Denver	7	6	2	4		4	2	1
Total	105	105	70	100	79	90	86	127
Per cent	30.9	24.9	20.6	23.7	23.2	21.3	25.3	30.1
II. Unfavorable to Equal Suffrage								
A. State officials	7		1		3		1	4
B. Political workers—state	9	5	2	2	10	5	4	4
C. Other citizens—state	33	4	8		32	8	47	7
D. Delegates—Denver	7	14	1	1	8	14	6	21
E. Prominent citizens—Denver	1					1	2	
Total	57	23	12	3	53	28	60	36
Per cent	31.3	25.6	6.6	3.3	29.2	31.1	32.9	40
III. Indifferent to Equal Suffrage								
A. State officials	4	3	2		3		4	2
B. Political workers—state	2	3		1	1	8	4	4
C. Other citizens—state	12	3	6	3	11	5	34	13
D. Delegates—Denver		3	1	4	2	4	4	17
E. Prominent citizens—Denver	3						1	
Total	21	12	9	8	17	17	47	36
Per cent	22.3	16.4	9.6	11	18.1	23.3	50	49.3
Grand total	183	140	91	111	149	135	193	199
Grand per cent	29.6	24	14.7	18.9	24.2	23.1	31.5	34

personal qualities, and apparently the "woman's woman" is nearly if not quite as often found in politics as the "man's woman." As one of the women county superintendents said: "Some women influence women and some influence men; some men influence women and some influence men; equally divided." Evidently, however, as another well-informed woman said: "The source of strength of women politicians must be among men primarily, for the men have the power to give." She added, in regard to a woman of the opposite party: "Mrs. ——— was at first said by the women to be a man's woman, and this was held against her, but she stood up for the interests of the women and was able to win her points with the men, because she was popular with them. By her popularity with the men she won for the women representation on the state central committee."

E. Effect on Choice of Candidates

One of the most frequently mentioned benefits of equal suffrage is its effect on the selection of candidates for office. Though Table V does not show a very decisive public opinion upon this question, many well-informed people agreed with a wise woman of wide political experience who said: "It has exerted a good influence in many instances, though not always. The known immorality of a candidate is more of a bar to his success than formerly." Another prominent Denver woman added: "Generally better men morally; not always more efficient." The morality that is affected is not, indeed, political, but personal. A man

EQUAL SUFFRAGE

TABLE V

Question — What has been the effect of equal suffrage on the selection of candidates?

	Good effect		No effect[1]		No definite answer	
	Men	Women	Men	Women	Men	Women
I. Favorable to Equal Suffrage						
A. State officials	13	30	16	8	3	11
B. Political workers—state	17	66	12	19	7	19
C. Other citizens—state	104	44	81	8	57	43
D. Delegates—Denver	9	67	5	40	5	52
E. Prominent citizens—Denver	7	9	3	5	1	1
Total	150	216	117	80	73	126
Per cent	44.1	51.2	34.4	18.9	21.5	29.9
II. Unfavorable to Equal Suffrage						
A. State officials	2		8	3	2	1
B. Political workers—state	1	3	20	10	4	3
C. Other citizens—state	6	1	74	8	40	10
D. Delegates—Denver		5	20	33	2	12
E. Prominent citizens—Denver		1	3			
Total	9	10	125	54	48	26
Per cent	4.9	11.1	68.7	60	26.4	28.8
III. Indifferent to Equal Suffrage						
A. State officials	2	1	9	2	2	2
B. Political workers—state		6	4	8	3	2
C. Other citizens—state	7	3	25	4	31	17
D. Delegates—Denver		4	4	11	3	13
E. Prominent citizens—Denver	1		2		1	
Total	10	14	44	25	40	34
Per cent	10.6	19.2	46.8	34.2	42.6	46.6
Grand total	169	240	286	159	161	186
Grand per cent	27.4	41	46.4	27.2	26.2	31.8

[1] Seven persons classified as saying that equal suffrage has had no effect seem to have believed that, in one way or another, its effect has been bad.

of unclean private life is rarely nominated for office in Colorado, because politicians generally agree that, on account of the woman vote, such a man is a source of weakness to the ticket.

Women, however, when it comes to a contest in which sex lines are drawn, are more easily than men deceived and hoodwinked in regard to candidates. On one occasion the women delegates to a convention, after a long day's session, went home late in the evening in fancied security, and, as soon as they were gone, the men proceeded to nominate a candidate to whom they objected. It is, indeed, rather the fear of the woman's vote at the polls than the fear of her vote in the convention that affects the nomination of candidates. A county chairman said: "Do not see any difference in the selection of candidates, but do see a difference in the election." But doubtless, if he has the interests of his party at heart, this same chairman sees to it that the type of man who cannot be elected is not selected.

There can be no doubt but that in many communities men of notoriously unclean lives and men connected with saloons have been dropped from politics since women voted. A few experiences in which the names of such men were scratched from the party ticket by large numbers of women voters were sufficient to effect this reformation. As one woman from a mountain town puts it: "Before equal suffrage this mining-camp was governed almost wholly by the saloon element. Now it is almost impossible to elect a saloon man to office."

Outside of the question of personal morality and relation to the liquor business, however, women take little interest in the character of candidates. The majority of persons who gave any reason for their belief that equal suffrage has had a good effect upon the selection of candidates spoke of the standard of personal morality as improved, but not a dozen even so much as mentioned the standard of ability, business honesty, and public honor. Many persons, both men and women, complained that women have nothing to do with the selection of candidates, and five said that a woman's judgment is poor on this point. A prominent Denver man asserted that "women are known to work for the election of their friends, rather than for the best candidates"; and a woman from a small town, who had had no political experience, voiced the time-worn opinion that woman is prone to consult her heart rather than her head. Except for this one case, however, the answers to the question gave no evidence of even a suspicion on the part of either sex that woman's more emotional and impulsive nature has had any ill effect on the selection of candidates for public office. The conclusion is therefore unavoidable that, while women have often caused men of clean personal lives, not connected with the saloon or gambling interests, to be nominated in preference to men of notorious immorality, equal suffrage has had no effect whatever upon the other qualities required of candidates for public office.

F. Effect on the "Slate"

Closely related to the question of candidates is that of the effect of equal suffrage on the "slate," or the set of candidates agreed upon by the party managers. The answers to the question concerning the making and breaking of the slate at political conventions were especially difficult to classify. In many cases it was not

PARTY MACHINERY

possible to tell definitely from the answer whether the effect was considered good or bad, though doubtless in most instances the former was meant. A large proportion, however, of all the persons who answered the question-blank, 55 per cent. of the men and 33.7 per cent. of the women, believed that equal suffrage has had no effect upon the making or breaking of the slate. Nearly 17 per cent. of the women, and nearly 10 per cent. of the men believed that women have some influence over the slate. But 49.6 per cent. of the women and 35.4 per cent. of the men gave no definite answer. The question, however, was ambiguous, and a considerable number of answers could be classified only as "Indefinite." Nine men and four women answered that women have the same influence as men over the making and breaking of the slate.

In truth, the influence of women on this point, as on the previous ones relating to political conventions, depends upon local conditions, the number of women at the convention, their interest and ability as compared with that of men, the attitude of men toward them, and other factors. But the consensus of opinion that women generally have more influence over the choice of candidates than over the slate tends to the conclusion that their influence over the choice of candidates is not direct, through their representation at conventions, but is, as before stated, indirect, through the desire of the party leaders not to alienate their votes. As one woman said, women, when they do not like the slate, have a remedy in their ability to scratch the ticket, and this they use freely.

There is convincing testimony in the answers to these questions, as well as to others, to the effect that women, more often than men, vote split tickets. For instance, a Weld County man said: " In small communities they have been known to aid materially in breaking a slate by their votes. In the recent municipal election at this place there was a case in evidence when a candidate for mayor on the only regular ticket was defeated by writing another's name on the ballot."

G. Women Candidates

There is some unwillingness manifested by men toward allowing women to be nominated for any political office except for state and county superintendent of schools and for certain offices in small towns where the salary is no object. Women have also been nominated and sometimes elected county or city clerk or treasurer.[1] This unwillingness is due to two causes—first, the feeling that men are needed in the positions, and, second, the idea that the paying jobs should by rights go to men, who normally provide for women.

The office of county superintendent, however, in many counties is given to a woman as a matter of course, and the tendency is to take this office out of politics. In many of the smaller counties, indeed, the candidate for county superintendent does not need to be a politician in order to win. This office has for years been filled by a woman in a number of localities where women take little or no part in politics except to vote. Some of the women county superintendents, according to their own assertions, have never so much as attended a political convention as spectators. Originally the concession of this office was made to the women voters, but it seems gradually to have become simply a recognition of woman's peculiar interest in all matters pertaining to education.

[1] See chap. iv, sections 4 and 5.

PARTY MACHINERY

When one political party nominates a woman for county superintendent the opposing party usually finds it a wise policy to follow the example, though this is not invariably the case, for women voters do not always stand by a woman candidate.[1] Personality is a more important factor than sex, and party more important than either. In 1906, however, out of twenty-six counties from which it was possible to obtain information, six had men candidates for county superintendent on both tickets, fifteen had women candidates on both tickets, and in only five cases did a woman run against a man. In two of these cases the women, and in three the men, were successful.

It is often said that, if the suffrage is really equal, sex should not be considered as a point either for or against a candidate for public office. One prominent woman from outside of Denver went so far as to say: "Women do not distinguish as to sex in my party or the others to my knowledge. The strongest candidates in the judgment of the party in convention are nominated. The candidates are supposed to represent the party and stand upon its platform, not to represent a sex." Although women voters probably do not hold as closely to sex as to party lines, and although the strongest candidate, in the opinion of the convention, is doubtless nominated, nevertheless in practice sex is taken into consideration as one of the elements of strength or weakness, and women therefore become, politically, another "interest" to be represented or conciliated. Sex, however, is merely one of numerous interests, most of which women

[1] For the vote for women candidates, see chap. iii, section 7.

share with men, and these other interests induce the majority of women to affiliate with men on party lines. There is a tendency, especially evident in nominating candidates for the State Legislature, to consider the sex interest less than was done in the early years of equal suffrage, and as a result it seems to be increasingly difficult for women to obtain these nominations.

As for the method of nominating the woman candidate, the answers to the question, "Do the women agree on their candidates for offices conceded to them by the men, and, if so, will the men accept their candidates?" were decidedly unsatisfactory. The question was ambiguous and misunderstood or not understood at all by many. Nevertheless, the general opinion seemed to be that women, either in convention caucuses, or in their local organizations, social, literary, or political clubs, agree upon candidates conceded to them, and that the men accept their choice. Of all the men answering the blank, 27.6 per cent., and of all the women, 29.4 per cent., gave this opinion. About 14 per cent. of all the men and 10 per cent. of all the women, principally those from outside of Denver, believed that the men select the candidate without consulting the women, and about 12 per cent. of the men and 10 per cent. of the women asserted that women find it impossible to agree. One man said: "My observation is that they have about as much trouble reaching an agreement as to their candidates as do the men. There is quite a little human nature in both." Under 3 per cent. of each sex testified that women agree, but the men do not accept their candidate. A prominent Denver woman said: "If a woman must be chosen, I think the men are glad to have the women settle their difficulties among themselves." But nearly half, 44.3 per cent. of the men and 46.5 per cent. of the women who answered

PARTY MACHINERY

the blank, gave no definite reply to this particular question.

In the majority of counties, where no women or less than half a dozen are present in conventions, the plan usually followed is described by one of the county chairmen as follows: "Generally a candidate, whether man or woman, is discussed and approved by the party workers as such without leaving it to either sex alone." But in the Denver conventions the women hold separate caucuses to settle upon their candidates and their policy.

One Denver woman gave the following facts in regard to the choosing of candidates: "The women of the Democratic Party (to which I belong) meet and select their women candidates and nominate them from the floor of the convention. They must take their chances with the men. In last fall's election four women were chosen in this way for the lower house of the legislature; some twenty-three nominations were made from the floor of the convention, including men and women, and eleven delegates were chosen from the twenty-three, three of whom were women." It should be added that at this convention the women made a vigorous but unsuccessful effort to have their four candidates nominated by acclamation before the other candidates were voted upon. One man, in supporting their proposition, said that "caucuses name candidates—caucuses in which no woman is allowed to raise her voice."

The Democratic County Convention of Denver in 1906 was nearly unanimous in the choice of county superintendent. But in the State Convention the women did not agree so well. In fact, the contest for the superintendency of public instruction was three-cornered, and one of the hottest of the convention. Of this contest a prominent woman delegate said: "In the State Convention the women were divided on state superintendent and the men nominated the younger, prettier woman." In the Republican

EQUAL SUFFRAGE

County Convention of 1906, in Denver, the candidate for county superintendent favored by the women's political clubs was presented too late in the day, after the slate had been made up by the men, and was consequently defeated in the convention. At the Republican State Convention the slate candidate for state superintendent had no real opposition, though there was abundant grumbling from the women of the faction opposed to the slate.

H. EFFECT ON THE PLATFORM

Upon the platform adopted, according to Table VI, equal suffrage has had considerably less influence than upon the candidates selected. A prominent Denver woman said that women "can get planks inserted if they desire," and this is doubtless true, provided they make sufficient effort and their plank does not arouse strong opposition on the part of the men. As a general rule, however, neither men nor women take much interest in the platform, and there has been no very good reason why equal suffrage should have had, on ordinary occasions, any special influence. Women have sometimes aided the adoption of humanitarian and other reform planks in the state platforms, but the results along this line can best be studied under the subject of legislation.[1]

In the framing of local platforms women usually give strong support to the temperance cause, and doubtless often influence local conventions to adopt anti-saloon planks.[2] A number of persons complained that, though certain planks are put in platforms to catch the woman vote, just as others are put in to

[1] See chap. vi, section 2. [2] See chap. vi, section 3.

PARTY MACHINERY

TABLE VI

Question — What has been the effect of equal suffrage on the platform adopted?

	Good effect Men	Good effect Women	No effect[1] Men	No effect[1] Women	No definite answer Men	No definite answer Women
I. Favorable to Equal Suffrage						
A. State officials	7	17	19	13	6	19
B. Political workers—state	9	47	19	21	8	36
C. Other citizens—state	69	23	93	14	80	58
D. Delegates—Denver	5	47	8	42	6	70
E. Prominent citizens—Denver	5	7	4	6	2	2
Total	95	141	143	96	102	185
Per cent	27.9	33.4	42.1	22.7	30	43.9
II. Unfavorable to Equal Suffrage						
A. State officials	2		8	3	2	1
B. Political workers—state		4	20	10	5	2
C. Other citizens—state	5	1	73	6	42	12
D. Delegates—Denver	2	1	15	35	5	14
E. Prominent citizens—Denver		1	3			
Total	9	7	119	54	54	29
Per cent	4.9	7.8	65.4	60	29.7	32.2
III. Indifferent to Equal Suffrage						
A. State officials	1	1	8	2	4	2
B. Political workers—state		4	5	3	2	9
C. Other citizens—state	4	1	27	5	32	18
D. Delegates—Denver			4	13	3	15
E. Prominent citizens—Denver	2		2			
Total	7	6	46	23	41	44
Per cent	7.5	8.2	48.9	31.5	43.6	60.3
Grand total	111	154	308	173	197	258
Grand per cent	18	26.4	50	29.5	32	44.1

[1] Two county chairmen who were opposed to equal suffrage, here classified, stated that they believed its effect has been bad.

catch the votes of the church people, they are entirely disregarded after election. "This is a condition, and not a theory."[1]

Upon the whole, however, the effect of equal suffrage upon the actual work of political conventions has been slight. Drunkenness, profanity, and even occasional fistic encounters still occur, and many men smoke and wear their hats in the presence of women delegates. In short, men act much as they would at home if there was some unusual cause of excitement. Those who are gentlemen at home are so at political conventions, and those who are the reverse are not made over by the refining influence of the "woman delegate." The "woman delegate," indeed, is often little more than a figure-head, just as is the man who is not in the "inner circle." One woman delegate who believed in equal suffrage said that the men "have it fixed up," and there is "no use in 'bucking' at conventions for those who do don't get a chance to go again." Another woman, who did not believe in equal suffrage, said: "I went as a delegate to the last convention and sat there like all the rest, as a dummy, while this one was nominated

---

[1] Only two persons who replied to the question under consideration thought that the effect of equal suffrage on political platforms has been bad, and these were both county chairmen who were opposed to equal suffrage. One of them said: "Women's influence occasionally causes the adoption of certain planks, sometimes to the detriment of the party." The other answered: "It has produced more freak expressions and the catering to impractical policies." Weighed against the opinions of the one hundred and eleven men, not to mention the one hundred and fifty-five women, who said equal suffrage has had a good effect, these two unfavorable opinions sound decidedly weak.

and that one seconded—all in favor say 'yes.' No one got a chance."

3. Political Committees

Under this title must be considered the activity of women as compared with that of men in the permanent state, county, and city organizations which carry on the official party work. There is within each party a representative system, each grade of which rests upon the grade below until "the people" are reached. At the top stands the chairman of the State Central Committee, and from him the organization spreads downward to the party caucus of the individual precinct in which the local committee man is elected. The work at the top is primarily executive, while at the bottom good "hustlers" are needed to canvass the precinct and to see that the voters are brought to the polls on election day. Leaving this last part of the work for Section 6, consideration will now be given to the representation of women upon state and county central committees, and the general verdict of public opinion upon their efficiency as precinct committee women and in the canvassing of precincts.

For their representation at conventions women have always competed side by side with men, and have not asked for any special system to aid them in securing their fair proportion of delegates. But a different plan has prevailed in the case of state committees and—in Arapahoe County, at least—of county committees, on which women have been far more in danger of securing no recognition whatever. From the beginning of equal suffrage the Populist Party organized its committees upon the basis of one man and one woman from each representative district, whether county or precinct, but in the other parties women have been obliged to bring pressure to bear to secure this dual system of representation.

Trouble early arose on this subject in the Republican Party of Arapahoe County. When women first came into politics, in 1894, the Republican State Central Committee was reorganized to admit one woman as well as one man from each county. The state committee then proceeded to appoint as members of the Arapahoe County Republican Central Committee one woman from each precinct. The county committee refused to admit these women. The latter promptly joined with the Business Men's League in a fight at the primaries upon the committee. The reports of the result are conflicting, but the upshot was that the women perfected a complete organization auxiliary to that of the men.

In 1900 there were 19 women and 175 men members of the Arapahoe County Central Committee of the Republican Party, all regularly elected as the only representatives of their precincts. But two or three years later this plan was changed to the present dual system under which each committee man selects a committee woman for his precinct. Since 1894 it has been the custom for the Republican County Chairman of Arapahoe County to appoint a woman as vice-chairman—the woman usually being selected by the Republican women's clubs.

The history of the Democratic Party in the matter

PARTY MACHINERY

of women on its committees has been quite different. When women were first enfranchised, this party was weak, and struggling, on the one hand, against Populism, and, on the other hand, against Republicanism. Partly, doubtless, as a result of these early difficulties and the greater necessity for patient loyalty, the women of the Democratic Party did not secure equal representation with the men upon committees until the fall of 1906. Another reason for this, perhaps, was that the Democratic Party was originally less favorable to equal suffrage than the others, and consequently expected less aid from the women. In the fall of 1906 the matter was brought up, first in the Denver City and County Convention, and later in the State Convention, and it was settled that women should have the same representation as men upon the central committee. The Democrats, moreover, elect their committee women in the same way as their committee men, instead of having the woman appointed by the man, as in the Republican Party. This measure was carried, however, against considerable opposition. Before its adoption at the county convention there had been only one woman member of the county central committee.

At the present time, then, the State Central Committee and the Denver County Central Committee of both parties are composed of an equal number of men and women, one of each sex from each representative district, with a man for chairman and a woman for vice-chairman. This plan is in use in several other counties, but is not by any means general in either party. The usual scheme of organization provides for only one representative for each precinct, and this representative is generally a man. In El Paso County, including Colorado Springs, the Republican County Central Committee in 1906 was composed of two women and about twenty-two men. Most of the other counties, with the exception of Pueblo, had no women upon the local central committee of either party.

One of the questions upon the blank sent out to political workers and others related to the greater or less efficiency of women as members of these committees. In the summary of the answers to this question in Table VII, there is evident a wide divergence of opinion between the men and the women, the largest number of men believing that women are less efficient, and the largest number of women believing that they are more efficient. There are, also, disparities in opinion which seem to be due in part to prejudice for or against equal suffrage. In every case the largest proportion of women thought them more efficient, but among the women who were indifferent to equal suffrage a much higher proportion believed them less efficient than among the women who believed in equal suffrage. Precisely the same difference is observable among the men.

Considering separately each of the eight counties under special investigation, outside of Denver, it was found that, except in San Miguel, Teller, and Weld counties, where women seem to be considered particularly inefficient, the proportions did not differ widely from those for the state as a whole. But from all these counties the testimony was that women rarely serve upon the central

TABLE VII

Question—Are women more or less efficient than men as committee women?

	More Men	More Women	Same Men	Same Women	Less Men	Less Women	No definite answer Men	No definite answer Women
I Favorable to Equal Suffrage								
A. State officials	7	4	8	22	8	13	9	10
B. Political workers—state	4	22	9	42	13	19	10	21
C. Other citizens—state	39	23	59	17	62	13	82	42
D. Delegates—Denver	4	100	5	36	6	8	4	15
E. Prominent citizens—Denver	4	7	5	4	1		1	4
Total	58	156	86	121	90	53	106	92
Per cent	17.1	34.6	25.3	28.6	26.4	12.7	31.2	24.1
II. Unfavorable to Equal Suffrage								
A. State officials	1	1	2	1	6	1	3	1
B. Political workers—state		4	5	3	14	8	6	1
C. Other citizens—state	10	3	17	4	55	4	38	8
D. Delegates—Denver	3	18	6	15	10	6	3	11
E. Prominent citizens—Denver		1	1		2			
Total	14	27	31	23	87	19	50	21
Per cent	7.7	30	17	25.6	47.8	21.1	27.5	23.3
III. Indifferent to Equal Suffrage								
A. State officials	1		3		5	2	4	3
B. Political workers—state		3	1	2	4	6	2	5
C. Other citizens—state	2	2	10	4	22	3	29	15
D. Delegates—Denver	2	13		8	2	3	3	4
E. Prominent citizens—Denver	3		1					
Total	8	18	15	14	33	14	38	27
Per cent	8.5	24.6	16	19.2	35.1	19.2	40.4	37
Grand total	80	201	132	158	210	86	194	140
Grand per cent	13	34.1	21.4	27.1	34.1	14.9	31.5	23.9

committees. A man from Boulder County said: "I do not think any ever served in Longmont." A Delta County man replied: "We see so little of their work along these lines in here it would be impossible to say." Three Huerfano County men gave answers similar to the following: "Never knew of a committee woman." A La Plata County man stated: "It is a number of years since we have had a woman on a political committee." Two Las Animas men said: "Have never tried them." Three persons from San Miguel County asserted: "There are none here." And three Weld County persons testified substantially as follows: "Women have not been on committees here but twice since woman suffrage that I know of, and that is years ago."

Many answers declared that it depends on the individual whether men or women are more efficient, and this is obviously true, though it begs the question. A few said that those women who take part are better than the average man, but that few take part. Many gave lack of experience as a cause of less efficiency on the part of women, while several gave answers similar to the following, from a member of the State Legislature who believed in equal suffrage: "They seem to have less executive ability; otherwise I believe they are more careful in what they do." One prominent Denver woman said: "Less. A committee man can work at all hours, a woman generally only during certain daytime hours." A Denver woman delegate to a political convention complained: "They are more effective and efficient as workers in any department of political work than men, but women do the work and the men get the money and position nine times out of ten." Some persons said that

PARTY MACHINERY

women do not attend the committee meetings as regularly as do men, while others said they attend more promptly and more regularly. Evidently this, too, depends on the woman, but it doubtless also depends upon the number of women on the committee, and whether or not they are made to feel as if they are "freaks."

The first experience of women in the canvassing of votes was before the spring city elections of 1894, but since that time a large part of this work has been done by them. The opinion prevailed among both sexes, according to Table VIII, that women are more efficient than men at this work. Of the men, 35.4 per cent., and of the women, 53.6 per cent., gave this answer.[1] Only 16.2 per cent. of the men and 5.5 per cent. of the women considered them less efficient. About half of the remaining answers were to the effect that men and women are equally efficient, and the other half were indefinite. Canvassing is paid work, and in many localities it is the custom to appoint as canvassers, and also as election officers, needy widows with children to support, seamstresses, or laundresses, to whom the $3.00 to $5.00 a day so easily earned about election time is a welcome addition to an uncertain income. One milliner, for example, said she was committee woman for a number of years until her business demanded her whole time.

In the larger places, such as Denver and Pueblo, the work of canvassing is almost wholly given over

[1] This percentage is based, as in all cases, on the total number of answers to the blank, whether or not a definite answer was given to this particular question.

to women; but in the smaller rural and mining communities, such as Delta, Huerfano, San Miguel, and Weld counties, women are rarely or never employed. In Boulder, La Plata, and Las Animas counties, however, they do a large part of the work, while in Teller County one woman asserted that they are employed almost entirely. In short, the evidence appears to prove that, where the size of the community justifies canvassing in any systematic way, women are employed in somewhat larger numbers than men.

The efficiency of women in this work depends, not merely upon their personal characteristics, but also upon the character of the district to be canvassed. In residence precincts it is often found that it is easier for women than for men to get into the houses. There is, however, some complaint, especially from small towns. As a Weld County man put it: "They are not less efficient than men, but they cannot make a success among their sisters because of social distinctions. If the canvasser does not belong to the same social clique as the women on whom she calls, she is at once squelched and probably has all kinds of bad things said about her, not by the men, but by the women she calls on, not in the same clique." A Boulder woman of some political experience gave another view: "They are really better, for they love to get into a house that they have never been in and find out all they can, political and otherwise."

A Denver woman who was opposed to equal suffrage added another side-light when she said: "The women are more thorough. Men hurry through and get the money, thinking it won't be known." But women, too, are, of course, after the money. A prominent Denver politician thought there was not a woman working in Colorado politics who was not paid for it in one way or another, but

PARTY MACHINERY

TABLE VIII

Question — Are women more or less efficient than men in the canvassing of precincts?

	More Men	More Women	Same Men	Same Women	Less Men	Less Women	No definite answer Men	No definite answer Women
I. Favorable to Equal Suffrage								
A. State officials	11	21	14	12	1	7	6	9
B. Political workers—state	12	48	10	39	8	5	6	12
C. Other citizens—state	101	33	51	15	25	8	65	39
D. Delegates—Denver	14	124	3	17	1	1	1	17
E. Prominent citizens—Denver	7	10	3	4			1	1
Total	145	236	81	87	35	21	79	78
Per cent	42.7	55.9	23.8	20.6	10.3	5	23.2	18.5
II. Unfavorable to Equal Suffrage								
A. State officials	3		3	2	4	1	2	1
B. Political workers—state	9	6	6	6	7	4	3	
C. Other citizens—state	30	5	26	6	31	1	33	7
D. Delegates—Denver	8	32	5	7	5	2	4	9
E. Prominent citizens—Denver		1			3			
Total	50	44	40	21	50	8	42	17
Per cent	27.5	48.9	21.9	23.3	27.5	8.9	23.1	18.9
III. Indifferent to Equal Suffrage								
A. State officials	4	1	5		1	1	3	3
B. Political workers—state	1	9	1	1	3	2	2	4
C. Other citizens—state	11	8	12	1	11		29	15
D. Delegates—Denver	4	16	1	7			2	5
E. Prominent citizens—Denver	3		1					
Total	23	34	20	9	15	3	36	27
Per cent	24.5	46.6	21.2	12.3	16	4.1	38.3	37
Grand total	218	314	141	117	100	32	157	122
Grand per cent	35.4	53.6	22.9	20	16.2	5.5	25.5	20.9

this is undoubtedly a somewhat exaggerated statement, and, with the modifications which would make it true, would be quite as applicable to men.

4. WOMEN'S POLITICAL CLUBS

As soon as the women of Colorado received the ballot they began to form political clubs, separate and distinct from the men's clubs, to which they have never asked admission. These clubs, though unofficial, are strong factors in a political campaign. In their private meetings the members discuss legislation, questions of representation, and other matters affecting the interests of women, but their most conspicuous work is the holding of receptions and rallies for candidates, at most of which men, as well as women, are invited to speak to an audience composed of both sexes.

In the smaller towns there is usually only one club of each party, often including members from all parts of the county, but in the cities it is customary to have, in addition to one large general club, a smaller local organization of the women in each district or ward. Sometimes a large club is formed in a geographical section of the city including several wards. These organizations are naturally most active during political campaigns, and many of them fall to pieces after election, especially if their party is defeated. But many have lived on for years, holding more or less regular meetings, with a more or less fluctuating membership.

The Populist women organized clubs in some places

PARTY MACHINERY

even before they were enfranchised, and in February, 1894, formed the Women's Industrial League. This was a secret order, with branches throughout the state, the most important of which was the Woman's Populist League of Denver. The organization continued in the field until the decline of Populism.

The Colorado Women's Democratic Club was organized in May, 1894, and, owing to the split in the party, was recognized by the National Committee as the only straight Democratic organization in the state. One of its charter members was appointed organizer, and formed twelve women's clubs in as many different towns. An editorial in the *Rocky Mountain News*, August 26, 1894, asserted that whatever there might be of harmony in the Democratic Party belonged to the new voters, who were not in politics for the spoils of office; and in September this club of women was largely instrumental, through its intermediate position, in bringing the two factions of the party together in one state convention.

In June, 1894, the annual convention of the National Republican League Clubs was held at Denver, and this seems to have furnished the incentive for the organization of the Republican women. A woman was put in charge of that work, under the direction of the State Central Committee, and Women's Republican Leagues were established in many towns throughout the state and in every district in Denver. The two most powerful organizations in Denver were the East Capitol Hill Women's Republican League, which at one time had a membership of one thousand, and the East Denver Women's Republican

EQUAL SUFFRAGE

Club. During the fall campaign of 1894 several large mass-meetings for both sexes were conducted by these clubs.

At first organized along strictly party lines, the women, because of the lessons learned during this campaign, created considerable feeling in favor of non-partisan politics, and in the spring of 1895 the Civic Federation was formed. This was a non-partisan association of women which at first confined its direct political activity to endorsing candidates for nomination for city offices and for the State Legislature, with the idea of securing a clean city government and the passage of legislation desired by women. It was fairly successful, and in the spring of 1897 formed a union with the Taxpayers' Party, composed of men, and with other similar organizations, which nominated and elected a non-partisan ticket. The ensuing administration was one of the best Denver has ever had, though it failed to fulfil the high expectations of many of the enthusiasts. After one or two less successful elections, however, the Civic Federation languished and died. But one of its outgrowths was the Educational Alliance, which for several years aided materially in electing women to the school-board and keeping that board free from partisan politics.

By 1900 most of the women had returned to party lines. The Woman's Democratic Club of Colorado claimed in that year a membership of 10,000. The principal local organization was the Woman's Bryan Club of Denver, though there were many others scattered through the state. The Woman's Bryan Club was said, in November, 1900, to have two thousand registered members,[1] and its "Silver Rally" at the Broadway Theatre, in Denver, a few nights before election, was called the largest audience of women voters ever assembled in Colorado.[2] In addition to rallies, many receptions and parlor meetings were held by the Democratic women throughout the campaign.

The Woman's Republican League of Colorado, perhaps the largest and most powerful political organization of women that has ever existed in the state, was formed in 1900. Branches of this league were soon organized in every district of Denver and in every part of the state, including the towns of Rocky Ford, Longmont, Delta, Victor, Silverton, Akron, La Junta, Colorado City, Boulder, Glenwood Springs, Cripple Creek, Silver Cliff, Montrose, and Golden. The *Denver Republican* of October 1, 1900, says that never before had the women taken such a lively interest in politics as in that year, and that they no longer treated the subject "with the disrespect that arose when the right was first given them." Many receptions and rallies were held during the course of the campaign, including a reception to Senator and Mrs. Lodge. The activity of the league is further evidenced by the fact that in one week it announced nine different meetings to be held under its auspices.[3] This organization held its power until the fall of 1902, when it went to pieces as the result of trouble with the new state chairman, who superseded the president

---

[1] *Rocky Mountain News*, November 2, 1900.
[2] *Ibid.*, November 3, 1900.
[3] Appendix B gives some of the circulars issued by the Woman's Republican League to women voters.

of the league by appointing a woman vice-chairman of the State Central Committee, to whom he gave charge of the work among women. This led to a change in method, but the women's Republican clubs continued their successful work.

In the fall of 1906 there was a Woman's Republican Club of Colorado and women's Republican clubs in every ward in Denver, as well as in many of the smaller towns. A Colored Woman's Republican Club, which was organized in 1901, gave occasional rallies, with both white and colored speakers of both sexes. There was also an Italian Women's Republican Club with about forty members, a Swedish-American club with about sixty members, and a German club. The oldest political organization of women then existing in the state was the Woman's Eagle Republican Club, which was founded in Denver in 1896, and incorporated in 1897.

The most important of the Democratic women's organizations in 1906 was the Jane Jefferson Club, which was founded about 1898. The Democratic women, apparently, do not pay as much attention to local precinct organizations as do the Republican, but concentrate all their efforts upon the one large club.

During the campaign of 1906 these clubs all held rallies, receptions, or parlor meetings. Usually there were two or three speakers, more often men than women, and at the close refreshments and a social hour were enjoyed. Music, too, was often added to the programmes, and sometimes a dance or a lawn-party was given by a political club. The meetings were generally held in the evenings, and were attended by nearly as many men as women, not to mention the children.

Outside of Denver, in 1906, the political woman's club movement was decidedly weak. Except in Pueblo, Colorado Springs, Cripple Creek, and possibly one or two other places, indeed, it has been found impossible to hold these organizations together from one election to another. As a result, even the Republicans have practically given up their original idea of forming permanent organizations in the small places. In this attempt, however, the women were trying to effect a far more thorough political organization than the men maintain, and the effort was doomed to failure. That they have been able to arouse as much interest as they have is surprising.

Of the Denver women of political experience who answered the question-blank in 1906, 53.9 per cent., as compared with 88.9 per cent. of the men, had at one time or another belonged to a political club. Of the experienced women outside of Denver, 36.4 per cent., as compared with 48.2 per cent. of the men, had belonged to political clubs, and of the women county superintendents, 35.3 per cent., as compared with 70.9 per cent. of the men state legislators, had belonged to political clubs.

5. Campaign Meetings

Closely allied to the subject of political clubs is that of general campaign meetings, the attendance of women as compared with men, and the active part taken by them, *i.e.*, the number and efficiency of women speakers. In regard to the attendance, the answers to the question, "What proportion of women, as compared with men, attend political meetings?" show that, except among the men who were unfavorable or indifferent to equal suffrage, the opinion prevailed that women form from one-fourth to one-half of the total attendance at such meetings.

A large proportion of those who believed in equal suffrage, however—25.9 per cent. of the men, and 27.2 per cent. of the women—testified that as many women as men attend political meetings. In all, 25.5 per cent. of the men and 25.8 per cent. of the women who gave any answers to the question-blank, whether definite or indefinite on this particular question, said that women form from one-fourth to one-half of the total attendance; 20.1 per cent. of the men and 24.6 per cent. of the women said that there are as many women as men; 31.5 per cent. of the men and 14 per cent. of the women said that they form less than one-fourth of the attendance; 2.3 per cent. of the men and 6.2 per cent. of the women said that more women than men attend; 2.9 per cent. of the men and 0.3 per cent. of the women said that no women attend; and 17.7 per cent. of the men and 29.1 per cent. of the women gave no definite answers.

Some local differences are evident. Not a single person from Denver, for instance, said that no women attend political meetings, but twenty persons from other parts of the state made this assertion. In several cases persons from the same county contradicted one another on this point. For example, one woman from San Miguel County said that no women attend political meetings there; while another, probably more accurately, stated that usually about 25 per cent. of the persons present at large meetings

PARTY MACHINERY

are women. Many of those, however, who said that no women attend seem to have understood "meetings" to mean "conventions." The true attendance of women, then, is probably somewhat higher than indicated in the table. It would seem from the testimony that in almost every part of the state an important political rally with good speakers will bring out an audience of at least one-third, and in some localities nearly one-half, women. In point of fact, however, such meetings were well attended by women before suffrage was granted. On the other hand, the attendance of women at meetings where only local speakers are to be heard naturally varies according to local customs and according to the issue involved.

A Delta County woman suggested still another difference when she answered, "In more intelligent communities, half, I should think, are women; where the standard is lower, a smaller number." But this may also be said, with equal truth, of men. In Huerfano County, for instance, women rarely attend political meetings, but these gatherings are infrequent because other methods than the appeal to reason are used to control the vote.

A Las Animas County man answered: "About 10 per cent. are women except in country precincts. There the women attend well, as all meetings close with a dance." Another Las Animas man said: "About 25 per cent. are women. They seem anxious to secure information and enjoy the instruction and the speaking." A number of persons distinguished between married and unmarried women, and said that married women go with their husbands, while others testified that many girls under twenty-one are seen at political meetings, and that babies and young children are not lacking. As in the answers to many of the other questions, a number of persons asserted that the better class of women have nothing to do with politics.

Women speakers are few as compared with men, and the testimony, as shown in Table IX, was overwhelmingly to the effect that they are less efficient. The opinions of the men and of the women on this point were surprisingly uniform, 46.9 per cent. of all the men and 40.4 per cent. of all the women saying that they are less efficient, as against 21.3 per cent. of the men and 22.2 per cent. of the women who said that they are the same. This result can only in a small degree be due to prejudice against women in politics, for the same conclusion was reached by the men and women who believed in equal suffrage as by those who did not. A goodly proportion of those who gave no definite answer said that they had never heard any women speakers.

In the early years of equal suffrage more women were employed as campaign speakers than has been recently the custom, though before every election the state committees send out two or three women, in addition to the candidates, to talk to the members of their own sex in the smaller towns on the issues of the campaign. There are also in Colorado at least two colored women who occasionally make excellent political addresses. It has become customary, however, to have women speakers only at the parlor meetings, and not at the big political rallies at which, for various reasons, it is difficult to secure the best representatives of the sex, and where most women are at a disadvantage in the matter of voice.

Upon the whole, the following answer to the question concerning the efficiency of women campaign speakers is, perhaps, substantially correct: "A few

TABLE IX

Question—Are women more or less efficient than men as campaign speakers?

	More Men	More Women	Same Men	Same Women	Less Men	Less Women	No definite answer Men	No definite answer Women
I. Favorable to Equal Suffrage								
A. State officials	2	1	10	12	14	24	6	12
B. Political workers—state		5	8	35	21	40	7	24
C. Other citizens—state	4	3	53	16	100	30	85	46
D. Delegates—Denver		5	5	36	11	66	3	52
E. Prominent citizens—Denver	1	1	4	3	4	10	2	1
Total	7	15	80	102	150	170	103	135
Per cent	2.1	3.6	23.5	24.1	44.1	40.3	30.3	32
II. Unfavorable to Equal Suffrage								
A. State officials			2	2	6		4	2
B. Political workers—state		1	3	2	17	10	5	3
C. Other citizens—state	6		25	3	60	8	29	8
D. Delegates—Denver			3	11	16	25	3	14
E. Prominent citizens—Denver		1			3			
Total	6	2	33	18	102	43	41	27
Per cent	3.3	2.2	18.1	20	56.1	47.8	22.5	30
III. Indifferent to Equal Suffrage								
A. State officials			2		7	2	4	3
B. Political workers—state		1	1	1	4	8	2	6
C. Other citizens—state	2		9	4	24	3	28	17
D. Delegates—Denver			2	5	2	10	3	13
E. Prominent citizens—Denver			4					
Total	2	1	18	10	37	23	37	39
Per cent	2.1	1.4	19.1	13.7	39.4	31.5	39.4	53.4
Grand total	15	18	131	130	289	236	181	201
Grand per cent	2.4	3.0	21.3	22.2	46.9	40.4	29.4	34.4

women who have ability along this line are better, but the majority are not as good." A prominent Denver man said, "Women's voices are not as good, but they talk better sense"; and a Denver woman, whose opinion is based upon wide experience and a broad outlook, said, "Women's voices are hardly equal to general campaign work, but they have fine success as 'parlor speakers.'" A Boulder man added: "Women are more influential speakers because they get down to the issue and cut out mud slinging."

Some of the reasons suggested for the lesser degree of efficiency of women as campaign speakers are the following: weaker voices, lack of experience, lack of forcefulness, the fact that "women can't tell the open-faced lies that men can on a public platform," that "no woman can make a good campaign speech without appearing in a rôle that is not suited to her sex," and, again, that "where women aspire to the rostrum the world seems to feel that they step without their sphere and become mannish— that moment they lose their influence." The two latter sentiments are both quoted from men who did not believe in equal suffrage. Three answers stated that women speakers do not draw as large audiences as men, and one that they draw larger audiences. One of the county chairmen answered: "Women are not nearly as efficient as men for general campaign speakers because they do not hold the high positions, have not the reputation to draw crowds, and people do not care to listen to them." The opinion of a prominent woman of the state was as follows: "Women are naturally more timid in public than men, and few women are as gifted in eloquence as men. But talented, intelligent women speakers have more influence than men with audiences. It is unfortunately true that women are always personally attacked when they appear in public, whether as professionals, politicians, or what not. Abuse is aimed at their character always, and they are charged with the gravest sins, without grounds. This is done by men as well as women; it naturally lessens a woman's power for good."

6. Elections

The work of election-day is, roughly speaking, of two kinds: that of the judges and clerks, and that of the precinct workers who distribute cards and circulars or bring voters to the polls. Women are largely employed in many counties of Colorado as clerks of election, and they not infrequently serve also as judges. One of the women county superintendents said: "Many widows and other needy intelligent women are appointed judges and clerks."

In Denver, about one election officer out of every three is a woman. In the work outside of the polling-places women are even more numerous, forming in many Denver precincts two-thirds of the election-day workers. Just as in all other political work, they take less part outside of the larger cities. In Delta and Huerfano counties, for example, women rarely serve as election officers. But one woman from La Plata County testified that in her precinct there are always more women than men selected to serve in this capacity.

As to their efficiency as election officers, the consensus of public opinion from all parts of the state, given in Table X, seems to indicate that they are as efficient as men.

EQUAL SUFFRAGE

TABLE X

Question—Are women more or less efficient than men as election judges and clerks?

	More Men	More Women	Same Men	Same Women	Less Men	Less Women	No definite answer Men	No definite answer Women
I. Favorable to Equal Suffrage								
A. State officials	4	10	17	26	9	8	2	5
B. Political workers—state	6	11	19	67	9	5	2	21
C. Other citizens—state	29	17	110	37	34	6	69	35
D. Delegates—Denver	2	35	7	92	6	12	4	20
E. Prominent citizens—Denver	1	7	5	7	4		1	1
Total	42	80	158	229	62	31	78	82
Per cent	12.4	18.9	46.5	54.3	18.2	7.3	22.9	19.5
II. Unfavorable to Equal Suffrage								
A. State officials		1	8	2	4			1
B. Political workers—state	2	1	10	11	9	3	4	1
C. Other citizens—state	15		46	9	29	2	30	8
D. Delegates—Denver		6	8	18	11	15	3	11
E. Prominent citizens—Denver		1	2		1			
Total	17	9	74	40	54	20	37	21
Per cent	9.3	10	40.7	44.4	29.7	22.2	20.3	23.4
III. Indifferent to Equal Suffrage								
A. State officials	2		4	1	5	1	2	3
B. Political workers—state		2	4	4	2	5	1	5
C. Other citizens—state	5	2	22	6	13	1	23	15
D. Delegates—Denver	1	5	2	16	1	2	3	5
E. Prominent citizens—Denver	1		1		1		1	
Total	9	9	33	27	22	9	30	28
Per cent	9.6	12.3	35.1	37	23.4	12.3	31.9	38.4
Grand total	68	98	265	296	138	60	145	131
Grand per cent	11	16.8	43	50.6	22.4	10.2	23.6	22.4

PARTY MACHINERY

Of all the women who answered the question-blank, 50.6 per cent., and of all the men, 43 per cent., thought that women and men are equally efficient. Of the rest, the largest proportion of the women, 16.8 per cent., considered them more, and the largest proportion of the men, 22.4 per cent., considered them less efficient. Twenty-eight men and ten women expressed the opinion that as clerks they are equally or more efficient, but as judges less efficient. One woman said they "are not firm enough for judges."

Of those who thought them not as efficient, several added that this is due to lack of experience. One man complained that they cannot do so well as judges because they do not study the election law. A Boulder County woman said: "They do pretty well mixed in with men who understand the business." A woman county superintendent answered: "They rely too little on their own good sense. Last fall they allowed a scheming man judge to throw out a number of legal votes because they relied on his honor."

On the other hand, one of the prominent women of the state thought them "better because they are more cautious and particular about fraud being practised." A Boulder man added: "Equally as good as men, and I find it greatly improves the air about the polls to have them sitting in authority." A Las Animas man answered: "Very good. Their presence prohibits profanity, drunkenness, and heated debates." The testimony of a Delta man was: "They are much better, fairer in their decisions as judges, and generally more accurate as clerks."

There was considerable testimony to the effect that the time needed for counting the ballots, added to the hours of service at the polls, makes too great a strain to be easily borne by women. Two prominent Denver men and six Denver women spoke of the long hours—"often from twenty-four to thirty hours, which they cannot well stand." Two of the county chairmen stated that women rarely serve in their counties, because "the continuous labor, often lasting all night, is too trying on their physical strength." A Las Animas man said: "That will depend on the size of the precinct. If several hundred votes are cast, and it is desired to get the returns in promptly, a continuous session of perhaps twenty-four hours is necessary, but few could stand such work." This may seem an exaggerated statement of the time needed, but a Teller County man stated specifically: "They do very nicely, but a number of lady clerks and judges worked all night last fall counting the ballots—too long a strain for the average woman."[1] Another Teller County man remarked that, though they are good, "when it comes to carrying the ballot-box to the county or city clerk, men are needed."

The work of bringing in the vote on election-day is generally considered to be the women's special task, and many politicians say that they are far more efficient at this than men, or, as a prominent Denver politician put it, "The women bring in nine-tenths of the votes on election-day. Table XI shows that the general opinion, except among the men who were opposed or indifferent to equal suffrage, was that women are better at bringing in the vote, 31.6 per cent. of the men and 47.6 per cent. of the women who answered any question on the blank giving this answer. A number of replies, however, indicated that equal suffrage itself creates at least in part the very diffi-

[1] It is interesting to note in this connection that the tellers who counted the ballots at the election of the Daughters of the American Revolution, in Washington, D. C., May, 1909, were in session from nine o'clock one evening until about five o'clock the next evening.

PARTY MACHINERY

TABLE XI

Question—Are women more or less efficient than men in bringing in the vote on election-day?

	More Men	More Women	Same Men	Same Women	Less Men	Less Women	No definite answer Men	No definite answer Women
I. Favorable to Equal Suffrage								
A. State officials	13	25	12	14	2	4	5	6
B. Political workers—state	12	38	11	42	8	3	5	21
C. Other citizens—state	88	24	65	24	24	10	65	37
D. Delegates—Denver	12	113	6	24		2	1	20
E. Prominent citizens—Denver	8	8	2	4		2	1	1
Total	133	208	96	108	34	21	77	85
Per cent	39.1	49.3	28.2	25.6	10	5	22.7	20.1
II. Unfavorable to Equal Suffrage								
A. State officials	2	1	3	2	5		2	1
B. Political workers—state	5	6	4	6	10	3	6	1
C. Other citizens—state	29	6	30	4	26	2	35	7
D. Delegates—Denver	7	29	6	12	7	2	2	7
E. Prominent citizens—Denver	1	1			1		1	
Total	44	43	43	24	49	7	46	16
Per cent	24.2	47.8	23.6	26.7	26.9	7.7	25.3	17.8
III. Indifferent to Equal Suffrage								
A. State officials	4		5	1	1	1	3	3
B. Political workers—state	2	6	2	3	2	3	1	4
C. Other citizens—state	7	3	13	6	15		28	15
D. Delegates—Denver	3	18	1	4	1		2	6
E. Prominent citizens—Denver	2		2					
Total	18	27	23	14	19	4	34	28
Per cent	19.1	37	24.5	19.1	20.2	5.5	36.2	38.4
Grand total	195	278	162	146	102	32	157	129
Grand per cent	31.6	47.6	26.3	24.8	16.7	5.4	25.4	22.2

culty which women workers overcome by their activity. A county chairman, for instance, answered: "Women are more efficient than men, as it is the women's vote that it is hard to get out, and a woman generally has more influence with women, especially where they know one another." One of the county superintendents said: "Women do better than men in this work. I have known interested women to take care of babies and carry on housework so that the mother could go to vote."

In the cities and larger towns, where the women are otherwise active, they do a great part of this work, and it would seem, in general, that the larger the place the more completely is the work of bringing in the vote turned over to them. A Denver woman said: "In my experience the women have had entire charge of this work, and are very successful." In small towns like those of Huerfano County, however, they seldom take part.

Carriages and automobiles are used freely in the larger towns and cities to bring the voters to the polls, and in residence precincts a woman usually goes with each carriage. This fact gives rise to a number of bitter complaints and denunciations. A Weld woman said; "I hate this going after voters electionday; every American citizen should take pride in depositing his or her vote, and get there themselves." Another prominent woman from a small town answered: "In our town women frown on this. The best women will not ride in political carriages to the polls, as they consider it a *corrupt* practice."

Eight or ten persons complained that this work is

done merely for money and not for patriotism. The women who do it receive usually $5.00 per day, and a Denver woman delegate said that they are generally married women, who are very anxious to earn a little pin-money.

Other views of the subject are shown in the answers of two Delta County women. One said: "They [the women] are a veritable 'Ladies' Aid Society' in local elections." The other answered, "Where feeling runs high in some towns, more; but the more efficient some I have seen were, the less I have enjoyed seeing them do it."

7. Corruption in Politics

It is often said by equal-suffrage advocates that, if given the franchise, prostitutes would not vote, as they would not be interested and would not wish to give their names and addresses. This is a fallacy. True, they do not wish to vote. In the spring of 1895 they even sent a petition to the Woman's Republican Club of Denver, imploring the interference of that organization to prevent them from being compelled to register. But in spite of the request of the Republican women and the promise of the fire and police board, they were obliged to register and vote at the city election of 1895, and they have been obliged to register and vote at nearly every election since that date. Before Denver received her new charter it was said that this was one of the evils of police boards appointed by the governor, but the police department has usually seemed to be in politics "to win," whether controlled by the state or the city.[1]

Prostitutes generally vote, and their vote is cast solidly for the party in control of the police force. This is true not only in Denver, but usually in Pueblo, Cripple Creek, and Trinidad, and often in other cities. To any one familiar with practical politics, where "the end" is held to "justify the means," this fact is not surprising. The vote of these women, to whom police protection is essential, is regarded as one of the perquisites of the party in power.

Neither is it surprising to learn that the prostitutes vote not only once, but often more than once. Whenever "repeating" is to be done, their aid, naturally, is required. "Repeating" is usually effected on fraudulent registrations, though occasionally an innocent person goes to the polls to find that some one has already voted on his name, and that he is thereby disfranchised. Registration-books are most easily and unobtrusively "padded," as the saying is, in the rooming-house and red-light districts. Sometimes thirty or forty persons have been registered from small houses in this region where on investigation only six or eight legal voters could be discovered. Sometimes, when peculiar vigilance has been exercised, it has been made impossible for any one to vote on these fraudulent names, but undoubtedly the women of the "district" have often cast more than their fair proportion of votes.

---

[1] In justice it should be said that under the administrations of the late Governor Waite and of Governor Adams, prostitutes were not called into service at the polls.

All this, however, is far more a criticism of "politics as it is run" than of equal suffrage, for if the men and women are compared there can be no doubt but that a larger vote is cast by vicious men than by vicious women. Though prostitutes are probably more absolutely under the control of the police than men of the same grade of immorality, the latter are more numerous and more active. Women of this class rarely do more than vote, while men keepers of low saloons and resorts often exert a certain degree of real political power.

As for repeating, two-thirds of this, at least, and probably even a larger proportion, is done by men. We find, for instance, on a list of fraudulent registrations published in 1900 by the chairman of the Arapahoe County Republican Central Committee, the names of 1772 women and 3512 men, or only about one-third women. The names of men and women appear in nearly the same proportion in every ward and precinct in Denver, showing that the fraudulent registrations of women were not confined to certain precincts and wards, but were distributed in the same ratio as those of men over the entire city. This was a year of unprecedented political corruption in Denver, especially in the matter of padded registration-rolls. Even in 1906, however, the work of purging the registration-books from fraudulent names, this time all from the lower wards, including the red-light district, involved four hundred and nineteen names, one hundred and thirty-eight of them of women. None of these women, moreover, appeared before the court to resist the challenge of their votes. In every investigation that has been made for years in Colorado of alleged election frauds, women have been implicated in one way or another. But not half a dozen have ever been arrested for any form of political corruption. Ex-Congressman John F. Shafroth, now Governor of Colorado, said, in 1905, in an interview on the subject of the frauds in the congressional election which caused his withdrawal from the contest: "Of the persons implicated very few were women—not more than one in ten at the outside."

The prevailing opinion that women if admitted to political life would be less corrupt, on the average, than men in their exercise of the franchise seems to be confirmed, moreover, by the testimony of many other Colorado people who have seen how it actually works. According to Table XII, 44.3 per cent. of all the men and 55.5 per cent. of all the women, inclusive of those who gave no definite answer to the question, thought them less corrupt. But 29.9 per cent. of the men and 26.2 per cent. of the women failed definitely to answer this question. A majority, then, of both men and women who answered considered women less corrupt. A goodly number, however—20.5 per cent. of the men and 14.9 per cent. of the women—thought them just about the same; while a few—5.3 per cent. of the men and 3.4 per cent. of the women—considered women more corrupt in politics than men. Fifty-three persons in all answered "more," but thirty-five of these were opposed to equal suffrage, and some of them were doubtless prejudiced. On the other hand, the prevailing opinion, above mentioned, together with a belief in equal suffrage, probably ac-

PARTY MACHINERY

TABLE XII

Question—Are women more or less corrupt than men in politics, and why?

	More Men	More Women	Same Men	Same Women	Less Men	Less Women	No definite answer Men	No definite answer Women
I. Favorable to Equal Suffrage								
A. State officials..................			5	8	19	37	8	4
B. Political workers—state.......		2	3	8	25	75	8	19
C. Other citizens—state.........	5	2	32	11	134	53	71	29
D. Delegates—Denver...........	1	2	2	11	9	109	7	37
E. Prominent citizens—Denver...			1	6	6	8	4	1
Total........................	6	6	43	44	193	282	98	90
Per cent.....................	1.8	1.4	12.6	10.4	56.7	66.8	28.9	21.4
II. Unfavorable to Equal Suffrage								
A. State officials..................	1		6	1	4	2	1	1
B. Political workers—state.......	3	2	9	5	10	6	3	3
C. Other citizens—state.........	13	4	30	6	31	1	46	8
D. Delegates—Denver...........	5	5	5	18	5	10	7	17
E. Prominent citizens—Denver...	1	1	1		1			
Total........................	23	12	51	30	51	19	57	29
Per cent.....................	12.7	13.3	28	33.3	28	21.1	31.3	32.3
III. Indifferent to Equal Suffrage								
A. State officials..................			3	2	5	1	5	2
B. Political workers—state.......	1	2	2	2	3	9	1	3
C. Other citizens—state.........	3		20	4	19	6	21	14
D. Delegates—Denver...........			3	5	2	8	2	15
E. Prominent citizens—Denver...			4					
Total........................	4	2	32	13	29	24	29	34
Per cent.....................	4.2	2.7	34	17.8	30.9	32.9	30.9	46.6
Grand total.......................	33	20	126	87	273	325	184	153
Grand per cent...................	5.3	3.4	20.5	14.9	44.3	55.5	29.9	26.2

counts for many of the answers in the "less" column. A number of other persons whose answers appear in the "less" column frankly confessed that they thought the reason that women are less corrupt is because they have less opportunity or "because they don't know the game."

It is both interesting and profitable to study the reasons given for the belief that women are more corrupt in politics than men. These may be grouped in eight classes, and, leaving out of consideration a half-dozen answers which gave no reason for the opinion expressed, the classes are fairly evenly represented. First were the answers which said simply that a bad woman is worse than a bad man, or that "their finer sensibilities when once blunted soon become extinct."

The second class, which is somewhat more largely represented than any other, was to the effect that women are bought cheaper than men. One of the Denver women delegates who did not believe in equal suffrage said: "More, because they will work cheaper. Five dollars looks bigger to a woman than it does to a man." One man said that women can be bought "with a compliment," and a woman put it "with a smile." A Denver woman delegate told of a woman who made a practice of exchanging a hair tonic of her own concoction for votes; and a county chairman who did not believe in equal suffrage said: "Last fall I knew of a number of women voters in the county who sold their votes for dress patterns, etc., and refused to vote for certain candidates who did not bring them candy or gum." A San Miguel County woman said: "There are a class of women who do not realize the sacredness of the responsibility of doing their part to elect good men and women to office, and who will sell their vote for a box of candy or less, while the same class of men will sell theirs at a little higher price."

PARTY MACHINERY

Closely allied to this as a reason for the belief that women are more corrupt was the statement that more often than men they are in politics for money. A Teller County man, who was unfavorable to equal suffrage, said: "Women are more corrupt, more easily bought up, because, as a rule, a large percentage of the better class of women will not actively engage in political work, and a large percentage of those who take active interest do so for selfish reasons." A county chairman who also did not believe in equal suffrage answered: "Yes, because the women who take the most interest are from the lower classes and always look for the money." A considerably larger number of answers, however, were to the effect that women are less corrupt because they have less financial interest at stake than men.

The fourth reason given was that they are more petty. For instance, a La Plata County woman said: "More so, I am sorry to say, so far as my observation goes. They stoop to petty, unwomanly gossip, and stop at no scandal by which they can defeat a candidate against whom they have a grudge, and merit is not considered."

Fifth, was the belief that women are more reckless than men. One of the Denver men delegates who did not believe in equal suffrage said that women "will do boldly things a man might also do, but would try to hide," and a Teller man who did not commit himself on the suffrage question suggested that women "do not figure on the fact that there will be another election some time." A La Plata man who believed in equal suffrage accounted for this greater recklessness by the fact that women are less familiar with the laws and are encouraged by "the amenities shown to the sex." Other persons, however, testified that women are less corrupt than men in politics because they are more timid.

A sixth reason was the assertion that women are more easily influenced than men, and a seventh that their code of honor in such matters is defective. A Teller County man who believed in equal suffrage thought that women are more corrupt, "as they do the men's bidding"; and a La Plata County woman who also believed in equal suffrage said: "Women are more corrupt because of inexperience and short-sightedness. They will do without knowing it is dishonorable an act considered in men's code below the mark."

Lastly was the belief expressed by several that women are often deceived or tricked into acts and methods which, if they were more experienced, they would recognize as corrupt. For instance, a Pueblo man who believed in equal suffrage answered: "They are more trusting or gullible, more partisan, less reasonable, and cheaper purchased. I have known women of standing, church-members, housewives, and mothers, in the employ of the machines at two to three dollars per day, to go from house to house and promulgate among the women the most vile and false and slanderous tales about candidates, and yet such women doubtless believe the stories which they tell." A woman of wide political experience remarked: "From what I have observed, human nature is apt to show up in both sexes in politics as elsewhere. I should say that men are more openly and intentionally corrupt, but women, from long lack of necessity for acting on their own judgment, often blind themselves or permit others to blind them, with the result that they do fully as questionable things as the men." In Pueblo, in January, 1905, a woman testified in court that she had assisted a man in making out dozens of fraudulent registration-sheets, and had received pay for this work on his assurance and her own belief that there was nothing wrong about the proceeding.[1]

Those persons who believed that women are more corrupt are, however, only fifty-three out of over

[1] *Denver Times*, January 18, 1905.

twelve hundred. Though some women are doubtless more easily tempted than some men, and many instances of corruption can probably be given, the sum total of the evidence seems to prove conclusively that, as a whole, women are less corrupt than men.

In a careful consideration of the question of corruption, it should be noted that there are two points involved: first, the corruption of the ordinary citizen through the sale, in one form or another, of his or her vote; and, second, the corruption of workers in party politics through the buying of votes or through some other kind of dishonesty. There can be little question but that the average woman is much less likely to dispose of her vote for a consideration than the average man, but it is highly probable that men and women politicians do not differ so widely. There are many incorruptibly honest politicians of both sexes in Colorado, but there are also many persons who are in politics for revenue only, to whom the political game means war, with supreme faith in the old adage, "All is fair in love and war."

Even under the "rules of the game," indeed, the line between the fair and unfair is somewhat loosely drawn. It is not uncommon, for instance, for a Democratic woman to work for pay for the Republican Party, or the reverse, but this is not usually considered dishonest, even by her own party. The woman candidate for state representative, for instance, who received the largest number of votes in the Democratic Convention in Denver in 1906, had appeared as a canvasser for the Republican Party before the committee which investigated the gubernatorial election in 1904.

It is safe to say, in general, that even active women politicians are less corrupt than active men politicians. For one thing, they are rarely trusted with the corruption funds. Then, too, for the most part, they simply follow the lead or obey the orders of the men, and, consequently, whether the women of any particular locality are corrupt depends upon the political honor of the men of that locality. It is noticeable, however, that in several communities where political corruption is common, such as Huerfano County, women take practically no part except to vote.

Another noticeable thing is that whatever corruption exists among women is confined almost wholly to those who are engaged in the lowest grades of political work. Women candidates for office are almost invariably above reproach on this ground, and necessarily so, for the double standard prevails in public opinion to such an extent that a woman with an unsavory record, in either public or private life, would not be tolerated in any conspicuous position. A man of very doubtful honesty may be nominated and elected, but not a woman.

8. Conclusion

The influence of equal suffrage over the machinery of party politics, though apparently not great, has probably been beneficial. Women have been slack, even more so than men, in the fulfilment of political duties other than voting. Few of them attend cau-

PARTY MACHINERY

cuses or primaries, but more serve as delegates to conventions, and their presence has a slight tendency to improve political platforms and the selection of candidates. "Planks" are sometimes introduced to "catch the woman vote," but they are no more lived up to than the planks introduced to catch other classes of votes. Saloon-keepers and men of questionable personal morality are usually, but not always, tabooed as candidates. This, however, does not necessarily improve the standard of public efficiency or honor. Few women, compared with the number of men, are corrupt in politics, but the red-light district is freely used by the party in power, and its women are compelled, not merely to vote, but often to repeat. Some complaint has been made that equal suffrage, by adding a large number of uninterested voters to the electorate, has strengthened the hold of professional political manipulators. A Denver man, for instance, said that equal suffrage "increases the facilities of the 'ward heeler,' instead of neutralizing his force, as was expected." But there is little evidence to warrant such an assertion. Upon the whole, party politics appears to be upon a somewhat higher plane in Colorado since women have voted.

The most superficial consideration, however, of the evidence produced in every section of this chapter reveals the heavy handicap placed upon women's influence by the caucus and convention system. Under the existing machine methods in politics, women, though nominally admitted, are not yet truly enfranchised so far as the nomination of candidates is concerned. Practically their only influence on the selection of party candidates is due to their power to scratch the ticket at the ensuing election. As a result, their influence, even in elections, is only negative—the empty option of choosing between two candidates often equally obnoxious or inefficient, nominated by the bosses of two "machines." Plainly, in such a case they can make their influence felt only by scratching the candidate whose personal immorality or allegiance to saloons is well known. They have no opportunity of taking into account the finer qualities and the independent character of a candidate, which might give him the preference in the nominations.

This disfranchisement at caucus and convention is not an evidence of women's political incapacity. Such incapacity marks the best kind of men wherever the system prevails. Both sexes stay away from caucus and convention because they know they are helpless, and that they can succeed only by debasing themselves to the level of hired political workers. The caucus and convention are arranged long in advance. Corporations, the saloon element, and special interests that seek control can afford to furnish the bosses abundant funds to hire these professional workers, and both men and women who value their honor and patriotism will not descend to these mercenary methods. Their only refuge is to run an independent candidate after the regular nominations are made, and this requires such herculean efforts that it is not undertaken unless under keen provocation and actual insult to their ideals of citizenship. Women are especially handicapped by these secret and devious methods, which succeed by persistent, continuous, and professional activity. Their influence tells only in the open and aboveboard. It is the appeal to publicity and public opinion. As long as the caucus and convention are practically closed against them they are ineffective.

The machinery of nominations is just as vital for the influence of the better elements as the machinery of elections. Women's influence would be nullified in the elections if bribery and corruption prevailed as they did before the secret ballot was effectually installed.[1] The only machinery of nominations that will enfranchise women and give them, as well as the better class of men, an effective share in government, is the system that makes the caucuses and conventions really open to all the voters on equal terms. That this condition is becoming more and more evident is shown by the answers to questions looking toward the system of direct nominations at primary elections. This system, if properly devised, especially with the second-choice feature, gives women and men the free opportunity of making independent nominations on petition within the party lines, regardless of the contrivings of hired workers.

Women have shown their capacity for breaking away from party lines when moral issues became apparent. They need only the right kind of nominating machinery in order to express their rightful influence within party lines. It is no reflection, then, on equal

---

[1] See chap. vi, section 3.

suffrage to show women's incapacity to cope with the existing machinery of nominations. Equal suffrage, indeed, serves to show, in the most striking way, the essential rottenness and degrading character of the existing system.

III

STATISTICS OF ELECTIONS

AS no separate record of the sexes is kept, it is difficult to obtain exact figures in regard to the proportion of women, as compared with men, who vote in Colorado. For past years, indeed, the registration and poll-books have been destroyed in the majority of counties and cities,[1] and only contemporary estimates are available. A statement which has been persistently circulated is that, in 1894, women cast 52 per cent. of the entire vote of the state. This assertion is said to be based on actual returns furnished by the county clerks. But familiarity with the laborious and conscientious work necessary to obtain accurate figures on this point inclines one to doubt seriously whether the so-called statistics fur-

[1] The law provides that poll-books used in state and county elections shall be preserved for two years, and that those used in municipal elections, for which only one set of books is necessary in the smaller places, shall be kept in the ballot-boxes until the next election, which may be in a year. In cities and towns where permanent registration-books have been used, the records are often kept for a number of years, but, after each election, the names of the persons not voting are stricken off, frequently to be re-entered before the next election. As a result of this complicated system it is practically impossible to secure any record except of persons registered at the last election at which the books were used.

EQUAL SUFFRAGE

nished by uninterested clerks were anything more than rough estimates. A comparison, moreover, of the total vote at the election of 1892 with that at the election of 1894 indicates that only about 47 per cent. of the vote in the latter year was cast by women, and it is probable that in 1896, at the first presidential election after equal suffrage was adopted, women did not cast more than 48 per cent. of the total vote.[1] The most that can be fairly claimed from the evidence now in existence is that probably at these early elections between 47 and 48 per cent. of the vote was cast by women. Even this, however, was considerably more than their proportion of the voting population, for, assuming an even rate of increase for both sexes between 1890 and 1900, it is estimated that women constituted, in 1894, only 38.5 per cent., and in

[1] In 1892, 93,756 votes were cast for governor, and in 1894, 180,983, or 87,227 more than in 1892. Assuming that the men's vote neither increased nor decreased, and that the natural falling-off because of the fact that 1894 was not a presidential year was offset by the great importance attached to the contest between the Republican and Populist parties, it would appear that women cast something over 48 per cent. of the vote. But, in spite of the effect of the panic of 1893 upon the population of the state, there was doubtless some increase in the vote of men, which would reduce this figure. Assuming, indeed, that the increase in the voting population of men from 164,920 in 1890 to 185,708 in 1900 was evenly distributed over the ten years, and that the same proportion, about 55.5 per cent., of the men cast ballots in 1894 as in 1892, it appears that, in 1894, 96,145 votes were cast by men, leaving only 84,837, or under 47 per cent. of the whole, to the credit of women. In 1896, the next presidential year, 188,373 votes were cast for governor, an increase of 94,617, or a little more than 50 per cent. over the vote of 1892. But by the last method only 89,920, or about 47.7 per cent., of these votes can be credited to women. It is possible, moreover, that equal suffrage may have stimulated more men to vote, which would still further reduce the proportion of the total vote cast by women.

STATISTICS OF ELECTIONS

1896 only 39.9 per cent. of the persons twenty-one years of age and over in Colorado.[1]

A much larger proportion, indeed, of the women than of the men who were entitled to the ballot appear to have availed themselves of their privilege at these early elections. If the increase between 1890 and 1900 in the voting population of men was evenly distributed, only about 55.5 per cent. of the men of voting age cast their ballots at the state election of 1892. A statement made in 1898 in defence of equal suffrage [2] says that between 85 and 90 per cent. of the women of Colorado voted at the election of 1894. This is somewhat exaggerated. But a comparison of the approximate vote of men and of women, as previously estimated, with the estimated voting population of each sex, shows that between 75 and 80 per cent. of the women of the state probably voted in both 1894 and 1896.[3] In 1900, more-

---

[1] The census of 1890 shows that there were in the state in that year 93,471 women over twenty years of age, including those classified under "Age unknown." (Eleventh Census, Population, Part II, p. 105.) Deducting one-fifth of the number between the ages of twenty and twenty-four, it is found that there were approximately 89,740 women of voting age in Colorado in 1890. By the same method it is found that in 1900 there were about 136,340 women of voting age in Colorado. (Twelfth Census, Population, Part II, p. 111.) Assuming that the increase between 1890 and 1900 was evenly distributed through the ten-year period, it is found that, in 1894, there were about 108,380, and in 1896 about 117,700 women of voting age.

[2] See Appendix K, II.

[3] The estimated number of votes cast by women in 1894 was 84,837, which is 78.3 per cent. of the estimated number of women of voting age in that year, and in 1896 it was 89,920, or 76.4 per cent. of the estimated number of women of voting age in that year.

over, when women constituted 42.3 per cent. of the entire population of voting age, only about 68 per cent. of the possible vote of both sexes together was cast for governor.

Again, for the 1900 election, it was estimated that in the state, as a whole, women cast over 41.5 per cent., and in Denver about 42.5 per cent. of the total vote.[1] Upon what authority this estimate was based is not stated, but the results of the present investigation seem to indicate its substantial accuracy. It is of interest to note, too, that in the same year, according to the estimated figures already given in the foot-notes, women constituted only 42.3 per cent. of the total population of voting age in Colorado.

Figures quoted by ex-Governor Adams, in a speech before the National Woman Suffrage Convention in 1904, show, moreover, that in his own residence precinct in Pueblo, at the 1902 state election, 46 per cent., and at the 1903 municipal election 44 per cent., of the total vote was cast by women. He also stated that at the former election 73 per cent. of the men and 76 per cent. of the women who were registered voted, and at the latter election 81 per cent. of the men and 73 per cent. of the women who were registered voted.[2]

This represents actual figures, and not a mere estimate, as does also the table given by Mr. Lawrence Lewis in the *Outlook* for January 27, 1906. Mr. Lewis' statistics cover for the state election of November, 1904, fourteen typical precincts, eight in Pueblo City and six in the agricultural and ranching portion of Pueblo County, and, for the city election of April, 1905, the same eight city precincts.

[1] Susan B. Anthony and Ida Husted Harper, *History of Woman Suffrage*, p. 525.
[2] At the state election of 1902 there were 794 persons, and at the municipal election of 1903, 760 persons, registered in this precinct.

STATISTICS OF ELECTIONS

These are the most extensive statistics derived from actual count of the names on the registration and poll books which have been heretofore published.[1] They show that the proportion of the total vote cast by women ranged from 46 per cent., at the municipal election in the best residence precinct, to 25 per cent., at the state election, in an agricultural and horticultural region. It appears from these figures that a considerably larger proportion of the women of the leisure-class residence districts register and vote than of the women of the working-class or than of the women of the lodging-house and "disreputable" section, and that, roughly, the proportion of women to men decreases as the degree of intelligence and morality lessens. The truth of this generalization is confirmed by the results of the present investigation.

1. REGISTRATION AND VOTE

Owing to the impossibility of making for this investigation an accurate count of the names on the registration and poll books of the entire state, the examination of these books was confined to nine counties, which it is believed are typical of the state as a whole.[2] All of these counties except Delta and Huerfano contain towns for which detailed facts in regard to tenancy, conjugal condition, and occupation of voters were obtained; and one, Teller County, has three such towns—Cripple Creek, Goldfield, and Victor. The cities of Boulder and Longmont are in Boulder County, Durango in La Plata, Greeley in Weld, Telluride in San Miguel, and Trinidad in Las Animas.

[1] The table given in Mr. Lewis' article is extensive and complicated, but its most important figures are given in Appendix C.
[2] For a description of these counties, see chap. i, section 2.

EQUAL SUFFRAGE

Table XIII gives the vote and registration of these counties and cities in 1906, the population, with proportion of men and women according to the 1900 census, and the vote by counties on the equal-suffrage amendment in 1893.[1] The figures for the

---

[1] The registration for Teller and Weld counties could not be secured, and, as Teller County was part of El Paso in 1893, its vote on the equal-suffrage amendment could not be stated. Goldfield, Longmont, and Telluride were so small in 1900 that their population was not separately given in the census.

Four sources of error arise in connection with these figures. First, the census gives no statistics from which the proportion of women of voting age may be estimated by counties. Though in 1890 females constituted 40.5 per cent. of the entire population of Colorado, it has been estimated that they formed only 35.2 per cent. of the voting population, and in 1900, though they constituted 45.3 per cent. of the entire population, it has been estimated that they formed only 42.3 per cent. of the voting population. Second, the movement shown by these figures doubtless continued, so that the proportion of women to men was higher in 1906 than in 1900. Third, the figures for the registration and vote are not entirely satisfactory, as in some cases it was not possible to determine by the given name whether the voter was male or female, and in even more numerous instances only initials were given. Where the name did not reveal the sex, errors in one direction were likely to be counterbalanced by errors in the other, but the names to which only initials were attached were necessarily considered as belonging to men, though a few of them may have belonged to women. The fourth source of error relates only to the figures for Goldfield and Victor. In these towns it was necessary to make the registration count from books in use since 1900. As a result, the vote, which was taken from the poll-books, appears to be larger than the registration. It is believed, however, that even for the registration the percentages are substantially correct.

Of these three sources of error, the second is calculated to cause a slight overestimate of the vote of the women as compared with the female population, and the first and third are calculated to cause a slight underestimate of the registration and vote of the women as compared both with their population and with the registration and vote of the men. The fourth affects the registration figures, but probably not the percentages, and has no in-

STATISTICS OF ELECTIONS

TABLE XIII

REGISTRATION, VOTE, AND POPULATION OF SELECTED COUNTIES AND CITIES

	Number and proportion of men and women registered, November, 1906				Number and proportion of men and women who voted, November, 1906				Population, 1900				Vote on Equal Suffrage, 1893	
Counties	Men	Perc't.	Women	Perc't.	Men	Perc't.	Women	Perc't.	Male	Perc't.	Female	Perc't.	For	Against
Boulder[1]	6,589	56	5,198	44	5,236	62	3,242	38	11,146	52.7	10,198	47.3	1,629	918
Delta[1]	3,222	64	1,738	36	2,056	70	894	30	2,914	55.9	2,573	44.1	471	197
Denver[2]	32,006	56	25,109	44	25,230	57.3	18,741	42.6	66,592	49.8	67,267	50.2	8,816[8]	7,001[8]
Huerfano[3]	3,583	61	2,314	39	2,092	66	1,062	34	4,530	54	3,865	46	328	837
La Plata[4]	2,814	62	1,753	38	1,851	63	1,087	37	3,857	52.1	3,259	47.9	463	818
Las Animas[5]	6,468	64	3,537	36	6,405	70	2,724	30	11,599	54.5	9,943	45.5	608	1,756
San Miguel	1,777	73	660	27	1,709	74	602	26	3,679	68.4	1,700	31.6	9	269
Teller[6]					4,961	64	2,757	36	17,087	58.9	11,915	41.1	207	9
Weld[6]					4,697	66	2,430	34	9,404	55.9	7,404	44.1	1,385	612
Totals	56,459	58.5	40,309	41.5	54,237	62.7	33,539	37.3	131,208	52.6	118,124	47.4	13,997	13,308
Cities														
Boulder	2,118	48	2,211	52	1,820	53	1,619	47	2,960	48.1	3,190	51.9		
Cripple Creek	2,228	61	1,600	39	2,055	63	1,205	37	5,000	55.2	4,547	44.8		
Durango	1,323	56	1,005	44	847	58	624	42	1,689	50.9	1,628	49.1		
Goldfield	224	63	132	37	323	62	201	38						
Greeley	1,831	58	1,357	42	1,251	60	859	40	1,431	47.4	1,592	52.6		
Longmont	1,366	58	990	42	762	59	532	41						
Telluride	583	67	284	33	535	66	274	34	2,661	49.8	2,684	50.2		
Trinidad[7]	1,529	54	1,315	46	943	58	692	42						
Victor	884	67	439	33	1,203	64	682	36	2,973	59.6	2,013	40.4		
Totals	12,086	56.5	9,333	43.5	9,739	59.5	6,688	40.7	17,314	52.5	15,654	47.5		

[1] Registration-books missing in precincts 8, 10, 14, 16, 23, and 34.
[2] The vote is not indicated in ward 1, precincts 2, 5, 6, 7; ward 3, precinct 8; ward 12, precinct 2; ward 13, precinct 6; ward 14, precinct 6, and ward 16, precinct 12.
[3] Registration-book missing for precinct 7.
[4] Registration and poll books lost in precincts 3 and 4.
[5] Registration-books missing in precincts 10, 14, 27; vote not given in precinct 39, ward 1.
[6] Registration could not be obtained.
[7] Vote in precinct 39, ward 1, not given.
[8] This vote is for Arapahoe County, which at that time included Denver.
[9] Teller County was a part of El Paso County in 1893.

103

nine cities, exclusive of Denver, which, for the purposes of the investigation, is considered as a county, are separately tabulated, though they are also included in the figures given for their respective counties.

It appears that in all of these counties taken together women formed 47.4 per cent. of the population, 41.5 per cent. of the persons registered, and 37.3 per cent. of the persons actually voting. A larger proportion, evidently, of men who were registered than of women who were registered voted. In the cities and towns, exclusive of Denver, which considerably increased the total percentage of women registered and voting, women formed 47.5 per cent. of the population, 43.5 per cent. of the persons registered, and 40.7 per cent. of the actual voters. According to these figures women register and vote in larger numbers as compared with men in the towns than in the country districts, but in neither do as large a proportion of registered women as of registered men vote. In only one county, however, did the vote of women fall below 30 per cent. of the total vote cast, and this one was San Miguel, in which women formed, in 1900, only 31.6 per cent. of the population, and in which their proportion of the vote was nearer their proportion of the population than in any other county except Denver and Teller.

The only counties in the list which voted against equal suffrage in 1893 were Huerfano, La Plata, and

fluence on the vote. The error, however, cannot be great, and it is believed that the proportions given here are substantially accurate and may be taken to represent, roughly, conditions in the state as a whole.

Las Animas. Of these, Huerfano and Las Animas contain a large proportion of Mexicans, and there are many Mexicans in parts of La Plata County. In each of these counties the proportionate vote of the women fell more than 10 per cent. below their proportion of the population, which was not true of any other county except Delta and Weld—the difference in the latter being only one-tenth of one per cent.

Comparing the cities with the counties and with one another, it is evident that a considerably larger proportion of women vote in Boulder City than in Boulder County, and a somewhat larger proportion than in any other city of which the population is given. The mining district in the western part of the county, where women take almost no interest, is mainly responsible for the lower record of the county as a whole. In Longmont, though women seem to take less interest than in Boulder, there is evidence that they take slightly more now than in previous years, for by actual count women constituted only 39.6 per cent. of the total persons registered there in the fall election of 1900 as compared with 42 per cent. in 1906. The vote of Longmont in 1900 was not obtainable.

The difference between the proportion of women who voted in the cities and in the country districts is strikingly shown by a comparison of the figures for the city of Trinidad and for the entire county of Las Animas. In this case, however, the lower vote of women in the outside precincts is in great part accounted for by the higher proportion of Mexicans.

Evidently the women of this race do not vote in as large numbers as the men.

The returns from the city of Telluride, where 34 per cent. of the total vote was cast by women as contrasted with 26 per cent. for the entire county of San Miguel, are accounted for in part by the fact, which does not appear in the table, that the proportion of women in Telluride is considerably larger than in the rest of the county. The unmarried miners, and those whose wives are not with them, generally live in large boarding-houses at the mines, while many of the married men live in Telluride and go out to their work.

In Teller County, on the other hand, the mines are in or close to the towns, and, consequently, no such discrepancy between the woman vote in the county and in the cities occurs. The women of both Cripple Creek and Victor seem to have been either more numerous or considerably more interested in politics in 1906 than in 1900. In Cripple Creek they constituted in 1900 only 32.3 per cent. of the persons registered as compared with 39 per cent. in 1906, and in Victor, in 1900, only 29.7 per cent. as compared with 33 per cent. in 1906. Statistics of the vote in 1900 are not obtainable.

In only two instances did the figures show that in 1906 the registered women turned out on election-day in larger proportions than the registered men. In Goldfield they constituted 37 per cent. of the total persons registered and 38 per cent. of the total vote, and in Telluride 33 per cent. of the total persons registered and 34 per cent. of the total vote. Some

STATISTICS OF ELECTIONS

TABLE XIV
REGISTRATION, VOTE, AND POPULATION OF DENVER

Wards[1]	Registration, 1906 Men	Per cent.	Registration, 1906 Women	Per cent.	Vote, 1906 Men	Per cent.	Vote, 1906 Women	Per cent.	Population, 1900 Men	Per cent.	Population, 1900 Women	Per Cent.
1	1,000	60.7	649	39.3	600[2]	72.2	231[2]	27.8	2,528	53.9	2,154	46.1
2	1,441	65.2	768	34.8	1,126	67.2	549	32.8	3,634	61.4	2,281	38.6
3	1,625	68.8	736	31.2	1,006[3]	72.5	381[3]	27.5	4,728	58.9	3,293	41.1
4	1,624	59.3	1,112	40.7	1,368	60.7	885	39.3	4,839	52	4,465	48
5	1,362	58.3	973	41.7	1,116	58.9	781	41.1	3,405	49	3,549	51
6	2,417	57.1	1,809	42.9	1,989	59.9	1,329	40.1	6,123	50	6,126	50
7	1,692	59.2	1,168	40.8	1,367	61	872	39	4,073	52.1	3,748	47.9
8	2,602	53.6	2,254	46.4	2,206	55	1,804	45	4,827	47	5,575	53
9	3,102	52	2,865	48	2,610	53.6	2,257	46.4	5,640	45.8	6,699	54.2
10	3,361	52.3	3,060	47.7	2,861	53.4	2,499	46.6	5,421	43.8	6,955	56.2
11	2,052	57	1,543	43	1,722	58.4	1,248	42	5,420	50.4	5,330	49.6
12	2,565	54	2,191	46	1,996[4]	54.5	1,588[4]	45.5	5,047	46.8	5,738	53.2
13	1,931	54.5	1,611	45.5	1,181[5]	52.6	1,065[5]	47.4	3,055	49.5	3,109	50.5
14	1,123	52.7	1,009	47.3	800[6]	53.8	688[6]	46.2	1,193	48.3	1,292	51.9
15	2,186	53.8	1,878	46.2	1,858	55.2	1,487	44.8	3,321	48	3,600	52
16	1,923	56.5	1,483	43.5	1,424[7]	57	1,077[7]	43	3,338	49.9	3,353	50.1
Total	32,006	56	25,109	44	25,230	57.4	18,741	42.6	66,592	49.8	67,267	50.2

[1] See "Description of Wards," page 108.
[2] Precincts 2, 5, 6, and 7, vote not indicated.
[3] Precinct 8, vote not indicated.
[4] Precinct 2, vote not indicated.
[5] Precinct 6, vote not indicated.
[6] Precinct 6, vote not indicated.
[7] Precinct 12, vote not indicated.

EQUAL SUFFRAGE

REMARKS ON TABLE XIV

DENVER

DESCRIPTION OF WARDS, 1906

Ward 1. Slum district, many saloons, mostly very poor and disreputable inhabitants.

Ward 2. About two-thirds low-class lodging-houses, and the other third good family apartment-houses. Some private houses.

Ward 3. Very low third-class hotels and lodging-houses for most part. Includes the greater part of the red-light district.

Ward 4. Includes part of red-light district. Low-class residences and rooming-houses, ranging to fairly respectable.

Ward 5. Second-class lodging and residence district. Small cottages of laboring-class.

Ward 6. Tenement housekeeping, rooming, and second-class residence district. Mainly respectable working-class. Includes Italian quarter.

Ward 7. Mainly laboring-class residence district, small private homes ranging from very poor to industrious, sober working-class.

Ward 8. Upper working-class to good residence district. Prevailing character of comfortable respectability, but not fashionable.

Ward 9. Second-class rooming to best residence district. Many cottages, but also elegant homes. Mainly good residences and apartment-houses.

Ward 10. High-class fashionable residence region.

Ward 11. Thrifty working-class inhabitants, mainly private homes.

Ward 12. Neat, small, private homes of clerks, small business men, etc. In part suburban. No saloons.

Ward 13. Same as 12. No saloons.

Ward 14. Residence district; largely high-class; sparsely settled.
Ward 15. Suburban, small houses, industrious, thrifty middle class.
Ward 16. Sparsely settled, laboring-class, ranging from skilled artisans to very poor people. Many Jews and Socialists. No saloons.

---

doubt, however, is cast on the figures for Goldfield by the discrepancy already mentioned between the vote and the registration. The larger proportion of registered men than of registered women voting in 1906 may be accounted for in part, at least, by the fact that a new registration law, providing for a house-to-house canvass, went into effect that year. By this method indifferent women were registered in larger numbers than indifferent men, who, not being at home in the daytime, were not reached. The law also provides that a new registration must be made for each election.

The following facts, though not of great significance, are of interest: Out of 470 illiterate voters, or persons "assisted," who cast ballots in Huerfano County in the fall of 1906, 41.5 per cent. were women, as compared with only 34 per cent. of the total vote cast by women. In Teller County, of 72 illiterate or "assisted" voters, 38.9 per cent. were women as compared with 36 per cent. of the total vote. But in Las Animas County, out of 869 illiterates, only 28.6 per cent. were women as compared with 30 per cent. of the total vote![1]

[1] There was, in 1900, very little illiteracy in Colorado, only 4.2 per cent. of the population ten years of age and over being illiterate, as compared with 6.3 per cent. for the Western division and 10.7 per cent. for the entire United States. Of the male population of Colorado ten years of age and over, 3.7 per cent. were

EQUAL SUFFRAGE

Statistics are given in Table XIV for the fall election of 1906 in Denver by wards, with descriptions of each ward. These figures answer conclusively the statement sometimes made that the better class of women do not vote, while the lower class go to the polls in large numbers. Precisely the opposite is found to be the case. Just as was shown in Mr. Lewis' figures for Pueblo, the proportion of the vote cast by women varies substantially with the respectability of the neighborhood, the best residence districts showing the largest percentage, and the slum, saloon, and cheap lodging-house districts the smallest. This does not mean, however, that the women who, as actual denizens of the red-light district, are under police surveillance do not vote.

The only figures available for city elections indicate that, except on extraordinary occasions, women

---

illiterate, and of the female 4.8 per cent., while in the Western division 6 per cent. of the males were illiterate and 6.8 per cent. of the females, and in the United States as a whole 10.2 per cent. of the males and 11.3 per cent. of the females. Considering only persons twenty-one years of age and over, and disregarding those whose ages were unknown, there were in the whole United States 2,302,100 illiterate males and 2,584,354 illiterate females, while in Colorado there were 7597 illiterate males and 7697 illiterate females. In Colorado, too, there were fewer illiterate males than females from ten to twenty years of age, 1085 as compared with 1219, though in the United States as a whole the rising generation of males contained more illiterates than the rising generation of females, 727,516 as compared with 580,154. Most of the illiteracy in Colorado, moreover, is among the foreign white population and the Mexicans. Thus, out of 17,779 illiterates ten years of age and over in 1900, 7264 were foreign white, and the six most distinctly Mexican counties—Archuleta, Conejos, Costilla, Huerfano, Las Animas, and Saguache—held 7286 illiterates, most of whom were doubtless Mexicans, as only 784 were foreign born. See *Twelfth Census*, vol. ii, pp. c–cii, 422–423, 471.

take little more interest in municipal than in county and state affairs. An estimate of the Denver vote in the city election of 1902 showed 24,000 women to 33,000 men, or 42 per cent. women. A count made by the Republican committee, moreover, from the poll-books used at the spring election of 1908 gave 40,453 men and 29,274 women, or, again, 42 per cent. women. In Durango, at the 1907 spring election, 515 women and 811 men voted, 39 per cent. women as compared with 42 per cent. the previous fall. In Greeley, on the other hand, in the 1907 spring election, 592 votes were cast by men and 455 by women, making 43.5 per cent. of the vote cast by women as compared with 40 per cent. in the previous state election.

Boulder had the saloon issue at the city election of 1907, and great interest and enthusiasm were aroused, with the result that 52.5 per cent. of the total vote was cast by women, and the town was carried by the "dry" element. Even in this instance, however, though an unusually large vote of both sexes was polled, the proportion of registered women who failed to vote was larger than the proportion of registered men, for women constituted 53.3 per cent. of the total registration.

2. Ownership and Tenancy

Interesting facts descriptive of voters, such as whether they were owners, tenants, or lodgers, native or naturalized citizens, married or single, and in what occupations they were engaged, were obtained from

EQUAL SUFFRAGE

the registration-books used in the towns and cities. The figures in regard to ownership and tenancy of persons registered at the November, 1906, election are given in Table XV, and in Appendix D the same points are brought out for Denver by wards. It should be noted that these statistics and those in Tables XVI, XVII, and XVIII are for all persons registered, regardless of whether or not they voted. These facts are found only in the registration-books, but in most cases the vote has to be obtained from the poll-books.

Other figures collected on the ownership and tenancy question are as follows:[1]

Cities and Elections	Owners Men	Owners Women	Tenants Men	Tenants Women	Lodgers Men	Lodgers Women
FALL ELECTION, 1900						
Cripple Creek	1105	770	2284	1006	426	56
Per cent	28.8	42.0	59.6	54.9	11.6	3.1
Victor	465	316	790	344	379	30
Per cent	28.5	45.7	48.3	49.8	23.2	4.5
Longmont	181	118	74	49	22	4
Per cent	65.3	69.0	26.7	28.7	8.0	2.3
SPRING ELECTION, '07						
Boulder	931	961	697	856	328	311
Per cent	47.6	45.2	35.6	40.2	16.8	14.6

[1] Before considering these figures it may be well to point out their precise meaning. Ownership refers, of course, to the residence from which the voter is registered. It is customary, in answering this question, to consider both the husband and the wife as owners if either has a legal title to the house. A daughter who lives at home is often counted in the same class, if the family residence is owned by her parents. In the case of a son who lives at home, too, though probably not as frequently, this is done. This fact tends to throw more women in the "owner" class at the expense of the "lodger" class. The figures cannot in any respect, however, be considered as proof positive, for they are liable to many errors from the ignorance or carelessness of the registration clerks and of the voters themselves.

STATISTICS OF ELECTIONS

TABLE XV

OWNERSHIP AND TENANCY OF PERSONS REGISTERD AT NOVEMBER, 1906, ELECTION

	Owner			Tenant			Lodger		
	Men	Per cent.	Women	Per cent.	Men	Per cent.	Women	Per cent.	Men	Per cent.	Women	Per cent.
Boulder	1,070	50.6	1,176	53.2	733	34.6	775	35	315	14.8	260	11.8
Cripple Creek[1]	688	31.2	611	38.6	1,172	53.2	889	56.3	344	15.6	80	5.1
Denver[2]	9,472	30.6	8,413	34.7	14,711	47.5	12,699	52.3	6,748	21.9	3,150	13
Durango	277	20.9	246	24.5	727	54.9	609	60.6	319	24.2	150	14.9
Goldfield	49	22.9	44	33.3	112	52.3	79	59.9	53	24.8	9	6.8
Greeley	630	34.4	570	42	689	37.6	508	37.4	512	28	279	20.6
Longmont	602	44.1	564	57	566	41.4	364	36.7	198	14.5	62	6.3
Telluride	134	25.3	120	41.1	205	38.7	128	43.8	191	36	44	15.1
Trinidad	532	42.3	465	41.3	522	41.5	522	46.4	205	16.2	138	12.3
Victor	85	9.6	92	21	617	69.8	311	70.8	182	20.6	36	8.2
Total	13,539	31.8	12,301	36.8	20,054	47	16,884	50.6	9,067	21.2	4,208	12.6

[1] Twenty-four men and twenty women in Cripple Creek not stated.
[2] One thousand two hundred and two (1202) men and eight hundred and ninety-two (892) women in Denver not stated.

EQUAL SUFFRAGE

Taking the table at its face value, it appears that in every town except one, Trinidad, the proportion of women owners exceeded the proportion of men owners. In every case, too, the proportion of women lodgers was less than the proportion of men lodgers, and the total percentage of women who were lodgers was not much more than half that of men who were lodgers. Among the tenants, in all but two cases, Greeley and Longmont, there was a larger proportion of women than of men, but the excess was slight compared with that of men lodgers over women lodgers. It would appear in general, then, that women voters are a more stable element in the population than men voters.

3. NATURALIZATION AND RACE

The proportion of foreign-born women as compared with foreign-born men voters is the next point of interest.[1] Table XVI gives a summary of the figures collected on this subject, with a rough classi-

[1] As to native and foreign-born population, Colorado differs little from the rest of the United States, having, in 1900, 16.9 per cent. foreign born, which is less than the average—20.7 per cent—for the entire Western division, but more than the average—13.7 per cent—for the United States. Between 1890 and 1900, however, the foreign born in Colorado increased only 8.5 per cent. as against an increase of 12.4 per cent. for the entire United States. In 1900 the foreign born of Denver constituted 18.9 per cent. of the total population. Of the whole foreign-born population in the state only a little more than a third, but in Denver nearly half, were females.

Negroes constituted, in 1900, only 1.6 per cent. of the total population of the state, and 2.9 per cent. of the population of Denver; but in the entire state nearly half, and in Denver more than half, of the negroes were females. See *Twelfth Census*, vol. i, Population, pp. c–cxxii. and 575.

STATISTICS OF ELECTIONS

TABLE XVI

NATURALIZED CITIZENS REGISTERED AT NOVEMBER, 1906, ELECTION

	German		Swede		Italian		Slavic		Miscellaneous		Total naturalized			
	Men	Women	Men	Women	Men	Women	Men	Women	Men	Women	Men	Per ct.	Women	Per ct.
Cripple Creek	86	28	46	16	1		22	9	168	43	323	77.1	96	22.9
Denver	1,601	861	956	526	272	136	838	540	2,698	1,685	6,367	63	3,748	37
Durango	85	30	23	8	23	1		1	110	43	241	74.6	82	25.4
Goldfield	6	3	7				7		32	6	52	83.9	10	16.1
Telluride	14	5	28	13	22	4			63	23	127	73.8	45	26.2
Trinidad	48	3	6	2	70	3	13	3	60	8	197	91.2	19	8.8
Victor	22	7	37	15			21	7	47	14	127	74.7	43	25.3
Total	1,862	937	1,103	580	390	144	901	560	3,178	1,822	7,434	64.8	4,043	35.2
Per cent	66.6	33.4	65.6	34.4	73.1	26.9	61.7	38.3	63.6	36.4				

115

fication, based on the character of the names, according to nationality. Boulder, Longmont, and Greeley are omitted, as the records in these places were too confused to yield even approximately accurate figures.

It appears that of the total number of naturalized citizens voting in Cripple Creek, Denver, Durango, Goldfield, Telluride, Trinidad, and Victor at the November, 1906, election, only 35.2 per cent. were women. This was about five per cent. less than the proportion of the total vote cast by women in the nine cities, as given in Table XIII, and two per cent. less than in all the counties studied. As may be seen, the proportions vary greatly in different localities. Thus in Trinidad only 8.8 per cent. of the naturalized voters were women as compared with 42 per cent. of all the voters, and in Goldfield only 16.1 per cent. of the naturalized voters were women as compared with 38 per cent. of all the voters. In Denver the proportion was the highest, 37 per cent. of the naturalized voters being women as compared with 42.6 per cent of all the voters.[1] The proportion of foreign-born women voters in every case, however, was considerably lower than that of foreign-born men voters.[2]

In the fall election of 1900 women cast only 8.2 per

[1] For an analysis of the Denver figures by wards, see Appendix D.
[2] These figures are doubtless roughly accurate, but it is possible that naturalized women may in some cases have been counted as native on account of the law which naturalizes a woman by the mere fact of the naturalization of her husband. This leads, in Colorado, to the curious anomaly that a foreign-born woman, without taking out papers of her own or expressing in any way her desire to become a citizen, may vote on exactly the same footing as a Daughter of the American Revolution.

cent. of the naturalized vote in Cripple Creek and 14.4 per cent. in Victor. According to the 1900 census, women constituted 39.5 per cent. of the foreign-born population of Cripple Creek, 34.7 per cent. of Victor, 43.8 per cent. of Durango, 44.5 per cent. of Trinidad, and 48.3 per cent. of Denver. Because of industrial conditions in the Cripple Creek district, the proportion of foreign-born women as compared with foreign-born men probably increased considerably between 1900 and 1906.

The colored vote is rarely distinguished from the white vote except in Denver, and it is, therefore, impossible to make even an estimate of its sex for any other city. In Denver, however, the registration-books used in the November, 1906, election contained the names of 1373 colored persons, 620, or 45.2 per cent., of whom were women. Women furnished, apparently, a larger proportion of the colored than of the total vote. This is partially explained, however, by the fact that, according to the census, there were in Denver, in 1900, 1881 male and 2042 female persons of negro descent. It is, therefore, evident that of the total colored population, not nearly as large a proportion of women as of men take advantage of the franchise privilege.

4. CONJUGAL CONDITION

The statistics collected in regard to the conjugal condition and occupations of women voters may be considered as only roughly indicative of the facts. Nevertheless, it is believed that, if the widowed and

EQUAL SUFFRAGE

married are taken as one class, a substantially accurate line may be drawn between the single, on the one hand, and the married and widowed on the other.[1] Table XVII gives the figures and percentages for the cities where it was possible to secure these facts.

TABLE XVII

CONJUGAL CONDITION OF WOMEN REGISTERED AT NOVEMBER, 1906, ELECTION

	Single		Married		Widowed	
	Number	Per cent.	Number	Per cent.	Number	Per cent.
Boulder........	484	21.8	1,559	70.1	178	8.1
Cripple Creek...	218	13.6	1,299	81.2	83	5.2
Denver[1]........	4,857	19.7	17,983	72.3	1,723	8
Durango........	146	14.5	805	80.1	54	5.4
Goldfield.......	13	9.8	118	89.4	1	.8
Greeley........	256	18.9	996	73.4	105	7.7
Longmont......	151	15.2	781	79	58	5.8
Telluride.......	55	18.8	214	73	24	8.2
Trinidad........	163	12.3	1,063	80.8	89	6.9
Victor..........	58	13.2	373	84.9	8	1.9
Total........	6,401	18.8	25,191	74.2	2,323	7

[1] The conjugal condition of five hundred and forty-six womens was not stated.

Taking the figures at their face value, it appears that in these ten cities 18.8 per cent. of all the women registered were single. But in the entire state, according to the census of 1900, only 16.5 per cent. of the women over twenty years of age were single,

[1] The distinction between the single and the married was doubtless drawn with substantial accuracy by the registration officers, but that between married and widowed seems to have been frequently neglected, and that between widowed and single was probably sometimes omitted. Most of the errors, however, would tend to increase the number of married at the expense of the widowed.

STATISTICS OF ELECTIONS

70.6 per cent. being married, 12.4 per cent. widowed or divorced, and 0.5 per cent. "unknown."[1] The registration figures for widows are too uncertain to compare with the census figures, but it appears from this rough comparison of ten cities with the entire state that the widowed and married together constituted a smaller proportion of the registered voters than of the total population. Precisely the opposite, however, appears to have been the case in Denver, for which the figures are probably more trustworthy. There, in 1906, only 19.7 per cent. of the registered women were single, though in 1900, of all women over twenty years of age, the single constituted 22.6 per cent., the married 61.7 per cent., the widowed and divorced 15.1 per cent., and the "unknown" 0.6 per cent.[2] In Denver, then, probably a larger proportion of the married and widowed than of the single women were registered.[3]

Further light is thrown on this question by the following figures, covering the registration of women in Cripple Creek, Victor, and Longmont in the fall

---

[1] The comparison is somewhat injured by the fact that the census age grouping makes it necessary to include in the population figures women from twenty to twenty-one years of age who are not, of course, included in the registration table. Moreover, the census gives the number of single, married, widowed, divorced, and "unknown" women only for the entire state and for Denver. In the registration-books the term divorced is rarely used, as a divorced woman is usually given as single or widowed. It seems best, therefore, for purposes of comparison, to add the divorced to the widowed.

[2] These percentages are derived from the *Twelfth Census*, vol. ii, Population, Part ii, p. 318, and those given above for the whole state are derived from the same volume, p. 261.

[3] For an analysis of the Denver figures by wards, see Appendix D.

election of 1900, and in Boulder in the spring municipal election of 1907:

Cities and Elections	Single		Married		Widowed	
	No.	Per cent.	No.	Per cent.	No.	Per cent.
FALL ELECTION, 1900						
Cripple Creek.......	272	14.9	1512	82.5	48	2.6
Victor..............	82	11.9	592	85.8	16	2.3
Longmont..........	11	6.4	152	89.0	8	4.6
SPRING ELECTION, '07						
Boulder............	580	26.0	1579	70.9	69	3.1

Except for the Boulder city election, which seems, through general interest in the saloon issue, to have brought to the polls an unusually large number of the unmarried, the proportions of single women shown in these figures are all lower than the proportion, 16.5 per cent., of single women in the population of the entire state.

5. OCCUPATIONS OF WOMEN VOTERS

Figures relating to the occupations of the women whose names appear on the registration-books are even more untrustworthy than those in regard to their conjugal condition. The occupation given is often a mere guess, and in many precincts no attempt at accuracy is made.[1] In Table XVIII, however, these figures, whatever they may be worth, are summarized. Under "no gainful occupation" are

[1] Married women are usually entered as housewives or housekeepers, unless they object and state another occupation. In one precinct the term housewife may be used exclusively, and in another the term housekeeper. Unmarried daughters living at home have their occupations given in some precincts merely as "family."

TABLE XVIII

OCCUPATIONS OF WOMEN REGISTERED AT NOVEMBER, 1906, ELECTION

	Boulder	Cripple Creek	Denver	Durango	Goldfield	Greeley	Longmont	Telluride	Trinidad	Victor	Totals	Per cent.
Agricultural pursuits...	5	2	9				4			1	20	.06
Professional service....	80	47	929	21	4	50	38	19	40	14	1,242	3.66
Domestic and personal service............	44	97	1,068			28	8	6	43	13	1,307	3.86
Trade and transportation	55	59	1,399	40	2	61	23	23	49	26	1,737	5.12
Manufacturing and mechanical pursuits...	43	23	733	7	3	36	18	6	23	3	895	2.64
Miscellaneous and indefinite.............	1	5	55		2	2			8	1	74	.22
No gainful occupation..	1,944	1,036	20,916	937	121	1,149	893	231	1,074	386	28,687	84.44

EQUAL SUFFRAGE

included "housewives" and "housekeepers," as no distinction could be drawn in the use of the terms. The proportion of women in this class is evidently somewhat higher than the proportion of married and widowed women given in the previous section.

The census of 1900[1] gives the following distribution of Denver females ten years of age and over engaged in gainful occupations:

FEMALES TEN YEARS OF AGE AND OVER ENGAGED IN GAINFUL OCCUPATIONS IN DENVER, 1900

	Number	Per cent.
Agricultural pursuits	22	.2
Professional service	1,695	13.9
Domestic and personal service	5,597	45.7
Trade and transportation	2,403	19.6
Manufacturing and mechanical pursuits	2,527	20.6
Total	12,244	100.0

Upon comparison, it seems evident that many women classed as "housewives" and "housekeepers" in the registration tables ought to be in the division "domestic and personal service." But no trustworthy conclusion can be drawn from these occupation figures.

6. SCHOOL ELECTIONS

Under the Colorado law no registration is required for school elections, and outside of Denver no records except of the total vote cast for and against particular candidates could be obtained. The following figures were secured for the vote at the school elections of 1904 and 1906 in School District No. 1, the principal district of Denver:

[1] See *Special Report on Occupations*, pp. 540–541.

STATISTICS OF ELECTIONS

Votes Cast at School Elections, Denver. District No. I	Men		Women	
	Number	Per cent.	Number	Per cent.
1904	6,970	52.9	6,204	47.1
1906	10,786	45.1	13,133	54.9

The total vote at school elections varies enormously, according to the heat of the contest. In Denver the standard issue relates to the disposition of the school funds, and the candidates are often said to represent the interests of different banks. Sometimes the newspapers try to arouse interest in their candidate by promising that he or she will favor the raising of teachers' salaries, and usually the personality of the candidate is a factor.

7. Vote Cast for Women Candidates

Women candidates, like men, sometimes run ahead and sometimes behind their tickets. The important factor is personal popularity rather than sex. In order, then, to determine whether, on the average, a woman runs as well or better than a man it is necessary to eliminate the personal element. This has been done, so far as the figures could be ascertained, by calculating the proportionate vote for men and for women candidates for state and county offices to the average for other offices for which about the same total vote was cast in the same party or parties in that year. Whenever there were two or more women candidates or two or more men candidates their votes were added together, so that the figures represent an average for the sexes. Thus, though in 1902 Mrs. Grenfell, candidate for superintendent of public instruction, ran nearly 7000 votes ahead of the average for her ticket and was the only candidate of her party elected to a state office, the proportion of votes cast for women candidates for that office to the average for state treasurer and secretary of state in the same parties was only 99.9. per cent. This means that the other women candidates ran far enough behind to a trifle more than counterbalance the lead of the successful candidate over her ticket.

It was found that in every year but one since women were enfranchised the total vote for state superintendent was somewhat less than the total vote for the other officers compared, usually state treasurer and secretary of state. Both men and women candidates for superintendent ran behind their tickets. Except in 1896 the men candidates for that office have belonged to one of the minor parties, and in that year the men ran further behind than did the women. Women candidates for state superintendent, indeed, except in 1894 and 1906, have always run ahead of men candidates for the office, and even in 1906 the woman who had been superintendent for two years was re-elected by a plurality over other candidates on her ticket of nearly five thousand votes. In order to retain a satisfactory official in this position there seems to be a tendency, perhaps primarily among women voters, to disregard party lines.

A woman candidate for lieutenant-governor in 1894 ran considerably ahead of the average vote for candidates

STATISTICS OF ELECTIONS

for governor and secretary of state on her ticket. The same may be said of a woman candidate for secretary of state in 1900, compared with attorney-general and state treasurer, and of a woman candidate for state treasurer in 1902, compared with secretary of state and attorney-general. But in both the latter cases the men candidates for the same offices also ran ahead of their tickets. On the other hand, women candidates for auditor in 1898 and 1904, compared with secretary of state and state treasurer, ran behind their tickets. In all these cases the women were candidates of minor parties.

For presidential electors, regents of the state university and state senators and representatives, figures were also calculated representing the proportionate vote for women candidates to that for men candidates for the same offices in the same party. The two women candidates for the office of regent of the state university in 1900 and 1902 ran ahead of their tickets, as did the woman candidate for state senator in 1902. Nevertheless, no woman has been elected to either of these offices in Colorado. The women candidates in 1902 for the House of Representatives from Arapahoe County, including Denver, on two tickets ran a trifle behind the men, on two a trifle ahead, and on the fifth exactly even. In 1906 the women candidates on the first ticket ran decidedly, and those on the second ticket somewhat, behind the men.[1] Two women candidates for Congress on the Socialist ticket ran, as compared with secretary of state and attorney-general, in one case behind and in the other ahead of the ticket.

In only twenty-six cases could the exact vote for women candidates for county offices be obtained, and in only nineteen of these did they run against

[1] The first ticket, as here used, indicates the ticket containing women candidates for which the highest number of votes was cast, and the second that containing women candidates for which the second highest number of votes was cast.

EQUAL SUFFRAGE

men. Of the latter cases, in six the women candidates, compared with two other county officers, in most instances clerk and treasurer, ran ahead of their tickets, and in thirteen they ran behind their tickets. Adding the seven cases in which there were no men candidates for the office desired by the women, the latter ran ahead of their tickets in eight instances, even in one, and behind in seventeen. Ten cases occurred in the year 1906, four in 1904, three each in 1895, 1897, and 1901, respectively, two in 1899, and one in 1903. In all but three of these the office was that of county superintendent. Two women candidates for clerk, in 1895 and 1897, and one for treasurer, in 1904, in Boulder County, ran further behind, as compared with the men candidates, than the average women candidates for county superintendent. In twenty-one cases out of thirty-nine, counting candidates of both sexes, the office of county superintendent failed to draw as large a vote as the other offices with which it was compared.

In Lake County the woman superintendent succeeded herself in office in 1906, and was the only person on her ticket elected, receiving a plurality of 1465 votes as compared with an average plurality of about 700 for candidates on the rival ticket. A Las Animas County man said that the only woman who ever ran for office in that county "came out ahead of her ticket in the city, but ran way behind in the country." Here, evidently, the Mexican vote was responsible for the weakness of the woman candidate. In Otero County the woman candidate for superintendent in 1906 received more than twice the majority given to the men on the same ticket. The same year in Jefferson County the woman elected superintendent ran somewhat behind the men elected to other offices, in Chaffee County far behind, and in El Paso County also behind. But in Montrose County the woman ran far ahead.

The only safe conclusion to be drawn from these few facts is that whether women candidates are a source of strength or weakness to a ticket "all depends on the woman." Upon the face of these figures more women have run behind than ahead, but unfortunately the three counties for which the most complete statistics could be obtained—Boulder, Delta, and San Miguel—cannot be considered as typical, because in the state as a whole more women than men have held the office of county superintendent, while in these three counties more men than women have been elected to that office.

IV

WOMEN IN PUBLIC OFFICE

WOMEN have served the State of Colorado in a variety of positions, from state superintendent of public instruction to park commissioner. The offices with which this chapter is especially concerned are, with the exception of places on the state boards and some of the city offices, elective, but women have served in even larger numbers in appointive positions. The latter offices, however, which seem to be primarily in the nature of "gainful occupations," are treated in the chapter on "Economic Aspects of Equal Suffrage." Consideration will here be given to elective offices and to appointive positions which carry no compensation or only sufficient to cover expenses.

A majority of the women who have served the public in Colorado have done so either in educational offices or on state and city boards. But in non-suffrage states, too, women have served in both of these classes of positions. In South Dakota, for example, in 1906, they held the office of county superintendent in eighteen counties out of fifty-three, and Illinois in 1905 had nine women out of one hundred and two county superintendents. In many states, too, women have served on boards of control of public charitable institutions. Illinois, for instance, had, in 1905, about a dozen women and over two hundred men, and New York had, in 1908, some fifty women and over three hundred men in such positions. More than half of these New York women were hospital managers, and a number of institutions for children had no women on their boards of control. Upon the whole, however, since 1894, a considerably larger part of the administrative work along educational and philanthropic lines has been done by women in Colorado than in non-suffrage states.

Even in the administration of justice, which, next to military service, may be considered as peculiarly man's sphere, owing to his greater physical strength, women have not been entirely lacking Colorado has had one woman police magistrate and two or three women deputy sheriffs, the latter appointed primarily to enable them to exercise greater authority in carrying on the work of the Humane Society. Women have also served on juries in a number of instances, though this is not customary. In theory and under the law they may be called upon for jury service just as often as men, but in practice their names are usually omitted in making up the panels, or, if drawn by mistake, women are generally excused from service on some technicality. There is more than one reason for this. The objections against locking up men and women together enter as one factor, but it is also considered that the duties of a housewife cannot be postponed during her service on a jury. In one case, however, which involved the fit of a woman's garment, the jury was composed entirely of women. It is not improbable, too, that the current agitation in favor of women on juries, especially in cases involving the interests of their own sex and of children, may ultimately result in the extension of jury service among the women of equal-suffrage states.

1. State Legislators

During the first decade of equal suffrage in Colorado ten women were elected members of the House of Representatives, one of whom served two terms, but the State Senate has never had a woman member. In the fall of 1894 three women representatives were chosen, two from Denver and one from Pueblo; in 1896 there were three women, all from Denver; in 1898 three women, two from Denver and one from Pueblo; and in 1900 and 1902 one woman in each year from Denver. After the session of 1903, however, there were no women in the State Legislature until the winter of 1909, when one woman, elected from Denver the previous fall, took her seat in the House. All of these women were married or widowed, several having grown or half-grown children. Most of them, too, were club-women of some local prominence, but only two or three had even state reputations before their election to the House of Representatives.

The record of women in the legislature has been fair, but not brilliant. They have averaged above the men members as a whole in intelligence, but no one of them could be classed with the most able of the men. On one occasion, however, a woman representative acted, creditably to herself and to her sex, as speaker of the House. In the number of committees on which they have served, of resolutions which they have offered, and of bills which they have introduced, they have averaged as high as the men. The character of bills mothered by them has been above the average of those fathered by the men. This is partly due to the fact that they have championed measures favored by women's organizations, which usually give careful and disinterested consideration to the subject of legislation.

As legislators, however, women have always been at a disadvantage because of their small numbers. A prominent Denver politician who, as a member of the legislature during most of the years in which women served, had every opportunity of forming an expert opinion, and who is protected from any accusation of prejudice by his ardent championship on every occasion of the woman's cause, said: "As legislators they are ineffective, because they do not attend caucuses, etc., where the real work is done. They don't attend these because they are not asked. They simply go on the floor and vote. There would have to be more of them to have any real influence."

2. STATE SUPERINTENDENTS OF PUBLIC INSTRUCTION

The office of state superintendent of public instruction has been held by women since 1894, and only once since that date has a man been presented by either of the two strongest political parties as a candidate for the position. Women are naturally most interested in this office, and it is the one least desired by male politicians. The salary is $3000 a year. In 1902, however, an unsuccessful effort was made by the Republican women to have a woman nominated for state auditor instead of for superintendent of public instruction, the reasons urged being as follows: "For eight years a woman has held that office [superintendent], and it is justly claimed along educational lines there should come influence from both men and women. It therefore seems wise at this time to place a man in nomination for the office of state superintendent of public instruction, thereby giving women an opportunity to show their ability in the conduct of other offices."[1]

Five women have served as state superintendent, two Republicans and three Democrats. Of these, the first was a widow with a grown daughter, and served only one term. She had been a teacher in early life, but not for many years previous to her nomination. The second was a teacher who married before the end of her term in office and died a few years later. The third was a married woman who had been a teacher, and who, after the death of an only child, had taken the position of superintendent of schools in her home county. From this she advanced to the office of state superintendent, which she held for three successive terms — the last as the only Democrat in any state office. She was succeeded by an unmarried woman, previously a teacher, who was

[1] Letter issued by the Woman's Republican League of Colorado, August 28, 1902, to County Central Committees.

twice elected on the Republican ticket, and defeated for a third term in the fall of 1908 by a Democratic woman who was also single and a teacher.

General supervision over the public schools of Colorado is vested in the state board of education, which is composed of the superintendent of public instruction, the secretary of state, and the attorney-general, with the first as president. The public school lands are managed by the state board of land commissioners, composed of the board of education and the governor. The state superintendent is also a member of the board of control of the state normal school, and is *ex-officio* state librarian. She has the appointment of two deputies, one of whom is acting state librarian and the other assistant state superintendent. Both of these offices have been held by women under the women superintendents. In addition to the duties here suggested and the general routine administration of her office, the superintendent of public instruction has the supervision of county superintendents, the preparation of blanks and lists of questions, the apportionment of funds among the counties, the visiting of schools, the holding of examinations for state diplomas, etc. Another duty falling to this officer under the law is the decision of cases arising under the school law. Finally, it naturally devolves upon the state superintendent to make a thorough study of the needs of the school system with a view to the recommendation of whatever legislation may be needed for its improvement In all of this work the women state superintendents have shown ability and good judgment, and under their management the public-school system of Colorado has grown and flourished until it is now one of the best in the United States.[1]

One of the most important, if not the most important, duties of the state superintendent is the management of the school funds and the school lands, and this furnishes the chief opportunity of the office, not simply for graft, but for the commission of blunders having serious and far-reaching consequences. But, instead of complaints of dishonesty, carelessness, and inefficiency, such as have spared no other state office in Colorado during these years, there is almost universal testimony to the honesty and efficiency of the state superintendents of public instruction. The leasing system applied to the school lands has brought excellent results, and, instead of present mismanagement of school funds, it is found that every superintendent's report since 1894 has called for legislation to provide for the return by the state of school funds invested in illegal state warrants in 1887, 1888, and 1889. The management of the women has evidently been better than that of the men who preceded them.

When the women first took control of the office, the state library was merely a roughly sorted and uncatalogued collection of documents. It is now an orderly and dignified library, with books carefully catalogued and the usual systematic provision for the

---

[1] See Appendix E for table showing number of teachers to 10,000 persons five to twenty-four years of age in Colorado and in other states. The school legislation of Colorado is considered in chap. vi, section 1.

convenience of readers. Much of the improvement would doubtless have been made by men if they had held control during the same years, but certainly the women have done well. No one thinks nowadays, however, of denying the ability of women to manage libraries. In 1908 ten other states, Georgia, Illinois, Louisiana, Maryland, Michigan, Mississippi, North Dakota, South Carolina, Tennessee, and Wyoming had women state librarians.

In the routine administration of the state superintendent's office many improvements have been made. New and excellent courses of study have been prepared. The biennial reports to the legislature have been greatly improved both in form and in substance. The decisions, too, of the women state superintendents have been, on the whole, at least as wise and just as similar decisions made by men.

Of the total school population of Colorado—*i.e.*, of children from five to eighteen years of age—94.71 per cent. were enrolled in the public schools in 1905-1906, which is a higher proportion than in any other state of the Union except Nevada, Idaho, and Washington. The proportion enrolled in the whole United States was only 74.43 per cent. In 1889-1890 only 72.20 per cent. of the school population of Colorado were enrolled, as compared with 68.71 per cent. for the whole United States, and in 1899-1900, 88.19 per cent. in Colorado, as compared with 72.43 per cent. in the whole United States. In Oregon, which seems a fair state for comparison, the percentage of school population enrolled in 1889-1890 was 74.78; in 1899-1900, 82.13; and in 1904-1905, the last year given, 88.92.[1] Although in 1889-1890, then, Colorado had a

[1] *Report of United States Commissioner of Education*, 1906, vol. i, p. 298.

smaller proportion of her school population enrolled than Oregon, in 1905-1906 Colorado's proportion was decidedly larger than that of Oregon in 1904-1905.

A comparison of the average number of days' schooling given for each child five to eighteen years of age in 1905-1906 shows that Colorado stands higher than any state in the Union except Massachusetts, Connecticut, Idaho, Washington, and California.[1] The actual number of days given in Colorado was 107.4 as compared with 101.8 in Oregon. The average daily expenditure per pupil in Colorado in 1903-1904, the last date available, was 26.4 cents, which is higher than in any other state except North Dakota, Montana, and Nevada.[2] In Oregon, during the same year, the average daily expenditure was 16.6 cents.

There seems, all things considered, ample warrant for the conclusion that the women who have held the office of state superintendent of public instruction in Colorado have made better records than the men who formerly held that office. Not by any means all of the improvement in the school system can, of course, be attributed to feminine management. The state had an excellent school system in 1893. But it has been rapidly improved and strengthened since that date, and it may be seriously questioned whether, if women had not been eligible for office during these years, the position of state superintendent would have fallen into as competent hands. It is generally conceded that in this office women have been more directly and indisputably successful than as state legislators.

[1] *Report of United States Commissioner of Education*, 1906, vol. i, p. 308.   [2] *Ibid.*, p. 310.

WOMEN IN PUBLIC OFFICE

Of Mrs. Helen M. Grenfell, the most famous of Colorado's women superintendents, an ex-governor of the state once said: "She is not only the best superintendent, but the best state official that Colorado has ever had." The following quotation serves to show, not merely the personality of the most prominent of Colorado's women office-holders, but also the type of woman who is calculated to win the greatest success in politics: "Mrs. Grenfell is strong, earnest, competent, yet womanly and inspiring. She has not made her office wait upon politics, and the result has amply justified her. . . . Mrs. Grenfell asks no special recognition on account of her sex, though she has always met with courteous treatment. She stands on her merits alone, as all women who are successful in public affairs must do, and on account of her reasonable and impersonal point of view has the faculty of working in harmony with the men associated with her."[1]

3. COUNTY SUPERINTENDENTS OF SCHOOLS

During the first twelve years after the passage of the equal-suffrage amendment, forty-seven out of fifty-nine counties in Colorado had women superintendents of schools.[2] Of these counties, in two the office was held by women for one term, in seven for two terms, in fourteen for three terms, in four for

[1] *Chautauquan*, 34:484. Raine, "Woman Suffrage in Colorado."
[2] The twelve counties in which women had not served in this office were: Boulder, Chaffee, Conejos, Costilla, Custer, Douglas, Las Animas, Montezuma, Rio Blanca, Rio Grande, Saguache, and Weld.

four terms, in seven for five terms, and in thirteen for the entire time since women have been eligible to office.

Until 1904 the county elections were held in the odd-numbered years, and consequently the change of superintendents did not begin as early in the counties as in the state, but in 1895 twenty-six counties elected women superintendents. At the next election only twenty-five women were elected, but in 1900 there were thirty women; in 1902, thirty-three women; in 1904, thirty-four women; in 1905, thirty-five women; and in 1907, thirty-six women. During this period forty-seven women and twenty-eight men have held the office for two terms, and nine women and fourteen men more than two terms.

One hundred and twenty different women have served as county superintendents. They have been elected by Republicans, Democrats, and Populists, and in one case a popular woman was elected county superintendent successively by the Populists, Populist-Silver Republicans, Populist-Republicans, Straight Republicans, and Democrats. It is not uncommon, moreover, for a woman to be nominated for this office by the Democratic Party and endorsed by the Republican, or *vice-versa*.

Of the fifty-eight women superintendents and ex-superintendents for whom the facts could be ascertained, nineteen were single, twenty-six married, and twelve widowed at the time of holding office. Of those who were married or widowed, twelve had no children, nine had one child, six had two children, five had three children, four had more than three children, and in three cases the number of children was not stated. Fourteen had at the time of holding office children under fourteen years of age, four had children from fourteen to twenty-one years of age, two had children over twenty-one, and seven did not state the ages.[1] Considering separately the twelve widows, three had no children, two had one child, one had two children, three had three children, two had more than three children, and one failed to state the number. On the other hand, at least one child of four of these widows was under fourteen years of age, three did not state the ages of their children, and the children of two were over twenty-one.

Fourteen of the fifty-eight women county superintendents and ex-county superintendents who answered the blank in 1906 gave their occupations as "housewife," twelve as "teacher," and twenty simply as "county superintendent." The rest named a variety of pursuits, such as "doctor," "librarian," "hotel-keeper," "farmer," with but one woman in each occupation. It should be said in this connection that in many counties which are small and sparsely settled the work of the office is not sufficient to occupy the entire time of the county superintendent. The salaries range from $100 to $2800, according to the population of the county.

The record of women county superintendents, like that of women state superintendents, is, upon the whole, excellent. It is true that some women have been put into office who did not have the ability, and one or two who did not have the character, to honor themselves and their constitutents by their public actions, but it would be very extraordinary if, among so many, there were not a few black sheep. The proportion, however, who have not been thoroughly successful has certainly not been as high as among

[1] See Table xxxvii.

EQUAL SUFFRAGE

men in other county offices during the same period. When women have been deficient, moreover, it has usually been from lack of the business ability requisite in such work as the organization of new school districts.

Of ninety-seven appeals against decisions of county school superintendents decided by the state board of education during the first ten years of equal suffrage, forty-five were against men and fifty-two against women superintendents. Of these, seven against men and ten against women were sustained, but three of the cases sustained against women were decided under peculiar conditions which make it at least possible that, in strict fairness, they should not be counted. In any event, considering that the women superintendents were in the majority during the period, this is a good record.

Women take an active and creditable part in the Association of County Superintendents of Schools, just as they do in the State Teachers' Association. And in a number of cases persons from different counties testify of their woman superintendent that she "has been the most efficient officer we have ever had in this county."

4. WOMEN IN OTHER COUNTY OFFICES

Little can be said about women in other county offices, save that in nineteen instances they have been elected county clerk, treasurer, or coroner, and in ten cases have been appointed as clerks of district or county courts, without apparent detriment to the public welfare or to themselves. Appendix F, I,

WOMEN IN PUBLIC OFFICE

shows the number of women who have served each county in Colorado, the office occupied, and the date of beginning duty. It appears that the office of clerk has been the favorite, for Logan County has retained a woman in that position since 1896, and women have served in five other counties. In two instances, however, they have acted as treasurer, and in two as coroner, a woman having served two terms in the latter office in Cheyenne County. In two counties women have acted as clerks of the district court, and in four counties—two terms in Arapahoe and four in Boulder—they have acted as clerks of the county court. Women have also frequently served as deputy county clerk, treasurer, or assessor. In some counties, indeed, it is the custom to appoint women to the latter positions.

5. Women in City Offices

In order to ascertain the number of women who have held city and town offices in Colorado, circulars were sent to the clerk or mayor of every city or town for which the State Directory of 1906 gave a population of over one hundred persons. Answers were received from all except four of the thirty-three cities credited with over two thousand population, and from more than half of the incorporated places in the state. Of the former class, the towns of over two thousand, thirteen reported that women had held city offices and sixteen that no women had ever served in such capacity. Only twenty of the incorporated places of under two thousand, however, answered that women had held city offices. This is not, of course, as in the case of the county positions, a complete census of women officials, but it is as nearly complete as could be obtained by repeated inquiry.

Appendix F, II, gives all the facts ascertained in regard to the number of women in city offices. It shows that they have served as clerks and recorders in twenty-five cities and towns, as treasurers in twenty-six, and as trustees in four. In Bellvue, a town of about one hundred population, women have been members of the common council, and in Greeley the office of city treasurer is always given to a woman.

The offices of clerk and treasurer in the smaller towns are appointive. In many of these places the salary attached is not more than fifteen dollars or so per month, or, in the case of the treasurer, a small percentage of the collections, and the offices are often given to needy widows. This is the case, for instance, in Altman, where women are always appointed to both these positions. This, however, is a mining community where men receive high wages, and can afford, in the distribution of public offices, to be generous to widows.

At Cañon City, in the spring of 1907, a woman physician was appointed health officer; a woman has served as park commissioner in Boulder; and women have acted as plumbing and health inspectors in Denver, wearing the star of the police department. There are doubtless other unrecorded instances of their holding similar appointive positions. Since women have voted, moreover, matrons have been installed at the Denver city-hall and at the larger city and county jails throughout the state. Women have also served on the Denver library board and art commission.

In the capital city no elective office, except that of school director, has ever been held by a woman, but three women were members of the first Charter Convention in 1903. These women were put, at their own request, upon the committee dealing with charities and corrections, and formulated an excellent plan for this work. Unfortunately, the charter framed by this convention was defeated at the polls. The second convention, however, had one woman member, who served ably and faithfully in assisting to frame the present charter.

6. Women on School Boards

Although the women of Colorado have been entitled to vote at school elections since the adoption of the state constitution in 1876, little interest seems to have been manifested until after their full enfranchisement in 1893. It has been impossible to discover, indeed, that during this entire period of seventeen years any women served on school boards. No records of school elections previous to 1894 have been preserved, but it is generally agreed that the women took little part except when aroused by some special issue.

One of the features of the agitation for equal suffrage in Denver in the early nineties, however, was the putting forward of women candidates for the East Denver school board. The first attempt was made in the spring of 1891, but, though probably more women voted at that election than ever before, the woman candidate is said to have received only three hundred out of about twelve hundred votes.[1] This defeat was partly due to the fact that the work was not begun early enough, and partly, doubtless, to the activity of men opposed to women on the school board. Two years later, however, at an unusually exciting election at which six thousand votes were cast for the four tickets in the field, another woman was elected by a majority of nineteen hundred votes.[2]

From 1893 to 1908 there was at least one woman on the School Board of District No. 1, or, since the Denver districts were consolidated in 1903, on the new Denver Board of Education. In 1895 a woman physician was added, but the next year the term of the woman elected in 1893 expired. Another woman was elected, however, in 1897, and these two served until 1900, when, their terms having expired, a fourth woman was elected after a lively contest. The latter served until the reorganization of the board in 1903, when Mrs. Margaret T. True was elected. Mrs. True was the only woman on the board, and served as its efficient president from 1906 to 1908, when she voluntarily retired and was replaced by a man.

During these years the second most important district in Denver, No. 17, has twice elected women to its school board, once in 1897 and again in 1901, but the third Denver district has never had a woman on its board.

[1] Susan B. Anthony and Ida Husted Harper, *History of Woman Suffrage*, vol. iv, p. 511. [2] *Ibid.*, p. 511.

WOMEN IN PUBLIC OFFICE

In other parts of the state many women have held school-board positions. It is difficult to secure accurate records for past years, but information at hand shows that of the larger towns women have been members of school boards in Colorado City, Cripple Creek, Georgetown, Greeley, Gunnison, Idaho Springs, Longmont, Ouray, and others. In at least half a dozen cases, and probably many more, women have been presidents of school boards, and they frequently serve as secretaries or treasurers. The custom of electing women to school boards seems to have become more common in recent years. In 1906, out of 4509 school directors in Colorado, 577, or 12.7 per cent., were women. In the same year, moreover, thirty-seven districts had two women on their school boards, and eleven had three women, the total membership in districts of the second and third classes.

In much of the work of school boards women are said to be more efficient than men because they take more interest and give more time. It is sometimes complained, however, that they shrink from business responsibility, and that when a school-house is to be built or bonds issued it is wiser to have men officials.

7. WOMEN ON STATE BOARDS

All of the previously considered positions, except court clerkships and town offices in small places, are elective, but women have also served as members of many of the boards of control of state institutions. These boards, with the exception of the regents of the University, are appointed by the governor. Though in several of the Western states, in which university regents are appointed, as in Illinois and Wisconsin, it has become customary or obligatory within recent years to place one woman on the board, no woman has ever been elected regent of the University of Colorado.

Previous to 1892 no woman had been appointed upon any state board, except that of the Home and Industrial School for Girls, which existed at the time, however, only in name. In January, 1894, moreover, out of about one hundred and forty such positions, women held only seven, one on the Board of Trustees of the Mute and Blind Institute, one on that of the State Industrial School, one on the State Board of Charities and Corrections, and two each on the boards of the Colorado Foundlings' and Orphans' Home and the State Home and Industrial School for Girls. Several new appointments were made early in that year, however, and by 1895 the number of women whose names appear on the lists had increased to seventeen.

In 1897 about twenty positions on state boards were filled by women; in 1899, fifteen; in 1901, sixteen; in 1903, fourteen; in 1905, twenty; and in 1907, twenty-one. The total number of positions on boards, which, as has been seen, was about one hundred and forty in 1894, had increased by 1906 to about one hundred and eighty-five.

Women served between 1894 and 1906 on fifteen of the twenty-six boards existing in the latter year. They have been in the majority on the Board of Control of the Girls Industrial School, and on that of the Home for Dependent Children. They have also furnished about one-third of the members of the Board of Charities and Corrections, and have usually had one member, in addition to the state superintendent, of the Normal School Board, and one or two of that of the School for Deaf and Blind. At least one or two women, moreover, have been members of the Board of Agriculture, the Board of Pardons, the Board of Arbitration, the Board of Health, the Board of Dental Examination, the Board of Horticulture, the Board of the State Industrial School, and the new Board of Nurse Examiners.

In these positions women have shown themselves quite as efficient as men, and in some instances they have signally distinguished themselves. Those who have served have belonged in many, if not in the majority of cases, to the leisure class, and could afford, without danger of neglect of other duties, to give much more time and attention to the work than could be given by the average man.

8. Conclusion

Though they have gained in their proportion of county superintendents and members of school boards, the women of Colorado seem, in other directions, since the early years of equal suffrage, to have lost ground in the distribution of elective offices. This is due, however, not to any record of dishonesty or inefficiency in office, but to three factors of an entirely different nature. First, there are many men who have a hankering for office; they are more experienced, and often less scrupulous politicians than women; and they are upheld by a powerful public opinion of both sexes that the woman should not take the man's job. Second, there are comparatively few women who desire office; those who do so are frequently deterred by distaste for the methods required to secure it; and they are seriously handicapped by the discovery that other women in voting cling much closer to party than to sex lines. Third, the normal political and economic motives were at first somewhat obscured by the uncertain element of the woman vote, and the men were not sure but they would be obliged to yield many offices in order to keep the new voters under the party whip. As things have settled down, however, they have discovered that the offices given to women may be quite narrowly limited without materially endangering party supremacy.

The record of women in office has been high. It is difficult to secure an adequate measure of the efficiency and honesty of individual office-holders, but the general opinion prevails that women have given, as a Weld County man put it, "more attention to business and less to wire-pulling than men." There is no record of a woman defaulter, though men defaulters in county and city offices have been distressingly common. Women office-holders have sometimes been accused of graft and of accepting bribes, but this has been only when charges of graft and bribery have been floating around in such numbers as to hit any one who stood in the lime-light. No such charge has ever been taken seriously enough to go beyond the opposition newspapers, and in only two or three cases have such accusations even gone beyond private conversation. In short, the record of women office-holders on the score of honesty is considerably above that of men office-holders.

Again, no woman has shown herself grossly inefficient in office, and several have made brilliant records — one, at least, attaining national eminence by reason of her excellent administration of the office of state superintendent of public instruction. In the matter of efficiency, then, women have made, on an average, better records than men. Their privilege of holding official positions has, moreover, brought out and developed talents which would otherwise have remained dormant and so have been lost to the state. It is unfortunate, however, that men and women rarely compete for the same office, because segregation along sex lines tends to hamper the selection of the fittest candidate. But, upon the whole, the administration of women in public office has been at least as successful, and, all things considered, probably more so, than the administration of men.

V

ECONOMIC ASPECTS OF EQUAL SUFFRAGE

AN important question concerning equal suffrage is its effect upon the work and wages of women. This problem is, however, incapable of entirely satisfactory solution—first, because adequate data on several important points cannot be obtained, and, second, because it is impossible to distinguish, in private employment at least, the influence exerted by equal suffrage from that exerted by other forces, such as trade-unionism.

The subject naturally divides itself into two parts—public and private employment. In the consideration of each, two questions arise: First—Has equal suffrage brought enlarged opportunities for employment? Second—Has it tended in any way to increase women's wages or to establish for women as compared with men "equal pay for equal work"? Another important question, however, is the influence of trade unions over wages. Twenty or thirty men, in answering the question-blank, endorsed the sentiment of a labor leader who gave the following answer regarding the influence of equal suffrage on wages: "Organized labor is the only force that has benefited the condition or wages of workers."

ECONOMIC ASPECTS

1. Public Employment

Many women in Colorado are employed as clerks, as stenographers in public offices, and as teachers. For the latter occupation fairly satisfactory information as to the number of each sex employed and their salaries in every year since 1885 may be obtained, but it is impossible to secure a definite basis of comparison by sexes of the numbers and wages of clerks and stenographers in the years before and after equal suffrage. The scattered facts available on this point, however, are given.

Considering first, then, public employees in appointive positions of a gainful character other than teachers, it is found that, according to the warrant register of 1890, there were regularly employed by the state in that year only two women, each at a salary of $90 per month. The register does not give the character of their work, but they were probably stenographers. During the same year there were fourteen men employed in unknown capacities at salaries ranging from $66.70 to $100, the average being $83.50.

In 1907, of all the employees in the capitol, 72, or 31 per cent., were women; and of the employees in purely clerical positions, 29, or 48 per cent., were women. It is interesting to note in this connection that in Ohio, in 1906, less than 15 per cent. of the employees in clerical positions were women,[1] and in New York, in 1908, only about 20 per cent. were women.[2]

---

[1] *Ohio Statistics*, 1906, pp. 34–62.
[2] *Legislative Manual, New York*, 1908, pp. 383–498.

EQUAL SUFFRAGE

Women clerks and stenographers in state offices in Colorado receive the same compensation as men for the same work, but the proportion of women in the higher positions is small compared with that in the lower. The salaries of state employees are fixed by law. All of the women employed in 1907, except fifteen, received exactly $100. Of the fifteen, three received $125, three $83, five $75, one $65, two $50, and one $25. The salaries of the men during the same year ranged from $65 to $300. Moreover, excluding elected officers, but including janitors and manual workers, most of whom were men, and all other persons employed in or about the capitol, the average salary of the women in 1907 was $93.92, and of the men $124.23.

For county offices in Denver, which before 1903 was the seat of Arapahoe, and since that date an independent county, no record of employees for any year previous to 1894 could be found except for the clerk's office. The abstract of employees in that office in 1892 shows six women, two at $90 and four at $100 per month, and eleven men whose salaries ranged from $75 to $125. In 1906 the Denver county clerk's office had twenty-five women with salaries of from $75 to $90, and only thirteen men with salaries of from $75 to $175 per month. Most of the work in this office is copying, which it is difficult to induce men to undertake at salaries which women are glad to receive. In the county assessor's office, however, where the work is difficult and particular, the proportions of the two sexes in 1906 were approximately reversed, there being fifteen women with an average salary of $75 and forty men with an average salary of $90. In the county treasurer's office, on the other hand, there were employed, in 1906, fifteen women and the same number of men. The salaries of the women ranged from $75 to $120 a month, the latter amount paid to an unusually capable woman of about twenty years' experience, and the salaries of the men ranged from $85 to $175 per month, the latter amount paid to the deputy.

The city records of Denver were destroyed by fire in 1903, so no information whatever could be obtained in regard to employees and wages previous to that date. In 1906 there were in permanent clerical positions eighteen women, with salaries ranging from $80 to $125, and an average of $88 per month, and nineteen men with salaries ranging from $90 to $175, and an average of $112.06 per month.

The other counties differ widely in the employment of women. Boulder County had, in 1906, two women stenographers employed in the county clerk's office, at a salary of $85 and $95 a month respectively. Before 1894 only $75 a month was paid. In La Plata County no women were employed in subordinate positions in 1906, and in Delta County two women deputies received $75 per month for the time they worked, which was not the entire year. In Las Animas County no women were employed in county offices until about 1903, but in 1906 there were two women in the treasurer's office, one serving as deputy at a salary of $125 per month, and one as clerk and stenographer at a salary of $80 per month. The City of Trinidad employed one woman stenographer at $75. In each of these cases the salary is said to be precisely the same as would be paid to men in the same positions, but the number of employees is too small to make possible any accurate comparisons of similar positions.

In Teller County the records for the treasurer's office show that between 1901 and 1906 six women were employed, one for a year and the others for periods varying from two to nine months, and that each received $80 per month. On the other hand, salaries for men in clerical positions in the treasurer's office of Teller County were given, in 1906, as $90 per month. The same difference was found in the county clerk's office, where women received $80 and men $90. Records of the early history of the county as far back as 1899 show that in the clerk's office twelve women were employed for varying periods of time, though for several years previous to 1906 there were none. In the latter year, however, two women were employed for six months each. The county assessor's office, too, in early years regularly employed a number of women, and in 1906 four—two at $80 and two at $75 per month. In 1893 a woman appeared upon the pay-roll as county assessor at $159.70 per month, but she merely received an honorary salary for nominally filling out the unexpired term of her deceased husband, and a deputy was specially appointed to do the work.

Weld County had, in 1906, five women employed in the county court-house at salaries ranging from $50 to $85, the latter sum paid to the deputy county clerk.

It is evident that, though in the smaller counties

women receive "equal pay for equal work," in those counties in which the amount of work is sufficient to justify a division of labor women are usually given the lower-salaried positions. Though it is almost universally asserted in Colorado that women receive the same pay as men in public employment, it is evident that this is true only as between very minutely classified positions. By overstepping the bounds of a reasonable classification, it may be said that women receive "equal pay for equal work," but, taking public employment as a whole, women receive considerably lower renumeration than men.

That as teachers, also, women receive lower salaries on the average than men is shown in Table XIX. Women who replace men in a school are not usually paid less than the men have received, but throughout the entire period included in the table, 1885–1906, women were apparently employed in the lower, and men in the higher, paid positions. That this is the custom, too, throughout the state appears in the table, given in Appendix G, of teachers' wages in 1906 by counties. Similar tables, moreover, for each year since 1885 show approximately the same conditions.

Comparing the wages of teachers in Colorado with their wages in sixteen other states, Table XX shows that the average monthly salaries of both men and women teachers in Colorado are higher than in any of the other states with the exception of Massachusetts for men and California for women.[1] It is noticeable,

[1] This is assuming that the figures derived from the Colorado state superintendent's report are strictly comparable with those of the United States Education Bureau for other states.

TABLE XIX

NUMBER OF TEACHERS IN GRADED AND UNGRADED SCHOOLS AND AVERAGE MONTHLY SALARIES IN COLORADO, 1885 TO 1906[1]

Year	Graded schools					Ungraded schools				
	Teachers		Salaries per month			Teachers		Salaries per month		
	Men	Women	Men	Women	Pr.ct. men's of women's sal.	Men	Women	Men	Women	Pr.ct. men's of women's sal.
1885	78	384	$106.39	$66.06	161.1	258	490	$51.26	$48.23	106.2
1886	76	394	113.33	71.71	158	271	565	51.03	45.21	112.9
1887	87	399	108.20	69.22	156.3	211	505	49.50	45.66	108.4
1888	80	283	99.53	64.95	153.2	283	830	49.41	43.05	114.8
1889	134	536	95.21	63.50	150	453	1,031	51.22	45.25	113.2
1890	144	614	96.80	62.78	154.2	478	1,139	51.84	44.48	116.6
1891	170	731	94.32	62.87	150	507	1,126	52.07	45.65	114.1
1892	170	838	103.91	64.28	161.7	495	1,250	51.25	46.29	110.7
1893	201	883	99.23	67.24	147.6	377	1,048	50.94	44.56	114.3
1894	...	...	...	(No figures	...	(given)	...	...	...	...
1895	...[2]	...	...[2]	...	...	643[2]	1728	60.84[2]	51.90	116.8
1896	...	...	...	(No figures	...	(given)	...	...	...	...
1897	279	1,194	88.88	64.62	137.5	434	998	49.14	42.81	114.7
1898	294	1,212	95.13	67.43	141.1	450	1,026	45.99	41.92	109.7
1899	331	1,331	89.43	61.84	144.6	408	1,038	45.76	42.50	107.7
1900	348	1,491	90.18	62.95	143.2	360	1,108	46.83	44.04	106.3
1901	339	1,502	91.04	63.33	143.7	374	1,173	48.35	44.18	109.4
1902	355	1,703	93.18	64.73	143.9	338	1,189	53.71	44.75	120
1903	359	1,728	89.22	64.34	138.6	342	1,207	50.09	46.10	108.6
1904	408	2,049	92.60	67.67	136.8	301	1,272	52.04	46.50	111.9
1905	425	2,067	91.61	64.10	142.9	261	1,410	54.69	45.99	118.9
1906	427	2,200	97.57	66.61	146.4	249	1,367	56.80	47.22	120.2

[1] From reports of state superintendents of public instruction.
[2] Figures for graded and ungraded schools not separately classified.

ECONOMIC ASPECTS

however, that men's salaries are higher proportionately to women's in Colorado than in the United States as a whole or in any division except the North Atlantic. That is, the difference in the salaries of men and women teachers in Colorado, instead of being unusually small, is unusually large. This is probably

TABLE XX

TEACHERS' SALARIES IN THE WHOLE UNITED STATES AND IN SEVENTEEN SELECTED STATES, 1905–1906

State or territory	Average monthly salaries of teachers [1]		
	Men	Women	Per cent. men's of women's salaries
United States................	$56.31	$43.80	128.6
North Atlantic Division........	64.95	44.11	147.3
Massachusetts...............	149.02	57.07	261.1
New York.................	86.72[2]	86.72[2]	.....
Pennsylvania...............	53.16	39.41	134.9
South Atlantic Division........	44.35	33.54	132.2
Georgia....................	33.83[2]	33.83[2]	.....
North Central Division.........	57.99	44.17	131.3
Ohio (1899–1900).............	45.00	40.00	112.5
Illinois.....................	74.57	57.54	129.6
Minnesota...................	62.86	42.85	146.7
Nebraska....................	60.78	43.49	139.8
Kansas (1904–1905)..........	48.00[3]	40.00[3]	120
South Central Division	46.35	38.10	121.6
Tennessee...................	39.00	35.00	111.4
Western Division..............	72.30	57.09	126.6
Idaho.......................	71.00	55.90	127
Wyoming...................	77.29	48.34	159.9
Utah.......................	77.79	51.96	149.7
Washington.................	67.86	53.50	126.9
Oregon (1904–1905)..........	54.22	42.05	128.9
California (1904–1905).......	80.00	64.60	123.8
Colorado...................	82.55	59.18	139.5

[1] All the figures except for Colorado are taken from the *Report of the United States Bureau of Education*, 1906, p. 305. The averages for the sections and for the United States are for those states reporting salaries. The figures for Colorado are not given in the *Education Bureau Report*, but are derived from the *Report of the Superintendent of Public Instruction of Colorado* for 1906. These seventeen states are selected for comparative purposes. It will be observed that all four of the equal-suffrage states are given.
[2] Average for both men and women.
[3] Does not include cities of the first and second class.

due to the greater proportion of men employed in the higher positions. But the conclusion is inevitable that, on the whole, men teachers are better paid in Colorado than women teachers.

There has been considerable agitation in Colorado, and especially in Denver, for an increase of teachers' salaries. The Board of Education of Colorado Springs in 1907 raised the maximum salary of grade teachers from $780 to $900. In Denver the actual yearly salaries paid in 1907 were: Two head teachers, $807.50; 376 grade teachers, $760; fifty grade teachers, $635; 28 grade substitutes, $570; 37 first assistants, $807.50; 30 alternating teachers, $950; 4 teaching German extra, $807.50; 1 assistant, $950; 1 assistant (German extra), $855; average yearly salary, $753.30; grand total, $398,497.50. It will be observed that no sum larger than $950 is even mentioned, and no regular grade teacher is paid over $760. The maximum salary of grade teachers in Seattle in the same year was $864; in Spokane, $1035; in Butte, $900; in Oakland, $942; in Chicago, $1000; in St. Louis, $840; in Boston, $1250; and in Detroit, $1000. It is evident that grade school teachers in Denver were not at that time as well paid as in many and possibly the majority of other cities.

More women than men are employed as teachers in Colorado, but this is universal throughout the United States. Table XXI shows, however, that the proportion of female teachers is somewhat higher in Colorado than in the United States as a whole, and higher than in the Western, the North Central, and both of the Southern divisions, though somewhat lower than in the North Atlantic Division. Of the seventeen states selected for comparison, Colorado

ECONOMIC ASPECTS

TABLE XXI

PER CENT. DISTRIBUTION OF TEACHERS BY SEX, 1890 AND 1900[1]

State or territory	Men 1900	Men 1890	Women 1900	Women 1890
Continental United States	26.6	29.2	73.4	70.8
North Atlantic Division	20.6	20.5	79.4	79.5
Massachusetts	15.8	14.5	84.2	85.5
New York	19.7	19.1	80.3	80.9
Pennsylvania	29.1	30.1	70.9	69.9
South Atlantic Division	31	36.1	69	63.9
Georgia	35.1	39.2	64.9	60.8
North Central Division	26.3	29.4	73.7	70.6
Ohio	35.8	39.2	64.2	60.8
Illinois	26	28.8	74	71.2
Minnesota	19	23.1	81	76.9
Nebraska	20.1	23.8	79.9	76.2
Kansas	28	33.9	72	66.1
South Central Division	38.1	44	61.9	56
Tennessee	41	46.4	59	53.6
Western Division	25.6	29.9	74.4	70.1
Idaho	30.7	35.7	69.3	64.3
Wyoming	16.6	20.7	83.4	79.3
Utah	39.1	39.6	60.9	60.4
Washington	29.7	35.9	70.3	64.1
Oregon	27.5	38.7	72.5	61.3
California	22.5	25.6	77.5	74.4
Colorado	22.8	27.4	77.2	72.6

[1] Part of table in *Census Bulletin* 23, Census Statistics of Teachers, p. 19. The seventeen states given separately are selected for comparative purposes. It will be observed that all four of the equal-suffrage states are included.

has a higher proportion of female teachers than any except Massachusetts, New York, Minnesota, Nebraska, Wyoming, and California. The ratio of female to male teachers, moreover, has steadily increased in Colorado since 1890. But it has also increased in the United States as a whole, and in all of the states given except Massachusetts and New York.

The report of the United States commissioner of education shows an even smaller proportion, 16.6 per cent. of the total for both sexes, of men teachers in

Colorado in 1905–1906. In 1889–1890 the proportion was 26.2 per cent., and in 1899–1900, 20.9 per cent. Meanwhile, however, the figures for the whole United States decreased from 34.5 per cent. in 1889–1890 to 29.9 per cent. in 1899–1900, and to 23.6 per cent in 1905–1906. In the Western Division the proportion of men teachers was 31.1 per cent. in 1889–1890, 24.7 per cent. in 1899–1900, and 19.5 per cent. in 1905–1906. For the state of Oregon the figures are 43.3 per cent., 28.4 per cent., and 20.3 per cent. for these years respectively.[1] The movement, then, for the increased employment of women as teachers in Colorado is evidently only a part of a general movement in the same direction all over the country.

2. Private Employment

As for the employment of women in private industry in Colorado, Table XXII shows the percentage of all females ten years of age and over engaged in gainful occupations in 1900, and their distribution by groups of occupations as compared with the whole United States, each geographical division separately, and seventeen selected states. The proportion in Colorado, 14.9 per cent., is a trifle less than that for the Western Division, 14.5 per cent., and considerably less than that for the whole United States, 18.8 per cent. In all states and geographical divisions the proportion engaged in domestic and personal service is highest, but in Colorado it is also higher than the percentage engaged in the same group of occupations in any other state or division except Minnesota, Tennessee, and Wyoming. The propor-

[1] *Report of the United States Commissioner of Education*, 1906, vol. i, p. 304.

ECONOMIC ASPECTS

TABLE XXII

PERCENTAGE OF TOTAL FEMALES, TEN YEARS OF AGE AND OVER, ENGAGED IN GAINFUL OCCUPATIONS, AND PERCENTAGE OF FEMALES ENGAGED IN EACH CLASS OF OCCUPATION OF TOTAL FEMALES, TEN YEARS OF AGE AND OVER, ENGAGED IN GAINFUL OCCUPATIONS, 1900 [1]

States and divisions	Per cent. of total females engaged in gainful occupations	Agricultural pursuits	Professional service	Domestic and personal service	Trade and transportation	Manufacturing and mechanical pursuits
Continental United States	18.8	18.4	8.1	39.4	9.4	24.7
North Atlantic Division	22.1	1.9	7.6	37.5	12.9	40.1
Massachusetts	28.1	.6	7.1	32.3	13.6	46.4
New York	23	1.9	7.7	39.5	14.3	36.6
Pennsylvania	18	2.5	7.5	40.6	12.2	37.2
South Atlantic Division	23.8	36.9	4.1	41.9	3.6	13.5
Georgia	27.5	45.9	3.	40.9	1.7	8.5
North Central Division	14.3	7.2	12.8	42.7	13	24.3
Ohio	15.1	6	10.2	40.4	13.8	29.6
Illinois	16.3	4.1	11	41.7	17.3	25.9
Minnesota	16.2	7	13.5	49.4	11	19.1
Nebraska	12.6	9.1	20.1	41.5	11.8	17.5
Kansas	10.4	11.9	19.1	39.8	11.1	18.1
South Central Division	19.6	50.7	4.4	35.1	2.6	7.2
Tennessee	15.8	29.2	5.	32.5	3.5	9.8
Western Division	14.5	7.8	15.2	43.1	13	20.9
Idaho	9.4	15.7	18.7	42.4	8.1	15.1
Wyoming	12.3	7.7	17.6	49.7	8.3	16.7
Utah	11.2	9.4	13.3	42	12.6	22.7
Washington	13	9.4	17.2	43.1	13.1	17.2
Oregon	13.3	8.5	18.2	40.6	13.2	19.5
California	16.5	5.5	15.4	40.6	15	23.5
Colorado	14.9	4.1	14.9	49.1	14.3	17.6

[1] Consolidation of parts of two tables in the *Twelfth Census*, Population, pt. ii, pp. cxxxi and cxli. The states given separately, seventeen in all, are selected for comparative purposes. It will be observed that all four of the equal-suffrage states are included.

tion engaged in trade and transportation in Colorado is precisely the same as in New York, and is higher than in any other state except Illinois and California. It appears elsewhere, too, that the proportion of saleswomen to salesmen in Denver is 27.3 per cent.,

EQUAL SUFFRAGE

which is lower than in New York, Philadelphia, Boston, Baltimore, or Washington, but higher than in Chicago, St. Louis, or New Orleans.[1]

In the proportion of women in professional service in 1900, Colorado ranks lower than the other Western states given, and slightly lower than the Western Division as a whole, but higher than any of the states farther east except Nebraska and Kansas. The proportion engaged in agricultural pursuits is lower than in any division except the North Atlantic, and very much lower than in the United States as a whole —4.1 per cent. as compared with 18.4 per cent. In manufacturing and mechanical pursuits, too, Colorado ranks lower than the whole United States, 17.6 per cent. as compared with 24.7 per cent., and lower than any of the other states given except Georgia, Nebraska, Tennessee, Idaho, Wyoming, and Washington.

The only occupation legally forbidden to women in Colorado is work in coal-mines, though in practice they are also excluded from metalliferous mines, smelters, and reduction-works. By police order, too, women have been prevented from serving as barmaids in Denver saloons. The women of Colorado are otherwise restricted in their choice of occupations only by their physical strength and their mental ability.

Public opinion was divided on the question of the influence of equal suffrage over wages and conditions of work. According to Table XXIII, of the men who

[1] *Statistics of Women at Work*, United States Census Bureau, 1900, p. 93.

ECONOMIC ASPECTS

TABLE XXIII

Question—What has been the effect of equal suffrage on the wages of women?

	Good Men	Good Women	None[3] Men	None[3] Women	No definite answer Men	No definite answer Women
I. Favorable to Equal Suffrage						
A. Political workers—state[1]	24	70	21	48	23	35
B. Employers and employees[2]	10		9		1	
C. Other citizens—state	85	31	84	26	53	38
D. Delegates—Denver	4	79	8	28	7	52
E. Prominent citizens—Denver	8	4	2	6	1	5
Total	131	184	124	108	85	130
Per cent	38.5	43.6	36.5	25.6	25	30.8
II. Unfavorable to Equal Suffrage						
A. Political workers—state[1]	6	5	23	13	8	2
B. Employers and employees[2]			3		5	
C. Other citizens—state	12	3	70	7	30	9
D. Delegates—Denver	3	8	16	20	3	22
E. Prominent citizens—Denver			3	1		
Total	21	16	115	41	46	33
Per cent	11.5	17.8	63.2	45.5	25.3	36.7
III. Indifferent to Equal Suffrage						
A. Political workers—state[1]	2	4	13	9	5	8
B. Employers and employees[2]			5			
C. Other citizens—state	7	5	24	5	27	14
D. Delegates—Denver		5	4	6	3	17
E. Prominent citizens—Denver	1		2		1	
Total	10	14	48	20	36	39
Per cent	10.6	19.2	51.1	27.4	38.3	53.4
Grand total	162	214	287	169	167	202
Grand per cent	26.3	36.6	46.6	28.8	27.1	34.6

[1] Includes state legislators, county superintendents, and chairmen, women workers, experienced and inexperienced, throughout the state.
[2] Includes employers and employees, socialists, and trade unionists.
[3] None of the persons answering the blank stated that they believed the effect bad.

answered any of the questions on the blank, 26.3 per cent., and of the women 36.6 per cent., believed that in general employment, without distinction between public and private, it has had a good effect. It was evident, however, that a considerable number of these answers were based on the increased opportunities to fill political positions—the "equal pay for equal work" in public employment already discussed —or on the general statement that wages have increased within the past ten or a dozen years. It may also be observed that out of one hundred and sixty-two men and two hundred and fourteen women who said that equal suffrage has had a good effect on wages and conditions of employment, one hundred and thirty-one of the men and one hundred and eighty-four of the women believed in woman's enfranchisement. Moreover, 46.6 per cent. of the men and 28.8 per cent. of the women considered that equal suffrage has had no effect on wages or employment, and 27.1 per cent. of the men and 34.6 per cent. of the women gave no definite answers. Public opinion, however, is not valuable on this question, because of the meagre information of the average person.

Such a large number of complicated factors enter into changes in wages during periods of time that comparisons of women's wages in Colorado before and since the adoption of equal suffrage are of no value. Some importance may be attached, however, to the relation between the wages of men and women in Colorado and in other states. Table XXIV shows this relation for manufacturing industries in 1905.

ECONOMIC ASPECTS

The table is arranged in the order of the proportion of men's to women's wages, with the states first which have the smallest percentage, and therefore the nearest equality in wages. Massachusetts leads with a percentage of 159.1, and the highest percentage, 278.1, is found in Utah. Colorado stands near the middle with a percentage of 194.5. Colorado is first, however, of these states in the amount of men's wages, Utah second, California third, Wyoming fourth, and Idaho fifth. The first five states in amount of men's wages are, then, the four equal-suffrage states and

TABLE XXIV

COMPARISON OF MEN'S WAGES AND WOMEN'S WAGES IN MANUFACTURING INDUSTRIES IN SEVENTEEN STATES AND THE UNITED STATES, 1905 [1]

State	Average wage [2] Women	Average wage [2] Men	Per cent. men's of women's wage
Massachusetts	$343.00	$546.00	159.1
Georgia	198.00	329.00	166.1
Wyoming	408.00	695.00	170.3
New York	321.00	579.00	180.3
Illinois	329.00	597.00	181.4
Nebraska	310.00	585.00	188.7
Washington	349.00	676.00	193.6
Colorado	365.00	720.00	194.5
Minnesota	280.00	548.00	195.7
Pennsylvania	275.00	546.00	198.5
Idaho	345.00	688.00	199.4
Ohio	274.00	547.00	200
Tennessee	199.00	408.00	205
California	334.00	703.00	210.4
Oregon	305.39	650.15	213.1
Kansas	258.00	560.00	217
Utah	255.00	710.00	278.4
United States	298.00	534.00	179.1

[1] This table is derived from *Census Bulletin* 57, Census of Manufactures, 1905, pp. 54–56. It will be observed that in the seventeen states selected for comparison all four of the equal-suffrage states are included.
[2] This means an average yearly *rate* of wages, and not average earnings, and is for men and women sixteen years of age and over.

EQUAL SUFFRAGE

California. Glancing down the column of women's wages, it is seen that the highest are received in Wyoming, the second highest in Colorado, the third in Washington, the fourth in Massachusetts, and the fifth in Idaho, with Utah well down toward the bottom. Of these states, then, the first five in amount of women's wages include three of the equal-suffrage states, Washington, and Massachusetts.

Table XXIV shows, however, only the average yearly rate of wages, and not average earnings. But in Table XXV there is summarized the median group and average weekly wages of men and women sixteen years of age and over engaged in manufacturing industries in these same seventeen states. As before, the states are arranged in the order of the proportion of men's to women's wages. Georgia comes first with a percentage of 158, and Utah last with a percentage of 250. Colorado comes farther down in the column than before, with a percentage of 207. In other words, the average weekly earnings of men were more than double those of women in manufacturing industries in Colorado in 1905. In actual amount of weekly earnings, moreover, Colorado ranks sixth of all the states of the Union for men, but only eighth for women.[1]

All that these tables seem to definitely prove, however, is that the wages of both sexes are comparatively high in the Mountain States. Whether equal suffrage has anything to do with this is a matter of conjecture.

[1] *Census Bulletin* 93, Census of Manufactures, 1905; Earnings of Wage-Earners, p. 38.

ECONOMIC ASPECTS

TABLE XXV

MEDIAN GROUPS AND AVERAGE WEEKLY EARNINGS OF MEN AND WOMEN IN MANUFACTURING INDUSTRIES IN SEVENTEEN STATES AND THE UNITED STATES, 1905 [1]

State	Women, 16 years and over — Median group of earnings	Women — Average weekly earnings	Men, 16 years and over — Median group of earnings	Men — Average weekly earnings	Per cent. men's of women's average weekly earnings
Georgia..........	$4 to $5	$4.24	$6 to $7	$ 6.70	158
Massachusetts...	6 to 7	6.91	10 to 12	11.15	161.3
New York......	6 to 7	6.54	10 to 12	11.79	180.2
Tennessee.......	4 to 5	4.37	7 to 8	8.17	186.9
Minnesota.......	6 to 7	6.27	10 to 12	11.75	187.4
Oregon..........	6 to 7	7.02	12 to 15	13.21	188.1
Illinois..........	6 to 7	6.54	10 to 12	12.37	189.1
Idaho...........	6 to 7	7.62	12 to 15	15.30	200.7
California.......	7 to 8	7.24	12 to 15	14.59	201.5
Pennsylvania....	5 to 6	5.68	10 to 12	11.53	202.9
Colorado........	6 to 7	7.14	12 to 15	14.78	207
Nebraska.......	5 to 6	5.60	10 to 12	11.66	208.2
Washington.....	6 to 7	6.69	12 to 15	14.13	211.2
Ohio............	5 to 6	5.43	10 to 12	11.49	211.4
Wyoming.......	6 to 7	7.18	15 to 20	15.93	221.8
Kansas..........	4 to 5	5.01	10 to 12	11.22	223.9
Utah............	5 to 6	5.34	12 to 15	13.35	250
United States.	6 to 7	6.17	10 to 12	11.16	180.8

[1] This table is derived from *Census Bulletin* 93, Census of Manufactures, 1905: Earnings of Wage-Earners, p. 36. It will be observed that in the seventeen states selected for comparison all four of the equal-suffrage states are included.

Other interesting facts in regard to the wages of men and women may be gleaned from the reports of the Colorado labor bureau. In 1902, for instance, it was found that the average yearly earnings of barbers in Colorado were $494.05, and of hair-dressers $333.56.[2] Figures for women's wages in other occupations in that year, and the number of women included who belonged to labor organizations, are given in Table XXVI.

The last published report of the Colorado labor bu-

[2] *Eighth Biennial Report of the Colorado Bureau of Labor Statistics*, pp. 42–43.

TABLE XXVI

STATISTICS OF WOMEN WAGE-EARNERS IN COLORADO, BY OCCUPATIONS, 1902 [1]

Occupation	Number of persons reporting	Average yearly earnings	Number belonging to a labor organization
Bindery girls	32	$347.79	32
Bookkeepers	18	595.06	
Clerks and saleswomen	98	369.01	46
Cooks	15	383.66	6
Cracker-packers	7	288.31	7
Chambermaids	23	201.76	
Factory operatives	53	251.43	
Garment workers	37	308.77	37
Housemaids	31	185.63	4
Laundry girls	48	300.35	19
Milliners	11	398.20	
Nurses	7	531.38	
Printers	9	316.35	2
Seamstresses	17	318.97	
Stenographers & typewriters	31	535.39	12
Taloresses	13	503.44	
Telephone girls	30	484.50	
Waitresses	59	285.05	34
Total and averages	558	$371.63	199

[1] *Eighth Biennial Report of the Colorado Bureau of Labor Statistics*, 1902, pp. 42–43.

reau shows [2] that in 1904 bindery girls received $7 to $10 per week; chambermaids, $12 to $25 per month, with board and room; housemaids, $15 to $25 per month, with board and room; milliners, $7.50 to $15 per week; trained nurses, $2 to $5 per day; seamstresses, $6 to $12 per week; and telephone girls, $35 to $50 per month. It also shows that laundry girls received $4 to $9 per week, and laundrymen $6 to $15 per week; taloresses, $10 to $18 per week, and tailors $13 to $25 per week; waitresses, $4 to $15 per week, and waiters $4 to $17.50 per week, both of the latter with meals. It is not stated upon how many schedules

[2] *Ninth Biennial Report of the Colorado Bureau of Labor Statistics*, pp. 41–44.

ECONOMIC ASPECTS

these figures were based or from what localities within the state the schedules were received.[1]

Figures in the Bulletin of the United States Bureau of Labor, too, furnish an interesting comparison of the wages and hours of women book-sewers and of men bookbinders in 1906.[2] In Denver the women worked only forty-eight hours a week, which is less by nearly two hours than in any of the twenty-eight other cities. Their wages, too, 17.5 cents an hour, were higher than in any other city except New York, where they were 18.6 cents. Male bookbinders in Denver also worked forty-eight hours a week,[3] less than in any of the other thirty-nine cities given except Butte, Montana, and Seattle and Tacoma, Washington, and received 39.6 cents an hour, which represents higher wages than in any of the other places except Albany, Butte, and Tacoma. Evidently, therefore, though the wages of the women book-sewers in Denver

---

[1] The Tenth Report of the Colorado Bureau of Labor Statistics, owing, it is said, to its radical character, has not been published, but the deputy commissioner in office during 1905–1906 furnished to the newspapers the statistics collected of daily wages of men and women in different occupations in Denver. According to these figures, in dye-works men received from $1.50 to $3.00, and women from $1.00 to $2.00; in paper-mills men received $1.66, and women 75 cents; in printing-houses men received 66 cents to $4.16, and women 66 cents to $1.66; in the manufacture of tents and awnings men received $2.00 to $3.33, and women $1.25 to $3.00; in making pickles and extracts men received $1.50 to $7.00, and women $1.00 to $2.00; in making cigar-boxes men received $1.75 to $2.75, and women $1.00; and in the manufacture of overalls and shirts men received $3.25, and women 75 cents to $1.25.

The department stores and laundries in that city paid as low as $3.00 a week to women workers. A great discrepancy between men's and women's wages is observable in all the occupations mentioned.

For the census figures of wages of men and women in different manufacturing industries in Denver and Pueblo in 1905, see Appendix H.

[2] *Bulletin of the Bureau of Labor*, No. 71, July, 1907, p. 154.

[3] *Ibid.*, p. 153.

were not half those of the men bookbinders, the chief differences were due to locality and not to sex.

The natural conclusion from these facts and figures seems to be that in Denver wages in some lines of employment are higher than in many other places. But the probability is, as a Denver employer put it, that "suffrage has nothing to do with the wages of either men or women. The wages of men and women in all fields of industry are governed by economic conditions." A member of the State Legislature from Denver added: "Three dollars a week in the big stores for women and girls does not look as though equal suffrage was a success in that line. In this connection it must be remembered that in the lighter employments the wages of both men and women in Colorado are sometimes depressed slightly by the fact that the state is largely used as a health resort for semi-invalids." This fact probably affects women's wages more than men's because they are more largely engaged in the lighter employments.

3. WOMEN IN TRADE UNIONS

Trade-union leaders who have formulated any opinion on the subject have usually been favorable to equal suffrage. As early as 1831, at a meeting of the "Association of Working People of Newcastle County," Wilmington, Delaware, a committee reporting upon the proposed new state constitution vigorously maintained that women should not be excluded "from the right of voting at the polls." [1] In

[1] *Carey's Select Scraps.* (Newspaper clippings made by Mathew Carey, and preserved in the Ridgway Library, Philadelphia.) Vol. xxxi, pp. 156–161.

ECONOMIC ASPECTS

the late sixties the equal-suffrage organ, *The Revolution*, was distinctly friendly to labor organizations, and William H. Sylvis, one of the presidents of the National Labor Union, repeatedly declared himself in favor of equal suffrage.[1] It is asserted, too, in the life of Richard Trevellick,[2] the last president of that organization, that he was a strong believer in equal suffrage, and that at one time, probably in territorial days, he stumped the state of Colorado on that issue.

The connection of the suffragists with the trade-union movement was weakened, however, when, in 1869, Susan B. Anthony advised women to take the places of striking New York printers. Because of this, though she had been a delegate to the 1868 convention of the National Labor Union, and had there made an effort to gain for women "the same wages for the same work,"[3] she was the next year denied admission as a delegate to that body. The equal suffragists made many attempts in those days to have their principles adopted by women's labor organizations, but usually without success, the working-women saying that it was not the ballot but a living wage that they wished.

It is interesting, too, to note that in the state of Colorado, where the experiment of equal suffrage under a republican form of government has been, perhaps, most thoroughly tried, the strongest labor organization, that of the miners, and many smaller

---

[1] Sylvis, *Biography of William H. Sylvis*, pp. 221-222, 398-400.
[2] *Life of Richard Trevellick*, p. 56.
[3] *The Revolution*, September 24, 1868.

unions, have endorsed equal suffrage along with the rest of the Socialist platform.

Women are generally much more difficult to organize in trade unions than men, and, once within the organization, they usually take less interest in its affairs. In unions by themselves, however, they take more active part than in mixed unions, where their rôle is usually a silent one, unless the proportion of women to men is very large. Unions almost universally demand "equal pay for equal work," which tends in some trades, it is said, to drive out the women, but at least equality is established in union shops. It has been found that women's unions usually flourish "in a locality where all trades are well organized and where the men workers have a strong union and women's work is supplementary rather than competitive with men's; in trades where a comparatively high standard of intelligence is found; where women are American born (though of foreign parents)."[1] These are undoubtedly far more powerful factors in stimulating the organization of women in labor unions than their power to vote.

A study of women in trade unions in Colorado reveals few facts of importance in an investigation of equal suffrage. As in other states, the number of women's unions which have succeeded is small in comparison with those that have failed, and it does not clearly appear that Colorado women are either more or less steadfast in this matter than those of other states. The record of Trinidad, for instance,

[1] Belva Mary Herron, *The Progress of Labor Organizations Among Women*, University of Illinois Studies, vol. i, No. 10, p. 67.

ECONOMIC ASPECTS

shows a cooks' and waitresses' union which lasted just four months; an organization of laundry workers, with five men and thirteen women members, which lived eight months; a retail clerks' union of both sexes, which held out nearly four years, and then disbanded, largely because of the difficulty of keeping the women organized; and a woman's auxiliary to the Trades Council, which, though primarily social, survived for only two years. In Cripple Creek the Woman's Auxiliary of the Western Federation of Miners was actively engaged in the distribution of relief during the "Labor War of 1904," but succumbed after the defeat of the Federation.

The first labor organization in Colorado to which women were eligible as members was Denver Local No. 49 of the International Typographical Union, organized in April, 1860.[1] It does not appear, however, how early in the history of this union women actually applied for membership. The second trade union in Colorado was that of the journeymen tailors of Denver, organized in June, 1871. One of the cardinal principles of this organization was equal pay for women, and it is probable that it contained the first women trade unionists of the state. The deputy labor commissioner said, in 1888: "The prices paid in union shops in Denver for vests—which are nearly all made by females—range from $2.50 to $3.50, according to quality. In non-union shops, prices for making articles of similar quality range from $1.25 to $1.75."[2]

---

[1] *First Biennial Report of the Colorado Bureau of Labor Statistics*, 1888, pp. 86–87.   [2] *Ibid.*, p. 89.

EQUAL SUFFRAGE

Cigar-makers' Union No. 129 of Denver, organized in August, 1884, also admitted women members.[1] This organization, from the beginning, succeeded in procuring for women the same rate of pay as for men.

Another union which early brought advantages to women workers was Waiters' Union No. 14 of Denver, which was organized in November, 1891. The deputy labor commissioner of Colorado reported, in 1900, that this union had reduced the hours from fourteen to eleven a day, and had raised men's wages from $9 to $10 and women's wages from $6 to $8.[2]

All of the preceding were unions organized and conducted by men, though women members were admitted; but in 1896 two new unions were started, one of garment-workers, composed principally of women, and one of bindery women, containing no men. The membership of the Garment-Workers' Union was at first made up exclusively of employees of the Underhill Overall Factory, and early in its history an agreement was entered into with the managers of that company by which only members of the union should be employed. This union started in 1896 with 35 members,[3] but in 1904 had a membership of 140,[4] and was in a flourishing condition. Its success has been due primarily to the fact that it is a "label" union, and the employers desire the use of the label because their goods are sold largely to union men who

---

[1] *First Biennial Report of the Colorado Bureau of Labor Statistics*, 1888, p. 74.

[2] *Seventh Biennial Report of the Colorado Bureau of Labor Statistics*, 1900, p. 36.   [3] *Ibid.*, p. 17.

[4] *Ninth Biennial Report of the Colorado Bureau of Labor Statistics*, 1904, p. 236.

ECONOMIC ASPECTS

demand it. Another garment-workers' union was started in 1900 as an offshoot of the tailors' union, with a membership composed largely of foreigners of both sexes, but this was unsuccessful, and is not now in existence.

Bindery Women's Union No. 58 of Denver was also organized in 1896,[1] and received a charter from the Bookbinders' Union. This, like the first Garment-Workers' Union, was still alive and flourishing in 1907.

The next trade organization composed exclusively of women seems to have been the Denver Council of the National Association of Women Stenographers, which was organized in June, 1898, by Miss Gertrude Beeks. The "Honorary Board" of this organization included some of the most prominent women in social and club circles in Denver, and its objects were literary and fraternal. In October, 1898, it formed an alliance with the Woman's Club of Denver, and together the two organizations arranged for the "Evening Extension of the Woman's Club," which any business-woman could join upon the payment of one dollar a year. The "Denver Council," however, existed for only two or three years.

The Colorado State Stenographers' Association was organized in May, 1900, and to its membership both sexes were eligible. Its objects were declared to be: "To advance and protect professional interests of members, to assist them in procuring employment, to encourage and develop their ability, and to elevate

[1] *Seventh Biennial Report of the Colorado Bureau of Labor Statistics*, p. 12.

the profession in general." [1] A stenographers' union had been organized in Denver about eight years before,[2] but was apparently short-lived. According to the census there were, in 1900, 776 stenographers and typewriters in Denver—230 men and 546 women. But in 1904 the Stenographers' Union had only one hundred members, and, evidently, little power.

To summarize the scattered facts. In 1892, so far as known, no trade unions composed exclusively of women existed in Colorado, though there were about sixteen organizations in six different towns and cities to which women members were eligible.[3] In 1900 there were two exclusively or primarily women's unions, both in Denver, and twenty-five or thirty unions to which women were eligible in eight or ten towns and cities.[4]

In 1904 in the entire state there were only eight unions which had women secretaries.[5] These were Bindery Women's Union No. 58 of Denver, Garment-Workers' Union No. 139 of Denver, Clothing-Makers' Union No. 16 of Denver, Stenographers' and Typewriters' Union No. 211 of Denver, two laundry-workers unions—one in Denver and the other in Leadville—and two branches of the Retail Clerks' International Protective Association—one in

[1] *Seventh Biennial Report of the Colorado Bureau of Labor Statistics*, p. 30.
[2] *Third Biennial Report of the Colorado Bureau of Labor Statistics*, p. 62.   [3] *Ibid.*, pp. 60–63.
[4] *Seventh Biennial Report of the Colorado Bureau of Labor Statistics*, pp. 41–49.
[5] *Ninth Biennial Report of the Colorado Bureau of Labor Statistics*, pp. 231–245.

ECONOMIC ASPECTS

Pueblo and one in Fort Collins. There were, also, two other laundry-workers' unions — one in Pueblo and one in Cripple Creek—and thirteen other branches of the Retail Clerks'—in Denver, Cripple Creek, Victor, Colorado Springs, Aspen, Trinidad, Leadville, Colorado City, Cañon City, Grand Junction, Salida, Florence, and Lafayette. The Typographical Union, moreover, had twelve branches in the state; the Cooks' and Waiters', eight; the Tailors', seven; the Bakers' and Confectioners', six, the Cigar-Makers', four; and about half a dozen other unions which admit women members, one each.[1]

It should be added, however, that there were, in 1907, in Denver, not appearing in the preceding list, unions of tobacco-strippers, of shirt-waist and laundry workers, of musicians, and of hotel and restaurant employees, including many women, as well as two women's auxiliaries and a woman's label league. The tobacco-strippers had in that year a membership of about one hundred, and the garment-workers a membership of 233.

For the most part, women's unions have not been aggressive, but in 1907 the Shirt-Waist and Laundry Workers' Union made a stand for an eight-hour day. Failing to secure trade agreements for the shorter hours, they appealed to the courts to enforce the eight-hour law for women which had been on the statute-books since 1903. They secured two convictions in

---

[1] No complete list of Colorado unions has been published since 1904, and it was impossible to ascertain, without far greater effort than seemed justified in a study of equal suffrage, the actual number of women members in these organizations.

the lower courts, but, on appeal, the law was declared unconstitutional. Later, the Woman's Club of Denver took up the matter, and the pressure of public opinion secured for women workers in many laundries an eight-hour day.

So far as the effects of equal suffrage on the trade-union movement are concerned, it is manifestly impossible, as in the case of wages, to isolate woman's enfranchisement as a separate factor. The history of trade-unionism among the women of Colorado does not differ materially, so far as can be discovered, from its history in other states. Only a minute study of the movement in several localities could reveal the points of difference between suffrage and non-suffrage states and cities, and no such study has yet been made. The only basis of comparison is furnished by *The History of Trade Unionism Among Women in Boston*, published by the Women's Trade Union League of Massachusetts. Conditions in Denver and Boston, however, differ in too many respects to warrant any deductions derived from a comparison of these two cities. It is highly probable, too, that the most careful and minute study of this point would result only in unsatisfactorily negative results.

4. Conclusion

The economic effect of equal suffrage during the first dozen years of its existence in Colorado has evidently been slight. The only clearly demonstrable results, indeed, appear to have been the opening-up to women of a few new avenues of employment, such as political canvassing and elective offices, their employ-

ECONOMIC ASPECTS

ment in somewhat greater numbers as clerks and stenographers in public offices, and the equalizing in most public positions of their salaries with those of men doing the same work. But the positions are graded, and men are given the best-paid places. The average wages, even of women teachers, are still decidedly lower than those of men teachers.

Considering the slight influence which equal suffrage can be clearly demonstrated to have exerted over the public employment of women, it would be surprising if their enfranchisement could be shown to have had any marked effect on their employment in private industry. As one women said, in answer to the question in regard to the effect of equal suffrage on the wages and conditions of employment of women, "It is the same old story of demand and supply in the commercial world." There is, however, some reason to believe that, through the slight influence exerted over their employment in public positions, equal suffrage may have affected for the better the opportunities, at least, if not the wages, of women in private industry in Colorado.

It should be noted, moreover, that twelve years is entirely too short a time for the influence of equal suffrage over economic conditions to have fully developed. To a certain extent this is true of its influence in other directions. But its effect, for instance, on the character of candidates nominated for office is direct, while it has almost unlimited possibilities of influencing economic life indirectly through legislation. The results of this opportunity are necessarily of slow development.

VI

INFLUENCE OF EQUAL SUFFRAGE ON LEGISLATION

TO ascertain the influence of equal suffrage on legislation is a peculiarly difficult problem, owing to the many factors and forces concerned in the success or failure of legislative measures. It is, indeed, impossible to determine exactly what effect the possession of the ballot by women has had in securing the passage or defeat of bills. Even an elaborate study of comparative legislation, which would occupy months of time and a separate volume, would hardly yield conclusive evidence on this point. The most that can be said is that Colorado has certain laws, some of them on the statute-books before women voted, thereby obviating the need for further legislation on the subjects involved, and others passed since they were enfranchised.

For the laws passed since 1894 the men and women of Colorado are jointly responsible. Not all the credit for good laws nor all the blame for bad laws should be given to either sex. Women have taken deep interest and active part in legislative affairs. Their share in the work, moreover, cannot be measured by the number and activity of women legislators, for the endorsement of an act by a powerful woman's

INFLUENCE ON LEGISLATION

organization exerts more real influence than its mere championship by women representatives. Wise legislators are keenly conscious of the ballots represented in women's clubs, and this consciousness not only affects their votes, but also induces them to introduce measures calculated to please these important constituents. The Colorado Federation of Women's Clubs is the chief organ through which the opinions of the women are expressed, though other clubs sometimes have lobbyists in the State Legislature for measures in which they are especially interested. The Colorado State Federation represents something like six thousand women, and its lobbyists are heard in the legislature.

1. LEGISLATION IN THE INTEREST OF WOMEN AND CHILDREN

The first concern of women in the matter of legislation, whether they be voting or non-voting citizens, is naturally to promote the interests of their own sex and of children. Legislation affecting these interests may be divided into six classes—those concerning property rights, those governing the labor of women and children, educational laws, measures concerning women and children as offenders against the law, measures concerning them as objects of offence, and laws governing the institutions which care for the women and children who, for one reason or another, are wards of the state.

Before the suffrage amendment was passed the property rights of Colorado women were, compara-

EQUAL SUFFRAGE

tively speaking, well recognized and protected. A series of legislative acts, beginning in territorial days, had gradually removed from the married woman the restrictions of coverture, and had made her, except for strictly marital obligations, very nearly as free as the single woman.

In buying and selling, for instance, making contracts, suing and being sued, etc., the married woman had, even before Colorado was a state, the same rights as the unmarried woman.[1] A married woman may carry on any trade or business or engage in any labor, except work in coal-mines, which is prohibited to all women,[2] and her earnings are her sole and separate property.[3] A woman, too, may become a special partner with her husband, or any other person, and in all suits arising from such partnership may be a witness for or against her husband.[4] In other business relations, such as loaning money, whether to her husband or any one else, a married woman stands in the same position as an unmarried woman. Dower and curtsey, and the common-law right of the surviving husband to exclusively administer his wife's personal estate have long since been abolished in Colorado. All of these laws stand substantially as enacted before women voted. Since before equal suffrage, too, a woman, whether married or unmarried, has had the same right to exemption of property from levy and sale on execution as has a man.[5]

Other laws, moreover, had been passed long before the suffrage amendment, providing that all property possessed by a woman before marriage, or which comes to her later

---

[1] Mills, *Annotated Statutes*, vol. ii, pp. 1684–1685.
[2] *Ibid.*, vol. ii, p. 1810.   [3] *Ibid.*, vol. ii, p. 1685.
[4] *Ibid.*, vol. iii, *Revised Supplement*, p. 822.
[5] A wage-exemption law was passed in 1893, amending a law of 1884. *Ibid.*, vol. iii, *Revised Supplement*, p. 724.

INFLUENCE ON LEGISLATION

by inheritance, gift, or purchase, shall be her sole and separate property, and shall not be subject to the control and disposition of her husband or liable for his debts.[1] On the other hand, the husband is liable for all the debts of the wife, except those contracted in her business.[2] He is liable, even, under a law passed in territorial days, for her debts contracted before marriage.[3] If a man fails to support his family, he can be compelled to do so, unless he is physically incapable or has some other good reason for his failure, under penalty of imprisonment for sixty days.[4] This law was passed by the Populist legislature of 1893. But under a law passed two years earlier, husband and wife are jointly or severally liable for the expenses of the family and the education of the children.[5]

As for inheritance, husband and wife, if of age, twenty-one for the husband and eighteen for the wife, have the same rights in making wills, but neither can will away from the other more than half of his or her separate property.[6] If no will is made and there are no children, the entire estate goes to the surviving husband or wife; and if there are children or the descendants of children, one-half of the estate goes to the survivor.[7] These provisions were in force long before the suffrage amendment.

Turning to laws affecting property rights passed since the women of Colorado were enfranchised, it is found that, probably because little was left to be done in this direction, few important additions have been made. In 1899 a law was passed exempting from execution a homestead to the value of $2000 for "the head of a family," and providing that such a

---

[1] Mills, *Annotated Statutes*, vol. ii, p. 1683.
[2] *Ibid.*, vol. ii, p. 1685. [3] *Ibid.*, vol. ii, p. 1688.
[4] *Ibid.*, vol. iii, *Revised Supplement*, p. 365.
[5] *Ibid.*, vol. iii, *Revised Supplement*, p. 821.
[6] *Ibid.*, vol. ii, pp. 1684–1685. [7] *Ibid.*, vol. i, p. 1017.

EQUAL SUFFRAGE

homestead cannot be mortgaged without the signatures of both husband and wife. To entitle it to exemption, it is necessary that the word "homestead" be entered on the margin of the recorded title, but this addition can be made at any time. By amendment, too, the husband can no longer sell the homestead without his wife's signature, but he has the same right in his wife's homestead that she has in his.[1] Whether he has the sole right to determine the family residence is doubtful. By removing, the homestead right is lost, but the husband cannot, by deserting his family, deprive them of the homestead, unless he acquires another in which they may share.

The first State Legislature which convened after the granting of the franchise to women passed a law making fathers and mothers joint guardians, with equal powers, of the children.[2] Since women voted, too, the former exclusive right of the father to inherit in case of the death, without will, of a child, has been abrogated, and now both parents inherit equally. A law of 1903 provides that a man who "wilfully fails, refuses, or neglects to provide proper food, clothing, shelter, or care in case of sickness for his wife or minor child, shall upon conviction, be deemed guilty of a misdemeanor and punished by imprisonment in the county jail for not more than ninety days nor less than thirty days."[3]

In 1901 a bill giving the wife a half-interest in all her

---

[1] Mills, *Annotated Statutes,* vol. iii, *Revised Supplement*, p. 603.
[2] *Ibid.*, vol. iii, *Revised Supplement*, p. 601.
[3] *Ibid.*, vol. iii, *Revised Supplement*, p. 822.

husband's earnings after marriage was introduced, but failed of passage in both houses.

In the matter of property rights, then, Colorado, even before the equal-suffrage amendment, had placed women on substantially the same footing as men. The few legal inequalities existing between men and women in 1894 have, since that date, been removed. But as the tendency had for years been strongly in the direction of absolute equality of the sexes in the matter of property rights, it would not be fair to the men of the state to attribute all recent improvements wholly to equal suffrage. In at least one respect women are exceptionally favored by the law, for they are exempt from the poll-tax. It is interesting to note, too, that for the purpose of voting it is not necessary that the wife's residence be the same as that of her husband.

On the other hand, Colorado is not as advanced as many of the Eastern states in the matter of legal protection for women and children in industry. But this is primarily due to the fact that manufacturing industries, which make necessary most of the legislation, have not yet been extensively developed. In 1900 there were only 1894 women and 243 children under sixteen years of age employed in manufacturing in Colorado,[1] as compared, for example, with 143,109 women and 12,556 children in Massachusetts.[2] Naturally, therefore, Colorado has not yet felt the same need as Massachusetts for a stringent factory code. But there are also engaged in trade and transpor-

[1] *Twelfth Census*, vol. viii, Manufactures, part ii, p. 61.
[2] *Ibid.*, p. 347.

tation in Colorado 3982 females ten years of age and over.[1] This includes the clerks, the telephone operators, etc. The problems, moreover, connected with women's work are bound rapidly to grow and multiply.

Practically the only law which regulates the labor of women or girls over fourteen years of age in Colorado, with the exception of those already mentioned, forbidding the employment of women in coal-mines and giving a married woman separate property in her earnings, was passed in 1885. This law provides that "every person, corporation, or company employing females in any manufacturing, mechanical, or mercantile establishments in this state shall provide suitable seats for the use of the females so employed, and shall permit the use of such seats by them when they are not necessarily engaged in the active duties for which they are employed."[2] This is practically identical with the Massachusetts law.

Before women voted a number of laws had been passed regulating the employment of children. By a law passed in 1885, and amended in 1891, Colorado forbade the exhibition, use, or employment of a child under fourteen "as an actor or performer in any concert-hall or room where intoxicating liquors are sold or given away, or in any variety theatre, or for any illegal, obscene, indecent, or immoral purpose, exhibition, or practice whatsoever, or for or in any business, exhibition, or vocation injurious to the health or dangerous to the life or limb of such child."[3] A similar Massachusetts law fixes the age limit for such employment at fifteen, and a New York law at "actually or apparently sixteen." Both of these other states, too, define more definitely than does Colorado the employments forbidden.

[1] *Twelfth Census*, vol. ii., Population, part ii, p. 509.
[2] Mills, *Annotated Statutes*, vol. ii, p. 1941.
[3] *Ibid.*, vol. i., p. 571, and vol. iii, *Revised Supplement*, p. 172.

INFLUENCE ON LEGISLATION

A law passed in 1883, and amended in 1885, provides that no boy under sixteen shall be employed in a coal-mine in Colorado unless he is able to read and write,[1] and, by a law passed in 1891, no person under eighteen can be employed as a railroad telegraph operator for train orders.[2]

As early as 1887 a law was enacted in Colorado forbidding the employment of children under fourteen "in any underground works or mine, or in any smelter, mill, or factory."[3] The employment of children in mercantile establishments, in street trades, and in other occupations not coming under the above law, is regulated, however, only by the compulsory education law, which was first passed in 1889, and applies to all children between the ages of eight and fourteen.

In 1903 an eight-hour law was passed in Colorado which applied to any woman engaged in an occupation requiring her "to stand or be upon her feet in order to satisfactorily perform her labors," and to children under sixteen employed "in any mill, factory, manufacturing establishment, shop, or store, or in or about any coal or other mines, or any other occupation not herein enumerated which may be deemed unhealthful or dangerous."[4] But in 1907 this law was declared unconstitutional.[5] Colorado has no provision for factory inspection.

Since women were granted the franchise, however, the compulsory education law of 1889 has been su-

---

[1] Mills, *Annotated Statutes*, vol. ii, p. 1810.
[2] *Ibid.*, vol. iii, *Revised Supplement*, p. 363.
[3] *Ibid.*, vol. i, p. 572.
[4] *Ibid.*, vol. iii, *Revised Supplement*, p. 757.
[5] *Burcher v. People, Supreme Court of Colorado*, 93 *Pacific Reporter*, p. 14.

perseded by a new and more effective law, passed in 1899, and since that date still further strengthened by amendments. The law, as now on the statute-books, provides that every child between the ages of eight and fourteen shall be required to attend a public, private, or parochial school for the entire school year during which the public schools are in session in the district in which he lives; and every child from fourteen to sixteen must attend school in the same way unless such child shall have completed the work of the eighth grade or "where its help is necessary for its own or its parents' support, or where, for good cause shown, it would be for the best interests of such child to be relieved from the provisions of this act."[1] A child instructed at home by a qualified person is not subject to the provisions of this law. Children between fourteen and sixteen years of age who cannot read and write the English language must attend school at least one-half of each day, or attend night school, or receive private instruction satisfactory to the county superintendent of schools. It is made the duty of employers to keep on hand for the inspection of truant officers evidence as to compliance with the school law for all children in their employment.[2] The school authorities, then, are the enforcing power, and, though localities differ, upon the whole the compulsory education law of Colorado works well.

The school law of Colorado has been strengthened also in other respects. Under the law passed in

[1] Mills, *Annotated Statutes*, vol. iii, *Revised Supplement*, pp. 1181–1182

[2] *Ibid.*, vol. iii, *Revised Supplement*, pp. 1182–1183.

INFLUENCE ON LEGISLATION

1899 one or more truant officers appointed by the school directors enforce school attendance in all districts of the first and second class, i.e., districts containing a school population of over three hundred and fifty.[1] For many years lessons have been required in hygiene "with special reference to the effects of alcoholic stimulants and narcotics upon the human body,"[2] and since 1901 on the subject of the humane treatment of animals.[3] Until 1901 habitual truants had to be sent to the boys' or the girls' industrial school, but in that year a law was passed providing that a truant school should be established in cities of over one hundred thousand population—i.e., Denver—and might be established in cities of over twenty-five thousand—i.e., Pueblo.[4] The truant or parental school, however, has been practically superseded by the probation system of the Juvenile Court.

As for measures especially affecting children as offenders against the law, Colorado has acquired, since women voted, perhaps the best legislation in the country. The Juvenile Court of Denver is deservedly famous, and its success has led to the enactment of laws extending in many ways protection to delinquent children. This work was begun under the school law of 1899 which, approved two months before the juvenile law of Illinois went into effect, contained practically the same features. In January, 1901, a system was established invoking the power

---

[1] Mills, *Annotated Statutes*, vol. iii, *Revised Supplement*, p. 1183.
[2] *Ibid.*, vol. ii, p. 2125.
[3] *Ibid.*, vol. iii, *Revised Supplement*, p. 1181.
[4] *Ibid.*, vol. iii, *Revised Supplement*, pp. 1176–1179.

of the County Court as a Chancery Court, aided by laws, passed in 1895, relating to dependent and neglected children.[1] In 1903, however, an elaborate set of laws was passed for the Juvenile Court,[2] with two important additions to previous legislation, the substitution of the detention school for the jail, and "the law holding parents and all other citizens to a rigid legal liability for any faults of children to which they may contribute."[3] In 1907, moreover, the Juvenile Court was made a separate and distinct tribunal.[4]

The success of the Denver Juvenile Court is due primarily to Judge Ben B. Lindsey, who framed the legislation under which it has carried on its special work, though public-spirited men and women of the city, especially women, have given him effective aid. The only support of the work, however, given by the enfranchised women, which their sisters in non-suffrage states cannot and do not give to Juvenile Court work, has been their earnest effort to retain and uphold Judge Lindsey in his political position. The sentiment on this subject, indeed, has been so overwhelming as to overcome much partisan opposition. When he ran for governor in 1906, though the women probably supported him in larger numbers than the men, there was a tendency among them to question the advisability of the change of office. But in the fall of 1908, doubtless because of the vote

[1] Mills, *Annotated Statutes*, vol. iii, *Revised Supplement*, p. 176 et seq. [2] *Ibid.*, vol. iii, *Revised Supplement*, p. 186 et seq.
[3] *The Problems of the Children. Report of the Juvenile Court of Denver*, 1904, p. 36.
[4] *Session Laws of Colorado*, 1907, pp. 324–331.

INFLUENCE ON LEGISLATION

of Colorado women, Judge Lindsey, as an independent candidate for Juvenile Court judge, scored over the candidates of both the Democratic and the Republican parties an overwhelming triumph. This fact alone, in the minds of many people, is sufficient to justify equal suffrage.

Turning to the subject of offences against women and children, it is found that before Colorado women were enfranchised a considerable number of protective laws were on the statute-books.

By a law passed in 1891 no woman can be supplied with liquor in a wine-room of any sort connected with a saloon.[1] Kidnapping women of any age, by force or fraud, for illicit purposes, is punishable by imprisonment for from one to six years, with or without hard labor.[2] Enticing any unmarried person under eighteen years of age to a house of ill-fame is punishable by imprisonment for from one to six months, or a fine of from $100 to $1000, or both, and the keeper of the house is subject to the same punishment.[3] Any person keeping an intelligence or employment office who sends female help to a house of ill fame may be fined $100 and imprisoned, and on conviction his or her license is revoked.[4]

Divorce, though easily obtained in Colorado, as compared with the average Eastern community, is more difficult than in neighboring states. Desertion for one year, cruelty, the infliction of either mental or bodily suffering, failure for one year to support on the part of the husband, and habitual drunkenness, are all grounds for divorce, but neither of the parties so separated can

---

[1] Mills, *Annotated Statutes*, vol. iii, *Revised Supplement*, pp. 355-356.
[2] *Ibid.*, vol. i, p. 895.
[3] *Ibid.*, vol. i, p. 935.
[4] *Ibid.*, vol. iii, *Revised Supplement*, p. 460.

re-marry within a year.[1] Except in special cases, too, an applicant for divorce must have lived in the state for a year. Alimony is settled by the court. Only minor changes have been made in the divorce law since 1893.

As for children, if a child under sixteen is abused, neglected or reared in vice it may be taken from the parents and made a ward of the state.[2] A law passed in 1891 prohibits the sale or gift of cigarettes or tobacco in any form to children under sixteen.[3] Selling liquor to minors is, of course, also prohibited, and as early as 1885 it was declared illegal to allow the presence of any minor, unless accompanied by parent or guardian, in any "saloon, barroom, billiard-hall, bowling-alley, gambling-house, house of ill-fame, or place where obscene plays are performed."[4] There is also a law prohibiting the circulation of obscene books and pictures.[5] In 1893, moreover, a law was passed forbidding insurance companies to insure the lives of children under ten on pain of criminal proceedings and forfeiture of charter.[6] All of these laws were passed before women voted.

In 1901 a law was enacted constituting the Colorado Humane Society a Bureau of Child and Animal Protection, and making this society the inspection bureau for the enforcement of the laws concerning children, as well as of those concerning animals.[7] During its biennial term ending in 1906, the bureau dealt with the cases of 4931 children. Nearly all of its agents, about seven hundred in number, are volunteers, a

---

[1] Mills, *Annotated Statutes*, vol. iii, *Revised Supplement*, pp. 397 et seq.
[2] *Ibid.*, vol. iii, *Revised Supplement*, pp. 174, 180–181.
[3] *Ibid.*, vol. iii, *Revised Supplement*, p. 173.
[4] *Ibid.*, vol. i, pp. 942–943. [5] *Ibid.*, vol. i, p. 934.
[6] *Ibid.*, vol. iii, *Revised Supplement*, pp. 361–362.
[7] *Ibid.*, vol. iii, *Revised Supplement*, pp. 175–176.

INFLUENCE ON LEGISLATION

large proportion being women, and they are located in all parts of the state. The head of the organization is a man, but its great success is doubtless largely due to the efforts of the women.

Another important law on the subject of offences against women—the first law, indeed, passed on the demand of Colorado women voters—raised the age of consent for girls from sixteen to eighteen.[1] In 1891 it had been raised from ten to sixteen. Though this is the most frequently cited legislative triumph of equal suffrage, and was undoubtedly desirable when a grown man was concerned, it was said often to work unjustly in the case of a young boy, since it applied to all males over fourteen. If the girl was seventeen and the boy only fourteen or fifteen, the girl was considered as the injured party, while the boy, under the law, was liable to confinement in the penitentiary for from one to twenty years. In 1907, however, an amendment to this law was passed providing that where the "male person" is under the age of eighteen years, and the girl employs solicitation, or is a prostitute, she may be found guilty of the statutory offence in the third degree and punished accordingly. The statute divides the offence into three degrees with considerable particularity, and provides also for the punishment of accessories of either sex.[2] It is believed that this amendment will lead to more frequent convictions.

The women of Colorado have taken great interest in the state institutions for the care of dependent,

[1] Mills, *Annotated Statutes*, vol. iii, *Revised Supplement*, p. 345.
[2] *Session Laws of Colorado*, 1907, pp. 355–359.

EQUAL SUFFRAGE

defective, and delinquent children. When they were first granted the suffrage, an industrial school for girls had been authorized, though not yet established, but soon afterward the Girls' Industrial School was opened in Denver. More than half of the members of the board of this school have been women, and women have always urged liberal appropriations for its maintenance. This is still, however, the only institution in the state not maintained by state appropriation, but by a fee for each inmate collected from the county from which the girl is sent. Women have tried through two or three sessions of the legislature to have the Industrial School for Girls placed on the same footing as the other institutions, but thus far without success. In 1895 women aided in securing the law establishing the Home for Dependent Children, and in 1897 in securing an appropriation for its support. In 1901, too, they urged and aided the passage of a measure permitting the State Board of Charities and Corrections to investigate private charitable institutions.

To sum up, the chief laws enacted in Colorado in the interest of women and children since the passage of the equal-suffrage amendment are: The law providing that a homestead cannot be mortgaged or sold without the wife's signature; the law making fathers and mothers joint guardians of the children, with equal powers; the eight-hour law, later declared unconstitutional; the revised compulsory education law of 1899; the law providing for truant schools; the Juvenile Court laws; the age-of-consent law and its revision of 1907; the law establishing the Home for

INFLUENCE ON LEGISLATION

TABLE XXVII

Question—What has been the effect of equal suffrage on legislation in the interest of women and children?

	Good Men	Good Women	None[1] Men	None[1] Women	No definite answer Men	No definite answer Women
I. Favorable to Equal Suffrage						
A. State officials	24	31	6	6	2	12
B. Political workers—state	25	80	8	9	3	15
C. Other citizens—state	149	52	42	5	51	38
D. Delegates—Denver	12	93	3	8	4	58
E. Prominent citizens—Denver	9	15	1		1	
Total	219	271	60	28	61	123
Per cent	64.4	64.2	17.7	6.6	17.9	29.2
II. Unfavorable to Equal Suffrage						
A. State officials	7		4	2	1	2
B. Political workers—state	6	7	13	4	6	5
C. Other citizens—state	29	5	50	7	41	7
D. Delegates—Denver	8	13	11	18	3	19
E. Prominent citizens—Denver		1	3			
Total	50	26	81	31	51	33
Per cent	27.5	28.9	44.5	34.4	28	36.7
III. Indifferent to Equal Suffrage						
A. State officials	7	2	3	1	3	2
B. Political workers—state	2	7	3	5	2	4
C. Other citizens—state	13	7	18	3	32	14
D. Delegates—Denver	4	4		3	3	21
E. Prominent citizens—Denver	4					
Total	30	20	24	12	40	41
Per cent	31.9	27.4	25.5	16.4	42.6	56.2
Grand total	299	317	165	71	152	197
Grand per cent	48.5	54.2	26.8	12.1	24.7	33.7

[1] Five persons complained of ill effects from the former "age of consent" law, enacted in 1904 and amended in 1906, but otherwise none of the answers expressed the belief that the effect has been bad.

EQUAL SUFFRAGE

Dependent Children; the laws granting appropriations for this institution and for the Girls' Industrial School; and the law permitting the State Board of Charities and Corrections to investigate private charitable institutions.

As for the influence which the enfranchisement of women has had on this legislation, Table XXVII shows that the general testimony was decidedly that the effect has been good—48.5 per cent. of all the men and 54.2 per cent. of all the women, inclusive of those who failed to answer or gave indefinite answers to this particular question, making this statement. Of the 165 men and 71 women who thought that it has had no influence, 81 men and 31 women did not believe in equal suffrage, and 24 men and 12 women did not give a definite answer as to their belief on that point.

A prominent Denver woman who did not believe in equal suffrage said: "Greatly improved legislation has been enacted in Colorado in late years, but I think that is due somewhat to the progressive spirit of our men, although woman's influence has certainly been felt here." Another prominent Denver woman who believed in equal suffrage was of the opinion that "all legislation along this line must be credited directly to the women." A prominent Denver man who did not believe in equal suffrage stated, in answer to this question: "Favorable, but again I say woman suffrage has nothing to do with this. Their influence would be just as great without it." On the other hand, a county chairman who believed in equal suffrage answered: "Very beneficial. Many laws have been passed by the legislature in the interest of women and children that could not have been passed without the influence of the women in politics. Politicians will always conciliate large classes of voters by enacting laws demanded, and women voters are no exception. They can procure the enactment of laws that would not be considered if they had no vote." It might be added, probably with equal truth, that they can secure the enforcement of laws that would be neglected if they did not have the vote.

2. GENERAL REFORM LEGISLATION

So far as the women of Colorado have expressed themselves upon general reform measures, they have almost universally been progressive rather than conservative. But in these matters there has been, doubtless, far more difference of opinion among the rank and file of women voters than on the subject of legislative protection for women and children. This is especially true of general labor legislation and of purely political reforms. The women have, however, been almost as united in support of measures designed for the protection of animals as in those designed for the protection of women and children.

In the matter of general labor legislation, Colorado is about on a par with other states of similar industrial development. Considering only laws enacted since the enfranchisement of women, it is found that on many measures, such as the bi-weekly pay-day law, the eight-hour law for miners, and the "boycotting and blacklisting" act of 1905, the women voters have divided up, so far as they have expressed

EQUAL SUFFRAGE

themselves at all, on practically the same lines as the men. One of the few measures, however, introduced in the State Legislature by a woman, which finally became a law, was the bill establishing the State Board of Arbitration.[1] It was not, however, the House bill, introduced by the woman representative, which was signed by the governor, but a similar Senate bill, introduced by a man. This law has frequently been cited as one of the triumphs of equal suffrage, but, in spite of amendments passed in 1903, it was one of the weakest arbitration laws in the United States, and in 1907 was repealed.[2] Another more successful labor law, however—the "frog blocking" law[3] for the protection of railroad employees—was materially aided in its passage through the House by a woman representative. The club-women of Denver, moreover, who for four years had maintained in that city a free employment bureau, succeeded, in 1907, in obtaining a law making this a part of the work of the State Labor Bureau.[4]

In measures of a purely political character, especially in primary-election reform, in the initiative and referendum, and in civil-service reform, many prominent women of Colorado have, since they obtained the ballot, shown deep interest. Bills on these subjects, and also one for indeterminate sentence for criminals, were introduced in the legislature of 1895, but they all failed of passage. The indeterminate-sentence bill,

---

[1] Mills, *Annotated Statutes*, vol. iii, *Revised Supplement*, pp. 744–748.   [2] *Session Laws of Colorado*, 1907, p. 219.
[3] Mills, *Annotated Statutes*, vol. iii, *Revised Supplement*, p. 1007.
[4] *Session Laws of Colorado*, 1907, pp. 292–295.

INFLUENCE ON LEGISLATION

however, which was generally favored by women, was passed in 1899,[1] and in the same year a law was enacted removing emblems from ballots.[2] In 1902, moreover, a constitutional amendment was passed providing for full citizenship of the United States and a year's residence in the state as requisites for voting.[3] A bill, drafted by Judge Lindsey, and designed to prevent frauds in registration, was passed in 1905,[4] and in 1907 a law was enacted putting the employees of all the eleemosynary, penal, and reformatory institutions of the state under civil-service rules.[5] The latter was urged mainly by the Civil Service Reform Association and the women's clubs. The "real Australian ballot," however, and the primary-nomination measure, doing away with the present convention system, have long been demanded in vain. A modified Australian ballot was adopted by Colorado in 1891,[6] and many persons testified that this has been more largely responsible than equal suffrage for the improved order at the polls.

The question of "home rule" for Denver, which was agitated for several years prior to the adoption in the fall of 1902 of the "home rule for cities" amendment to the constitution, evoked several petitions from women's organizations. "Home rule," indeed, received the endorsement of both the Re-

---

[1] Mills, *Annotated Statutes*, vol. iii, *Revised Supplement*, pp. 892–894. [2] *Ibid.*, vol. iii, *Revised Supplement*, p. 418.
[3] *Ibid.*, vol. iii, *Revised Supplement*, p. 405.
[4] *Session Laws of Colorado*, 1905, pp. 188 *et seq.*
[5] *Ibid.*, 1907, pp. 262 *et seq.*
[6] Mills, *Annotated Statutes*, vol. iii, *Revised Supplement*, pp. 407 *et seq.*

publican and the Democratic parties, of the Woman's Republican League of Colorado, the Woman's Bryan Club, the Civic Federation, the Denver Woman's Club, the Direct Legislation League, the Equal Suffrage Association, and the Citizens' League of Denver. Upon the precise method, however, by which the object should be attained there was a difference of opinion, following party lines, among both men and women.

Colorado probably has, all things considered, the most stringent and rigidly enforced laws dealing with cruelty to animals of any state in the Union, and nearly all of these laws have been passed since women have voted. In 1901, when the Colorado Humane Society was made a Bureau of Child and Animal Protection,[1] several other laws were passed forbidding cruel and inhuman treatment of dumb beasts. During the biennial term ending in 1906 the bureau cared, in one way or another, for 43,107 cattle, horses, mules, sheep, and burros. In 1903 an act to protect wild birds and their nests and eggs was added to the previous legislation on this subject, and in 1907 women were primarily responsible for the defeat of an effort to repeal the horse-docking law and to make the State Bureau of Child and Animal Protection a political board.

Among the other laws favored by women which have been enacted since their enfranchisement should be mentioned those providing for state appropriations for the travelling library, established by the

[1] Mills, *Annotated Statutes*, vol. iii, *Revised Supplement*, pp. 175–176.

INFLUENCE ON LEGISLATION

Colorado Federation of Women's Clubs in 1901, and an insurance law, endorsed by nearly every woman's organization in the state, and passed in 1901,[1] which provides that in cases in which an insurance company has to be sued for the amount of a policy, and upon trial a jury finds its defence to be frivolous or for purposes of delay, it must pay the costs of the suit, including an attorney's fee and 25 per cent. penalty. A pure-food law, long demanded by women, and generally endorsed by their clubs, was enacted in 1907,[1] but its success seems to have been due primarily to the stimulus of general public interest all over the country in the pure-food question. Minimum-salary and pension bills for teachers have long been vainly demanded.

The principal laws enacted in 1907, which were endorsed by the Colorado Federation of Women's Clubs, were: The pure-food law; a law establishing a school and workshop for the benefit of adult blind; one for the prevention of objectionable medical advertisements; one establishing free employment bureaus in Denver and Pueblo; a law making it incumbent upon any corporation or organization bringing a dependent child into the state to file a bond for the care and protection of such child; an amendment to the law on criminal assault specifying different degrees of punishment for different degrees of the crime; the local-option law; the civil-service law; the law providing for a parole officer for the penitentiary and reformatory; a law providing for the employment of

[1] Mills' *Annotated Statutes*, vol. iii, *Revised Supplement*, p. 634.
[2] *Session Laws of Colorado*, 1907, pp. 23 *et seq*.

prisoners; a law abolishing salary and mileage of boards of control and providing payment only for actual expenses of such boards; an appropriation bill for the travelling library; a law separating the Juvenile Court of Denver from the County Court; and bills providing for the permanent establishment of the detention house and for the erection of a building to serve also for the use of the Juvenile Court. At the same session a number of bills advocated by women failed, the principal ones being a primary-election bill; a bill providing for a minimum salary of $50 for teachers; one for teachers' pensions; a bill making school elections in cities of the first class biennial and providing for the registration of voters; and bills providing for the establishment of an institution for the care and education of the feeble-minded, and for the establishment of a State Bureau of Forestry.[1]

The consensus of public opinion in regard to the effect of equal suffrage on so-called "reform" legislation is shown in Table XXVIII. It appears that the persons who answered this question were fairly evenly divided between those who thought that equal suffrage has had a good effect and those who thought that it has had no effect. But there was a distinct difference of opinion between the men and the women, 35.2 per cent. of all the women who answered any of the questions on the blank replying that it has had a good effect, as against 28.7 per cent. of all the men, and 38.3 per cent. of the men replying that it has had no effect as against 17.4 per cent. of the women. But 33 per cent. of the men and 47.4 per cent. of the women gave no definite answers. Of the 236 men

[1] *Colorado Federation of Women's Clubs. Report of Legislative Committee*, 1907.

INFLUENCE ON LEGISLATION

TABLE XXVIII

Question—What has been the effect of equal suffrage on so-called "reform" legislation of other kinds?

	Good[1] Men	Good[1] Women	None Men	None Women	No definite answer Men	No definite answer Women
I. Favorable to Equal Suffrage						
A. State officials	19	20	9	11	4	18
B. Political workers—state	18	55	7	12	11	37
C. Other citizens—state	90	33	64	8	88	54
D. Delegates—Denver	6	60	9	19	4	80
E. Prominent citizens—Denver	7	11	3	2	1	2
Total	140	179	92	52	108	191
Per cent	41.2	42.4	27	12.3	31.8	45.3
II. Unfavorable to Equal Suffrage						
A. State officials	3	1	8	2	1	1
B. Political workers—state	2	4	18	8	5	4
C. Other citizens—state	14		64	6	42	13
D. Delegates—Denver	3	10	15	19	4	21
E. Prominent citizens—Denver	1	1	2			
Total	23	16	107	35	52	39
Per cent	12.6	17.7	58.8	39	28.6	43.3
III. Indifferent to Equal Suffrage						
A. State officials	4	1	4	1	5	3
B. Political workers—state	1	4	3	7	3	5
C. Other citizens—state	8	6	23	3	32	15
D. Delegates—Denver			4	4	3	24
E. Prominent citizens—Denver	1		3			
Total	14	11	37	15	43	47
Per cent	14.9	15.1	39.3	20.5	45.8	64.4
Grand total	177	206	236	102	203	277
Grand per cent	28.7	35.2	38.3	17.4	33	47.4

[1] About a dozen of these answers were to the effect that, since "reform" legislation itself is bad, the effect has been bad.

and the 102 women who believed it has had no effect, only 92 of the men and 52 of the women believed in equal suffrage; and of the 177 men and 206 women who believed it has had a good effect, 140 of the men and 179 of the women favored equal suffrage. A number of persons answered that women's clubs have had great influence in this matter, and others that women would have the same influence without the suffrage.

3. Municipal Regulations

Side by side with the influence of equal suffrage over legislation for the protection of children and of animals stands its influence over various forms of municipal activity, legislative and otherwise. The liquor question is, perhaps, most prominent, but it is not by any means the only subject of local concern in which women have taken deep interest. Outside of this question, however, their activity has generally taken the form of measures designed, like the state laws already mentioned, for the protection of women, children, and dumb animals. Such are, for example, the placing of drinking-fountains on the business streets of Denver, the furnishing of seats at corners where many people wait for cars, and the establishment of public playgrounds for children in the poor districts. It is certainly to the advantage of any modern industrial community that all of its members should be interested in the general welfare. This is particularly noticeable in view of the increasing development of what has been called "municipal housekeeping." Street cleaning and lighting, garbage disposal, and pure milk and water supply are matters of especial concern to women.

INFLUENCE ON LEGISLATION

Except in the regulation of the sale of liquor, however, the activity of women has been toward constructive rather than toward preventive measures. On gambling and other kindred evils, for example, the woman vote, though it has had some influence in the smaller towns, has had practically none in the cities and mining-camps. The problem here is not, however, the need of laws, but the need of their enforcement, and all that women can do is to vote and work for candidates pledged to such enforcement. On the social evil, too, it is impossible to see that equal suffrage has had any effect. Women, in fact, have made little effort in this direction. Previous to the spring of 1908, when the Market Street "cribs" in Denver were closed by the district-attorney, the social evil in that city, within the limits prescribed by the police department, was probably more brazenly open, and also, perhaps, owing to the floating population of miners and others who come to the city to spend their money, more extensive, than in almost any other city of the United States. But equal suffrage had about as much to do with this condition of affairs as a twelve-year-old child with the Constitution of the United States. The problem, indeed, seems to be too appalling and too fundamentally difficult for even the stoutest hearts and the clearest heads of experienced philanthropists.

The liquor question is not, of course, merely a local matter. From 1894 to 1907, however, little state legislation was passed on this subject. Among the bills introduced and advocated by the women in the 1895 session of the legislature was one providing for the Gothenburg system of control of liquor traffic, but it failed of passage. Before equal suffrage was granted, laws had been enacted prohibiting the sale of liquor on election-day and providing that polling-places should not be located within fifty feet of a saloon. No important change was made in the liquor laws of the state until 1907, when a local-option law was passed,[1] which, though not entirely satisfactory to women, as represented by the Legislative Committee of the Colorado Federation of Women's Clubs, has been put into force with some degree of success. This law threw the question definitely into municipal politics, where it had already been handled by the practice of pledging candidates on the subject. The latter method was weak, however, as there was no power to prevent the candidates from breaking their pledges. Though the passage of the local-option law was doubtless made less difficult by the fact that the women of the state vote, this, like other recent victories of the temperance cause. seems to have been primarily a result of the wave of temperance enthusiasm which has swept over the whole United States. The Woman's Christian Temperance Union has materially aided this movement, but the chief responsibility appears to have rested upon the men's organization, the Anti-Saloon League.

As early as 1897, however, the Woman's Christian Temperance Union reported that there were twenty-six municipalities in Colorado which prohibited the sale of liquor, as compared with two early in 1894. The latter places were Colorado Springs and Greeley,

[1] *Session Laws of Colorado*, 1907, pp. 495 *et seq.*

INFLUENCE ON LEGISLATION

in which liquor has never been legally sold. In 1907 there were in all fifty-eight "dry" towns, including Boulder, the seat of the State University, Cañon City, Delta, Longmont, and Rocky Ford. At Steamboat Springs, the same year, the woman's club nominated a ticket which received the endorsement of both political parties, and was successful. Their platform declared for high license and for confining saloons to a particular part of the town.

During 1908, out of forty-five Colorado towns in which the saloon was the issue, the temperance cause won in twenty-nine. In twenty-six the fight was made under the new local-option law, and in twenty of these successfully. In the other towns candidates were pledged.[1] The saloon was entirely eliminated in eight counties, including Delta and Weld. In Denver, moreover, where in the spring of the same year a hot fight was waged on the local-option issue, though the temperance cause was signally defeated in the down-town districts, two-thirds of the residence section was voted "dry." But in other states, too, the temperance cause, under the leadership of the Anti-Saloon League, met with many victories during that year. In Illinois, for instance, where conditions, however, may be more favorable than in Colorado, thirty-five counties were voted entirely "dry."

An unexpected and to some persons discouraging feature of this question is that equal suffrage has not materially increased the strength of the Prohibition Party. In 1892 the Prohibition candidate for governor received less than 2 per cent. of the total vote cast for that office,

[1] *American Issue, Colorado Edition*, April 25, 1908.

and in 1896 only a trifle over 2 per cent. of the total vote. A Denver woman accounted for the weakness of the Prohibition Party by the statement that women "would vote Prohibition if the party had enough male votes to do much good, but they do not like to waste votes on a losing proposition." Another Denver woman remarked: "The women are almost universally for total abstinence, yet the Prohibition Party never gets their vote, and by reason of its insignificance is obliged to file its ticket by petition. Yet none of the parties dare nominate a saloon-keeper for office, except possibly an alderman now and then in the slums." The latter part of this statement, that equal suffrage has had a blighting influence over the political careers of saloon-keepers, is indisputably true, but it does not seem probable that women "are almost universally for total abstinence." In several localities, indeed, women have frankly expressed a preference for the saloon over the drug-store sale of liquor, and the practice of "bootlegging," or carrying a bottle in the leg of the boot. Three or four persons who answered the question-blank, but were unfavorable to equal suffrage, thought that more women drink than before their enfranchisement. A Denver woman delegate, moreover, remarked that she had "heard women say they would not vote against liquor interests because they liked a glass of beer themselves."

The consensus of opinion, however, according to Table XXIX, was strongly to the effect that equal suffrage has had a good influence in improving temperance laws and their enforcement. The question asked, simply, What has been the effect of equal suffrage on the liquor interests? and the answers, consequently, were not absolutely definite, but they at least indicate the trend of opinion on the subject. About half of the replies from all the men and all the women, inclusive of those who gave non-committal answers to this particular question, expressed the opinion that equal suffrage has aided the

INFLUENCE ON LEGISLATION

TABLE XXIX

Question—What has been the effect of equal suffrage on the liquor interests?

	Good[1] Men	Good[1] Women	None Men	None Women	No definite answer Men	No definite answer Women
I. Favorable to Equal Suffrage						
A. State officials	27	31	4	11	1	7
B. Political workers—state	20	76	10	12	6	16
C. Other citizens—state	167	60	44	10	31	25
D. Delegates—Denver	8	73	5	35	6	51
E. Prominent citizens—Denver	7	10	3	3	1	2
Total	229	250	66	71	45	101
Per cent	67.3	59.2	19.4	16.8	13.3	24
II. Unfavorable to Equal Suffrage						
A. State officials	6	1	5	1	1	2
B. Political workers—state	3	8	19	8	3	
C. Other citizens—state	36	4	61	7	23	8
D. Delegates—Denver	3	6	15	29	4	15
E. Prominent citizens—Denver	1		2			1
Total	49	19	102	45	31	26
Per cent	27	21.1	56	50	17	28.9
III. Indifferent to Equal Suffrage						
A. State officials	6	2	2	1	5	2
B. Political workers—state	1	8	4	5	2	3
C. Other citizens—state	18	10	24	1	21	13
D. Delegates—Denver	2	5	2	7	3	16
E. Prominent citizens—Denver	2		2			
Total	29	25	34	14	31	34
Per cent	30.8	34.2	36.2	19.2	33	46.6
Grand total	307	294	202	130	107	161
Grand per cent	49.8	50.2	32.8	22.3	17.4	27.5

[1] "Good" here means that the influence has, in one way or another, been for increased temperance. Several men here classified stated that the effect has been bad, but, at the same time, clearly indicated that the reason for their statements was that they did not believe in the control of the liquor traffic.

temperance cause. Even of those who did not believe in equal suffrage, 27 per cent. of the men and 21.1 per cent. of the women thought that it has had a good effect.[1]

As the effect of equal suffrage on the liquor interests is primarily a local question, differences of opinion may be accounted for in part by local variations. A prominent Denver woman said: "In the cities of Denver and Pueblo the effect has been practically *nil*, save and except that saloon-keepers are no longer nominated for city offices. Throughout the state, in small towns and country places, the women have done much to curb or put it out of business entirely." Another Denver woman said: "Liquor interests are still paramount in defeating legislation, dominating elections, keeping the town wide open." There was, in fact, no specific testimony showing an appreciable effect in Denver or Pueblo, or in the strictly mining communities.[2] In smaller towns, however, progress has been made, and the general opinion was that "in municipal elections the women have been the force in voting out the saloons in many instances."

In spite, then, of the disappointment of the advocates of prohibition, the direct influence of equal suffrage on the liquor question is perhaps greater than on any other concrete political problem. A large

[1] Several men answered that the effect of equal suffrage on the liquor interests has been bad, because restrictions on the sale of liquor are not desirable; but these replies were classified under "good," as they merely expressed the same general opinion from another point of view.

[2] See Appendix I for the number of retail liquor saloons in Denver and in Pueblo, and in the five cities ranging next above and the five cities ranging next below each in population in 1903.

INFLUENCE ON LEGISLATION

number of the women voters apparently believe in temperance rather than in prohibition, and they have shown themselves inclined to accomplish their ends through local, non-partisan combinations rather than through adherence to the Prohibition Party. But it is impossible to doubt that equal suffrage has had great influence on the liquor question. A Weld County man, who did not definitely answer the question as to belief in equal suffrage, said: "There is doubtless a distinct gain here, and, so far as I have been able to discover, this is about the only gain." Another man who did not believe in equal suffrage thought "this the one question where women's votes count."

4. Conclusion

In conclusion, it is safe to say that the most conspicuous effect of equal suffrage has been upon legislation, and, though it is impossible to prove beyond the possibility of a doubt that the woman's club movement alone would not have brought about the passage of the same laws, it seems probable that the votes of women have effected the desired end with less effort and in less time than would have been required in non-suffrage states. When they were first enfranchised their influence may have been slightly stronger than at present, as they were then politically an unknown quantity, and the men, in order to win their votes, may have yielded more than later experience proved necessary. But they are still, to a certain extent, an unknown factor, as they split their tickets more often than men. For this reason, political bosses, as well as saloon men, are usually opposed to equal suffrage. They have never been known to favor "prize-fight" bills, or other laws of vicious tendency, and not more than twenty persons, in answering any of the questions relating to the effect of equal suffrage on legislation, expressed the opinion that it has been bad. Of these, nearly half thought stringent liquor laws, which they attributed to the woman vote, objectionable. Several of the others complained of the injustice of the 1895 "age of consent" law. Some persons considered the laws favored by women too radical, and others thought them too conservative.

Although the Colorado laws for the protection of working women and children might be greatly strengthened, and although the experience of older states furnishes a warning that such legislation should be enacted, if it is not to encounter grave difficulties, before urgent occasion for it has arisen, it is fair to say that, in other respects, no state has a code of laws better adapted to its immediate need for the protection of women and children, and that the influence of the enfranchised women has distinctly strengthened the cause of reform in this particular. The direct influence of women who have taken active part has been one factor, but the indirect influence of the merely voting woman, by materially strengthening the backing of the men who have stood for reform measures in the interest of women and children, has been even more powerful.

The influence of the social settlements and of the Juvenile Court is, of course, potent in securing many of the reforms which settlement workers have also

INFLUENCE ON LEGISLATION

secured in other states and cities. But the proportion of women interested in these matters is almost everywhere larger than the proportion of men, and in Colorado there is inevitably, in the consideration of such questions, a tendency to yield to the wishes of that large element of the political constituency, the women. This tendency is not as great as might be wished, and there are sometimes other more powerful interests to be conciliated. Whenever a Colorado woman, however, makes a demand in which she may reasonably be supposed to have the silent backing of the great mass of women who do not talk but vote, she inevitably has far less difficulty in obtaining her object than her sisters of the non-suffrage states. The possession of the ballot economizes for her both effort and time.

VII

EFFECT OF EQUAL SUFFRAGE ON THE WOMEN OF COLORADO

THE preceding chapters have dealt with the results of equal suffrage considered as a political reform. It has been seen that in active political work women take less part than men, but that a fair proportion of them fulfil their duty of voting on election-day. It has also been seen that the women who have been elected to public office have made as good records, and in some cases better, than the men. The economic influence of equal suffrage has thus far been slight, but its influence on legislation had undoubtedly been considerable, especially on legislation in the interest of women, children, and dumb animals, and against the free conduct of the liquor business. But there is another question which is, in the opinion of many, of even more importance and significance than the effect of women voters on politics. This is the question of the influence of politics on women. Equal suffrage is, indeed, a social as well as a political problem, and some of the most telling arguments against it are based upon the supposition that it tends to destroy womanliness.

A woman ex-member of the State Legislature answered the questions relating to the effect of equal suffrage on the moral character and intelligence of women and on the home and the children by saying that she did not "see any sense in these questions." Nevertheless, this is perhaps the most important side of the problem. Not only is it the chief point of attack by anti-suffragists, but, as has been seen, the arguments for woman's enfranchisement as a measure of political expediency are not strong enough to counterbalance any considerable degree of injury to the woman or to the home.

The chief points bearing upon the question which are considered in this chapter are: First, the extent of belief in the principle of equal suffrage among Colorado people, after twelve years' experience of its actual workings; second, the increase or decrease of women's interest in politics; third, the increase or decrease of their influence; fourth, the question of woman's political independence — *i.e.*, whether she merely doubles the vote by duplicating that of her male relatives; fifth, the effect of equal suffrage on the moral character of women; sixth, its effect on their intelligence and public spirit; and, seventh, its effect on the home and the children.

In considering each one of these subjects it must be remembered that there are at least two conflicting ideals of womanly excellence, and that opinions and answers to questions are dictated in large part by these ideals. As the replies do not admit of classification upon any basis of ideals, this naturally leads to some confusion and possible ambiguity. It is believed, however, that a fairly clear view of the situation may be obtained by assuming, throughout the following discussion, that the terms "improvement" or "good result," as used by the persons answering the question-blank, generally mean the enlargement of woman's mind or heart without any accompanying neglect of her traditional sphere.

1. Belief in Equal Suffrage

The first of these questions relates to the present attitude of the people of Colorado toward equal suffrage in general. It could not be considered, of course, that the answers to the circular sent out in the course of this investigation would indicate how a vote on woman's enfranchisement, if taken to-day, would stand. The blanks were sent almost entirely to men and women who were supposed to be particularly interested in politics, or at least in public affairs, and the answers may be assumed to have come from those who had the strongest opinions one way or the other, or who were most willing to aid, to the extent of their knowledge, in the investigation. Nevertheless, Table XXX shows that, of all the women, 72.1 per cent., and of all the men, 55.2 per cent., believed in equal suffrage. Of the remaining men, too, 15.3 per cent. did not give definite answers to the question, and less than 30 per cent. expressed an unfavorable opinion, while of the remaining women 12.5 per cent. gave no definite answers, and only 15.4 per cent. expressed themselves as opposed to equal suffrage.

Some interesting reasons were given for belief or disbelief in equal suffrage. A number of persons agreed with a Denver woman who answered that she believed

EFFECT ON WOMEN OF COLORADO

TABLE XXX
Question—Do you believe in equal suffrage?

	Yes Men	Yes Women	No Men	No Women	No definite answer Men	No definite answer Women	Total Men	Total Women
Members State Legislature[1]	32	49	12	4	13	5	57	58
County superintendents[2]	36	21	25	2	7	5	68	27
County chairmen[1]								
Women political workers—state								
Socialists and trade-unionists	16	11	2	2	1	4	19	13
Prominent women—state								
Employers[1]	4	18	6	3	4	3	14	24
Other women—state								
Boulder County {Political workers	42	16	13	2	4	2	59	20
{Other women	18	11	8	4	4	7	30	22
Conejos County {Political workers	18	2	8	2	4	2	30	6
{Other women	15	6	11	3	4	1	30	10
Delta County {Political workers	11	15	3	3	4	1	18	15
{Other women	19	159	22	50	7	28	48	237
Denver—prominent citizens		7	3	2	4	1	18	16
Denver—political workers								
Denver—other women								
Huerfano County {Political workers	10		3	1	4	1	17	1
{Other women	20	4	8	1	9	3	37	8
La Plata County {Political workers	17	6	14	1	6	1	37	8
{Other women		2		3				3
Las Animas County {Political workers	26	6	7	1	5	2	38	9
{Other women		3		1		1		4
Pueblo County {Political workers	14	4	12	1	3	1	29	6
{Other women		7		1		1		9
San Miguel County {Political workers	17	12	22	1	7	1	46	14
{Other women		5		1		3		9
Teller County {Political workers	43	23	14	1	12	3	69	27
{Other women		17		1		4		22
Weld County {Political workers								
{Other women								
Total	340	422	182	90	94	73	616	585
Per cent	55.2	72.1	29.5	15.4	15.3	12.5	100	100

[1] All men.   [2] All women.

217

in it "absolutely as a question of abstract justice, that has nothing to do with its present effect." But more made statements similar to that of another Denver woman who said: "I did not at the time it was granted, but do now." In several cases women who did not believe in equal suffrage stated that, nevertheless, they considered it their duty to vote. A number, too, who did not favor equal suffrage as a general proposition, added that they would fight against having it abolished. One woman answered, "It is a state law. I keep it." Another Denver woman: delegate to one of the conventions in 1906, believed "a woman has as much right to make a few dollars out of politics as a man has, and women need it more."

All of the more conventional reasons for woman's enfranchisement were given in answers to this question, as well as the conventional arguments on the other side, such as that woman "ought not to accept it for womanly reasons," that "suffrage demeans a woman," and that "by trying to place herself on the same level with man, woman degrades herself." There were a number of complaints similar to the following: "I believe in equal suffrage if women could learn to take the interest they should in politics, but they shirk every responsibility connected with it for a tea or a card party." Still others asserted that Colorado is such a corrupt state politically that it should not be taken as a fair example.

A far more serious complaint, made by a prominent, well-informed, and generally intelligent Denver man, was the following: "I have believed in equal suffrage all my life, but Colorado experience has been disappointing. Women will always have great influence on the legislation of the country with or without the ballot. Equal suffrage has brought a class of women to the front in political activity that hurts 'women's influence' in all respects. Perhaps longer experience will work improvement." It is true that in some instances undesirable women have been active in politics, but usually other women have been the first to repudiate them. There is another group of women, who, while perfectly respectable, intelligent, and well-intentioned, are hopelessly untactful, and antagonize instead of attracting the men with whom they work; but these, by their own methods, tend to eliminate themselves from active politics.

A wiser observation, perhaps, was made by another prominent Denver man, who said: "I did not expect the enfranchisement of women to work a revolution in our government, and I have not been disappointed." This answer, too, throws light on the replies of nineteen men who said that they voted for equal suffrage or advocated it when they came to Colorado, but after seeing how it worked changed their minds. One of these men said: "My mother was a pioneer suffrage worker, and I was taught to believe in and respect it, but my own experience, both as an office-seeker and participator in politics, together with eight years' observation as a newspaper manhas changed my views entirely." Another remark that throws light on the opposition of these nineteen men was made by a prominent woman experienced in politics outside of Denver, who said: "I have never heard an argument against it that would not apply equally to both sexes."

The truth is that both the ardent enthusiasts and the critics who have weighed equal suffrage in the scales of its own propagandists have found it wanting, and have sometimes, therefore, called it a failure. But meanwhile the measure has made converts among people who, having indulged in saner expectations, are thankful for what has been accomplished. A Boulder County man, for instance, said that he voted against equal suffrage when it was submitted, but was now in favor of it, "having observed the elevating effect"; and a Teller County man said that he believed in it "with all its disadvantages and ill effects, for I don't think men should have a monopoly in politics."

EQUAL SUFFRAGE

There has been considerable speculation as to whether Colorado is likely to do away with equal suffrage, but no reasonable person considers this within the range of political possibilities. Equal suffrage would have to be voted out just as it was voted in, first by the legislature and then by a referendum vote of the people. The legislature might possibly do its part, though the championship of such a bill would indicate almost unparalleled political recklessness. When it came to a vote, however, it is highly probable that a large proportion of the men would express their approval of the experiment, while no woman who has been favorable to equal suffrage would willingly yield her privileges, and a large number of those who have been indifferent or hostile would fight vigorously against their disfranchisement.

A shrewd, observant, and well-balanced man from Weld County gave the following statement as to his belief in equal suffrage and its permanence: "Yes, unqualifiedly. More than that, I am entirely satisfied with the results that have been achieved. I voted for woman's suffrage in 1893, at the time it carried in Colorado, but I did not expect the maturity of five per cent. of the promises made, and felt that extravagant predictions and radical claims were not only unwarranted but a positive harm. It is not only right that women should have power of suffrage, but it is an almost incalculable benefit to humanity as a whole. True progress is slow. Woman suffrage will not be done away with in Colorado."

EFFECT ON WOMEN OF COLORADO

2. Interest of Women in Politics

Actual experience of equal suffrage has undoubtedly increased the number of people who, not as a fad or a party measure, but as a reasonable conviction, favor its extension. There can also be no doubt but that equal suffrage has increased the interest of women in politics.

The answers to the question-blank, as given in Table XXXI, show that 51 per cent. of all the men, including those who gave no definite answer to this particular question, and 60 per cent. of all the women, believed that the interest of women has been increased. Of the men, 32.8 per cent., and of the women 41 per cent., said it has increased, but did not specify whether their basis of comparison was the time before equal suffrage or the time immediately following. The question failed to state the basis wished, and consequently the answers do not furnish any valid conclusion as to whether the women's interest has increased or decreased since the early years of their enfranchisement. Of the men 18.2 per cent., and of the women 19 per cent., definitely stated that the interest of women has increased since they have been granted political power. These answers, added to those of the men and women who did not specify their basis of comparison, furnish conclusive evidence that equal suffrage stimulates in women an interest in politics. About 20 per cent. of both sexes testified that women take less interest, but nearly all of these put their replies in such a way as to indicate that they meant, as one woman said: "Less than when first granted the right of suffrage."

The reasons given for interest in politics were many, but they may be roughly classified under patriotism; duty or responsibility for the proper exercise of political power; general intelligence or the routine interest of educated people in public affairs; the natural concern of the taxpayer; and other financial reasons indicating a desire to obtain money from political work or position. The largest proportion of men, 36.5 per cent., and also the largest proportion of women, 30.9 per cent., named patriotic motives, but of the men 25.7 per cent. considered interest in politics as a duty. The comparatively small proportion of women, 17.4 per cent., who named duty as a motive for interest is somewhat surprising, and may indicate that few women find suffrage an onerous burden. But 12.6 per cent. of the men and 9.4 per cent. of the women gave no definite answer to the question, and 2.7 per cent. of the men and 5.4 per cent. of the women said they were not interested. It is difficult, however, to draw the line between these reasons and to reach a definite conclusion.

Under "general intelligence" were placed such answers as these: "Because interested in humanity, economic justice, and civic progress"; "because I am a reasoning human being"; "political work has a great fascination to me"; "because it takes a woman out of the rut—fresh interest and opportunity to understand what is going on." A larger proportion of women than of men, 21.3 per cent. as compared with 14.8 per cent., named causes of this character. In cases where two or more reasons for interest were given, the answers were classified under that first or most prominently named. One woman said she was interested because she thought "it is high time the saloon was hung up to dry." The fact that they were taxpayers was given as a cause of interest by 1.4 per cent. of the men and 6 per cent. of the women.

More women than men, 9.6 per cent. as compared with 6.3 per cent., gave financial reasons for their interest. There is reason to believe, however, that a smaller proportion of men than of women were willing to confess, even when such was the case, to being interested merely "for the money that is in it." Women generally seek

EFFECT ON WOMEN OF COLORADO

TABLE XXXI

Question—Do women generally take more or less interest in politics than they did in previous years?

	More Men	More Women	More since suffrage Men	More since suffrage Women	Same Men	Same Women	Less Men	Less Women	No definite answer Men	No definite answer Women
I. Favorable to Equal Suffrage										
A. State officials	17	20	7	13	5	3	3	9	4	4
B. Political workers—state	12	16	11	37	5	8	4	6	4	7
C. Other citizens—state	106	46	64	28	34	5	16	3	22	13
D. Delegates—Denver	7	84	3	17	1	7	5	34	3	17
E. Prominent citizens—Denver	3	7	1		2	2	5	6	3	
Total	145	203	86	95	47	25	33	58	29	41
Per cent	42.7	48.1[1]	25.3	22.5	13.8	5.9	9.7	13.8	8.5	9.7
II. Unfavorable to Equal Suffrage										
A. State officials							6	1	2	2
B. Political workers—state	5	6	1	1	2	2	15	4	1	
C. Other citizens—state	25	5	2	3	27	6	36	4	20	4
D. Delegates—Denver	3	6	3	3	2	3	12	32	2	8
E. Prominent citizens—Denver	1		3		1	1		1		
Total	35	20	18	6	35	10	69	42	25	14
Per cent	19.2	26.7[1]	9.9	6.7	19.2	11.1	37.9	46.7	13.8	15.5
III. Indifferent to Equal Suffrage										
A. State officials	2	1		1			5		3	2
B. Political workers—state	1	6	1	2	1	2	4	1	3	2
C. Other citizens—state	15	9	3	5	12	2	14	4	19	7
D. Delegates—Denver	3	6		2		5	2	12	2	6
E. Prominent citizens—Denver	1	3	2		1					
Total	22	26	8	10	14	10	25	17	25	17
Per cent	23.4	39.7[1]	8.6	13.7	14.8	13.7	26.6	23.3	26.6	23.3
Grand total	202	240	112	111	96	45	127	117	79	72
Grand per cent	32.8	41.0	18.2	19	15.6	7.7	20.6	20	12.8	12.3
	51.1	60.1								

[1] These figures are the total percentages for the two columns "More" and "More since suffrage."

223

EQUAL SUFFRAGE

the appointive positions, while men are more often candidates for elective offices. Discretion of utterance is, consequently, not as essential to women as to men. This motive in both sexes is undoubtedly, however, greatly underestimated in the table.

A considerably larger proportion of women than of men interest themselves in politics in order to aid a relative, nearly always husband, father, or brother. The question was asked: "Have you any near relative active in politics, or who holds any position the salary or wages of which are paid from public funds, whose political affiliation is the same as yours?" Of the women who had done any political work, 16.7 per cent., and of the men only 9.9 per cent., answered "Yes" to this question. Moreover, the possession of such a relative was probably an accidental circumstance with more of the men than of the women. There is some complaint from both sexes that equal suffrage has obliged men politicians to make their wives and daughters enter politics in order to aid them against rivals whose women relatives would otherwise turn the balance. In 1906 a woman sat through the sessions of one of the long and tedious conventions in Denver with a nine weeks' old baby girl in her arms. Neither she nor her husband, who was with her, believed in equal suffrage, but her husband held a political position.

Twenty-four women and thirteen men, all of whom had at one time or another taken some active part in politics other than voting, said they were not interested. One of the women added: "But the work it has given me has added to the comforts of some very nice children which they would have had to do without otherwise." Another said, "I have a large family to care for"; a third answered, simply: "To help my husband"; and a fourth: "Because my husband asked me."

The increased interest of the women of Colorado in politics since their enfranchisement is doubtless due largely to their increased sense of responsibility in public affairs. As a Pueblo woman put it, they "have a personal interest, and study and learn more about government because they see the necessity of informing themselves in order to vote intelligently." Some persons who answered the blank thought that women candidates increase the interest among their own sex; others that husbands and brothers talk more about political affairs at home; and still others that interest is roused by contemplation of the good results of equal suffrage. A prominent Denver woman thought that women are taking more interest because, more and more, politics tends to enter into "everything concerning improvement of business conditions, education, and other things of vital interest to all classes." Several men and women cited the woman's club movement as a reason for increased interest in politics. Others thought that moral rather than political questions are now the issue, and that these particularly attract women. A number thought increased interest due merely to the fact that women are becoming accustomed to the franchise.

On the other hand, most of those who said that women take less interest than in the early years of equal suffrage alleged as a reason that the novelty has worn off. A prominent Denver woman added that women "realize that they are not able, with their short experience, to purify politics completely"; another gave as a reason "because the men do not accord them the importance they naturally feel they should command"; and a third said that women are "disgusted with dishonest methods." Similar opinions were given by others.

Some persons alleged that the better class of women are dropping out of politics, and others denied this, saying that, while some drop out, "they are not representative women." A Denver woman delegate to a convention in 1906 said that "those women who took it up as a fad naturally all dropped it when the novelty wore off," but she thought that women in general take more interest than when first enfranchised.

One of the county superintendents who believed that women take less interest than at first, nevertheless stated that they take as much interest as men who are not professional politicians. A prominent Denver man, too, thought that "their interest is sustained in about the same ratio as with the average male voter." Some answers were to the effect that the interest of women depends upon the issue, and several cited, in illustration of this, the great activity of the Boulder women in the city election of 1907. One woman said: "Among women of my acquaintance, voting is more general; actual attendance at primaries and conventions, less. Voting is a matter of civic duty. The other work is useless under the present system." Several others practically agreed with this opinion, and one woman added that women are also influenced "by the desire to avoid the turmoil, strife, and disagreeableness of political activity." A woman prominent in politics in a small town remarked: "To the older women politics was a new thing, and something for which they fought and worked. The young women take it as a right, and so do not talk as much." Another woman thought that they take more interest, but that there are "fewer women politicians than when suffrage was first granted."

A Weld County man answered: "Slightly more, but not as much as would be expected. I think the reason is they do not have the same natural interest in political matters as do men, and I believe another fairly sufficient reason is that they have never been sufficiently educated to manifest an interest in political and sociological matters as remote as have been most questions of general politics. The latest tendency in the political field is to bring political questions down to the personal element, and make it more a matter of the man and his character, and less a question of theoretical politics; and this fact will make the ordinary men and women both more directly concerned with the machinery of politics."

3. Influence of Women in Politics

Closely allied to the interest of women in politics is their influence and its increase or decrease. As in the preceding case, this question was so worded that it is impossible to show from the answers the verdict of public opinion as to the present influence of women as compared with their influence during the first years of their enfranchisement. In Table XXXII the replies of those persons who definitely stated that their influence has increased since suffrage was granted were separately classified. Disregarding this division, 40.5 per cent. of all the men who answered any of the questions on the blank, and 52.7 per cent. of all the women, believed that the influence of women in politics is increasing.

The proportion of both sexes who answered that it has not changed is somewhat small, 14.4 per cent. of the men and 9.6 per cent. of the women. A fairly large proportion of the men, 27.3 per cent., and only 17.4 per cent. of the women, believed that it has decreased. But of the 168 men and 102 women who answered "less," 99 men and

EQUAL SUFFRAGE

44 women did not believe in equal suffrage. The strong influence exerted over the answers to this question by the attitude toward equal suffrage is also seen in the large proportion of those who favored women's enfranchisement who answered "more."

Most of the persons who asserted that the influence of women has decreased were evidently comparing present conditions with those that prevailed during the early years of equal suffrage. A few, however, believed that the franchise itself has decreased their influence. A Boulder woman, for example, answered: "Decreasing in suffrage states, because they lose the quiet and more potential influence when they enter the public arena."

The chief cause cited for a decrease of influence was indifference, but many others were named. A member of the State Legislature said that women "lose their influence as soon as they are tied to party politics." There was some complaint from others of discouragement and slackened efforts. A prominent Denver man said: "Women's influence in politics is on the decline. 1. Because they are not posted on the issues involved. 2. Because men discourage their participation. Our politicians do not desire their influence, but they dare not say so." Several persons asserted that the "better class" of women, after a little experience, become disgusted with politics. Two or three of these added that, as the influence of the "better class" decreases, that of the lower class increases, because "the party in power controls the votes of the harlots and courtesans and women of questionable character, and compels them to vote their way." Another point was suggested by a member of the State Legislature: "Decreasing, except in local issues, due largely, I believe, to the fact that their influence has been less than thought to be, and that a fewer number are as active as anticipated." A prominent Denver woman said: "The fear of what women in politics will do is decreasing because the men see that, the excitement being over,

TABLE XXXII

Question—Is the influence of women in politics increasing or decreasing?

	Increasing Men	Increasing Women	Increasing since suffrage Men	Increasing since suffrage Women	Same Men	Same Women	Decreasing Men	Decreasing Women	No definite answer Men	No definite answer Women
I. Favorable to Equal Suffrage										
A. State officials	18	28	1		2	7	7	5	4	9
B. Political workers—state	24	78	1		5	11	4	7	2	8
C. Other citizens—state	139	63	13		36	7	21	22	33	15
D. Delegates—Denver	7	91	1	4	3	13	4	3	55	29
E. Prominent citizens—Denver	4	6			1	2	3	5	2	2
Total	192	266	16	11	47	40	39	42	46	63
Per cent	56.5	65.6[1]	4.7	2.6	13.8	9.5	11.5	10	13.5	14.9
II. Unfavorable to Equal Suffrage										
A. State officials	1	1			4		5	8	2	3
B. Political workers—state	2	3			1	4	16		5	1
C. Other citizens—state	19	3	1	1	15		59	6	27	10
D. Delegates—Denver	1	1			2	5	19	29	1	14
E. Prominent citizens—Denver	1	1			1		3	1		
Total	24	8	1	1	23	10	99	44	35	28
Per cent	13.2	10[1]	0.6	1.1	12.6	9	54.4	48.9	19.2	31.1
III. Indifferent to Equal Suffrage										
A. State officials					4	4	5	2	2	3
B. Political workers—state	2	7				2	3	3	3	5
C. Other citizens—state	1	10			12	4	17	3	22	7
D. Delegates—Denver	12	5			1	1	3	9	2	13
E. Prominent citizens—Denver	1				2		2	1		
Total	16	22			19	7	30	16	29	28
Per cent	17	30.1			20.2	9.6	31.9	21.9	30.9	38.4
Grand total	232	296	17	12	89	56	168	102	110	119
Grand per cent	37.7	50.6	2.8	2.1	14.4	9.6	27.3	17.4	17.8	20.3
	40.51	52.71								

1 "Increasing" and "Increasing since suffrage" added to obtain these percentages.

they are amenable to the same rules, if not methods, that have governed politics since the world began." Another prominent Denver woman suggested that the political machine is making both men and women helpless; and a Las Animas man said that the influence of women is decreasing, "because their husbands and sons work for corporations, and they cannot vote as conscience dictates." One woman asserted that women "lack the genius for leadership," and several others complained merely of a lack of leaders.

A number of both sexes asserted that women have not now and never had any influence whatever. Others testified that, owing to the continual advent of large numbers of Eastern women who take no interest until they are educated up to an appreciation of their privilege, the influence remains practically stationary.

The causes of increased influence are naturally much the same as the causes of increased interest, and the one is largely the reflex of the other. Additional reasons assigned for increased influence were that women now pay more attention to organization, that they have learned political methods and become generally familiar with political machinery, and that "the prejudice against women in politics on the part of both men and women is gradually disappearing." It was pointed out in some answers that women's influence cannot be measured by the number of candidates of their sex nominated. A Weld County woman of some political experience answered to this question: "Decreasing in outward manifestations, but increasing as a recognized factor, in the choice and election of candidates." Another experienced woman, from Boulder County, said: "Increasing, because they have studied the real issue and vote and work far more independently and not so much for the novelty." Several persons claimed that women study economic questions more than men.

A Denver woman suggested an important idea when she answered: "Increasing, as they can influence their children, growing into voting age, as well as others." Added to this suggestion is that of a Pueblo woman, who said: "At first it was a fad. Then interest decreased. But I think this is being followed by an increasing interest as the younger set come on who are educated in politics." A San Miguel woman stated that "young men consult their mothers more on political questions than their fathers." Only two or three, out of the twelve hundred odd people who answered the blank, asserted that women's influence in politics is evil. A broad-minded woman from Delta County said: "Increasing as the intelligence of women increases and broadens. Whenever any woman, however, so far forgets her womanhood as to raise her voice to a harsh note or do one ungentle thing, by that much it decreases."

4. POLITICAL INDEPENDENCE

In answer to the question in regard to the influence of women in politics, a number of persons gave as a reason for its lack that they merely repeat their husbands' votes.[1] Table XXXIII shows that, in

[1] One man somewhat illogically remarked that "no woman has any influence because she either votes the same way her husband does or else the other way, thereby killing his ballot." But

EQUAL SUFFRAGE

answer to a direct question, 73.2 per cent. of all the men and 53.2 per cent. of all the women stated that women usually vote the same tickets as their husbands, or, if unmarried, as their fathers. Many of those, however, who asserted that women usually vote with their husbands or fathers added that there are numerous exceptions, and others said that their so voting is due entirely to the fact that they are usually of the same political belief.[1] Fifteen or twenty women, however, answered that they themselves did not vote the same tickets as their husbands, and about an equal number thought independence in this matter increasing among women. A woman whose experience of Colorado politics gives her statement special weight, said: "An investigation made some five years ago showed ten per cent. as voting independent."

The opinions expressed in these answers, however, cannot be fairly weighed without first taking into consideration the probable result of a supplementary inquiry, which was not made, as to whether men usually vote the same tickets as their wives, or, if unmarried, as their fathers. It is highly probable that

---

this suggests that a man either votes the same way his neighbor does or else the other way, thereby killing his neighbor's ballot; and, if the argument is accepted as conclusive, manhood suffrage should logically be abolished.

[1] Answers which asserted that women vote "independently" or "according to their convictions" were classified under "No," though obviously their independence or their convictions might lead them to the same party affiliations as their husbands or fathers. Of the men, 13.5 per cent., and of the women, 34.4 per cent., gave answers of this kind. It must be remembered that the replies to this question were merely the expression of personal opinion and were considerably influenced, as the table shows, by the general belief or disbelief in equal suffrage.

TABLE XXXIII

Question—Do women usually vote the same ticket as their husbands, or, if unmarried, as their fathers?

	Yes Men	Yes Women	No Men	No Women	No definite answer Men	No definite answer Women
I. Favorable to Equal Suffrage						
A. State officials	25	20	7	18		11
B. Political workers—state	24	51	7	40	5	13
C. Other citizens—state	150	42	57	42	35	11
D. Delegates—Denver	14	80	2	68	3	11
E. Prominent citizens—Denver	5	9	4	6	2	
Total	218	202	77	174	45	46
Per cent	64.1	47.8	22.7	41.3	13.2	10.9
II. Unfavorable to Equal Suffrage						
A. State officials	11	2			1	2
B. Political workers—state	25	13		1		2
C. Other citizens—state	107	14	1	1	12	4
D. Delegates—Denver	20	36		9	2	5
E. Prominent citizens—Denver	3	1				
Total	166	66	1	11	15	13
Per cent	91.2	73.3	0.5	12.2	8.3	14.5
III. Indifferent to Equal Suffrage						
A. State officials	11	2		1	2	2
B. Political workers—state	5	11		1	2	4
C. Other citizens—state	41	13	5	7	17	4
D. Delegates—Denver	7	17		7		4
E. Prominent citizens—Denver	3				1	
Total	67	43	5	16	22	14
Per cent	71.3	58.9	5.3	21.9	23.4	19.2
Grand total	451	311	83	201	82	73
Grand per cent	73.2	53.2	13.5	34.4	13.3	12.4

the answers to such a question would be substantially the same as those to the question in regard to the women's vote. About twenty persons answered that daughters vote as their fathers in about the same proportion as do sons. One prominent Denver woman said: "Political opinion is largely a matter of interest and association. Families usually agree." Another remarked: "As a rule they vote alike, but which determines the double vote is another question." A member of the State Legislature asserted that "when you get the woman of the house with you, in seven cases out of ten you can count on the man." The influence is undoubtedly reciprocal.

A number of persons, in answering this question, distinguished between its two parts, some saying that unmarried women vote with their fathers, but married women do not vote with their husbands; and others that the married vote with their husbands, but not the unmarried with their fathers. Several said that women tend to follow the politics of their fathers, regardless of their husbands. Others distinguished between local and national politics. For instance, a Denver woman said that they usually vote the same tickets as their men relatives in national elections, but not in municipal. This is probably true, as party lines are not so closely drawn by either men or women in local elections. There was other testimony to the effect that "women are very independent in opposing or supporting a particular candidate of whom they approve. They scratch more than men." Several persons agreed with the Boulder County woman who said: "Uneducated and unread women vote as their husbands do. Educated and well-read women have a mind of their own and vote as they please." There was, too, a good deal of testimony to the effect that, as a Teller County man put

EFFECT ON WOMEN OF COLORADO

it, "they usually vote as their male relatives do except on liquor questions and other moral propositions."

Only three persons found it worth while to even mention the possibility of domestic discord in case the wife did not vote the same ticket as her husband. Fortunately, there are probably few men in Colorado who would take the position of the Weld County man who said: "I think the dutiful wife or child does. Especially I think the wife should not disagree with her husband as to politics. I know that I insist my own wife be a Republican, though born and bred a Democrat, and she gladly does as I desire in politics. However, she is not yet old enough to vote. Until she was married she knew no politics but that of a Democrat."

5. Effect on the Moral Character of Women

On the question, "What has been the effect of equal suffrage on the moral character and business and political honor of women?" there was little difference of opinion between the sexes, but a decided difference between those who believed in equal suffrage and those who did not. Thus, Table XXXIV shows that while of those who favored equal suffrage only 6.7 per cent. of the men and 3.9 per cent. of the women thought the effect bad, of those who did not favor it 30.8 per cent. of the men and 33.3 per cent. of the women asserted that the effect has been bad.[1] On the other hand, of those who believed in equal suffrage 31.8 per cent. of the men and 33.2 per cent.

[1] The percentages here, as in all cases, are based on the total number of each sex who gave an answer to any question on the blank, whether or not a definite answer to this particular question was given.

of the women alleged a good influence, while of those who did not believe in it only 3.3 per cent. of each sex gave this answer. Nevertheless, in every division, whether believers or non-believers or persons who did not commit themselves on the general question, with the single exception of the women who believed in equal suffrage, the largest proportion of both sexes answered that enfranchisement has had no effect on the moral character of women.[1] In view of the opinion expressed in most cases by the specific answers, that the bad influence has been solely over those women who have been active in political work, these figures may be taken to represent roughly, but perhaps as fairly as such things can be measured, the proportion of women upon whom the effect in this particular has been good, bad, or inappreciable.[2]

A dozen or so persons distinguished between moral character and business and political honor, and gave answers similar to this: "Has not changed the moral character; has increased the business and political honor." A woman who has done considerable work for her party in the state said: "Women are more liable to petty spite in voting than men. I know, because my husband has just been elected to office, and all the women who were mad at me voted against him." On the other hand, a Huerfano County man said: "I cannot say that it has

[1] In all, 38.8 per cent. of the men and 33.8 per cent. of the women gave this answer, as against 18.8 per cent. of the men and 26 per cent. of the women who answered "good," and 15.1 per cent. of the men and 9.2 per cent. of the women who answered "bad." Of the men, 27.3 per cent., and of the women, 31 per cent., did not answer the question.

[2] It seems approximately fair in making this estimate to add to the "none" column the indefinite answers.

EFFECT ON WOMEN OF COLORADO

TABLE XXXIV

Question—What has been the effect of equal suffrage on the moral character and business and political honor of women?

	Good		None		Bad		No definite answer	
	Men	Women	Men	Women	Men	Women	Men	Women
I. Favorable to Equal Suffrage								
A. State officials	7	18	19	19		2	6	10
B. Political workers—state	11	41	11	37	6	2	8	24
C. Other citizens—state	82	31	83	20	13	1	64	43
D. Delegates—Denver	5	49	6	55	3	9	5	46
E. Prominent citizens—Denver	3	1	5	8	1	1	2	5
Total	108	140	124	139	23	15	85	128
Per cent	31.8	33.2	36.5	32.9	6.7	3.9	25	30.3
II. Unfavorable to Equal Suffrage								
A. State officials	1		7	2	4	1		1
B. Political workers—state	1	1	11	12	6	2	7	1
C. Other citizens—state	4	1	55	5	33	6	28	7
D. Delegates—Denver		1	8	20	12	21	2	8
E. Prominent citizens—Denver			2		1			1
Total	6	3	83	39	56	30	37	18
Per cent	3.3	3.3	45.6	43.4	30.8	33.3	20.3	20
III. Indifferent to Equal Suffrage								
A. State officials	1		3		4	2	5	3
B. Political workers—state		3	3	6	1	2	3	5
C. Other citizens—state	1	4	22	6	8	2	32	12
D. Delegates—Denver		2	3	8	1	3	3	15
E. Prominent citizens—Denver			1				3	
Total	2	9	32	20	14	9	46	35
Per cent	2.1	12.3	34.1	27.4	14.9	12.3	49.9	48
Grand total	116	152	239	198	93	54	168	181
Grand per cent	18.8	26	38.8	33.8	15.1	9.2	27.3	31

improved the moral character of women, but I think it has made an improvement in men, both in morals and honor." A Pueblo County man who did not believe in equal suffrage answered: "Bad—during a campaign. I see men associate with women that they would not recognize under ordinary circumstances, and would not want their wives and daughters to know. Have also seen men of no moral character intrude themselves upon women who would not wish to recognize them, but must tolerate."

Upon the moral character and business and political honor of the great majority of the women of the state, however, equal suffrage has probably had no effect, nor is there any reason why it should have had. Moreover, although upon a few women who have taken active part the influence has apparently been bad, doubtless in most of these cases equal suffrage has not actually caused the woman to be disloyal or dishonest, but has merely enabled a woman who possessed these traits of character to display them more conspicuously. A prominent Denver woman said: "I have not noticed that it has changed them particularly. Many women with a low idea of honor have been prominent, but I have always felt that the political work simply made public the want of moral fibre inherent in the woman herself." The great majority of persons, indeed, who answered the blank seemed to agree substantially with the Denver woman who said: "The effect on the honorable woman has made no more difference than the effect of any other line of work that takes her among her fellow-creatures in a business way. It is the woman who has a flaw in her nature who allows suffrage to corrupt her."

Upon a few of these women, however, equal suffrage has undoubtedly had a bad effect by subjecting them to temptations which they were unable to withstand. Men, too, sometimes yield under similar circumstances. One woman thought that "a continuous political life, with its fierce temptations, will in time drag down any man who does not possess fireproof characteristics of the Rooseveltian order." A few answers claimed that woman's sense of honor has been blunted, others that the evil consists in their having been made bolder and more self-assertive, and several that the bad effect is confined to the cities. A county chairman, over his own signature, testified: "In the last campaign women sold their influence and agreed to work for both parties for cash—highest price paid, $25; lowest, $5. I myself bought one woman for $10 where the Democrats had paid her $15, and we have her endorsements on the checks."

On the other hand, there is evidence to show that upon the moral character and business and political honor of some women equal suffrage has had a good effect, in part by bringing them into contact with business and political ideals, and in part by developing dormant characteristics of a high order.

6. Effect on the Intelligence and Public Spirit of Women

The conclusion seems to be that on the moral side the influence of equal suffrage over the women of Colorado has been slight, but the evidence summarized in Table XXXV shows that on their intelligence and public spirit it has had a distinctly good effect.

There is greater difference of opinion between the sexes on this point, however, than on the preceding question, and nearly the same difference between those who believed in equal suffrage and those who did not. Of those who favored women's enfranchisement, 73.2 per cent. of all the men and 83.2 per cent. of all the women who answered any question on the blank thought the effect good. Of those who answered "No" to the general question, only 10.4 per cent. of the men, but a surprisingly large proportion, 32.2 per cent., of the women, also believed the effect good. Of all the men, only 5.2 per cent., and of all the women, only 1.4 per cent., testified to a bad influence, but of the 32 men and 8 women giving this answer 21 of the men and 7 of the women did not believe in equal suffrage. A good effect was observed by 47.6 per cent. of all the men and 71.3 per cent. of all the women. Upon the whole, then, the table indicates that a decisive plurality of the twelve hundred persons who answered thought that equal suffrage has had a good effect upon the intelligence and public spirit of women.

There was, moreover, no adequate reason suggested for the belief that it has had a bad influence. Criticisms of its moral and not of its intellectual effect were, indeed, practically the only remarks made in connection with these answers. For instance, a Teller County man who did not believe in equal suffrage said: "No appreciable effect, except to degrade. Women study politics and undertake to learn political methods. If they are good women, the more they learn the more disgusted they become. If they are otherwise, they accept the situation, adopt the political methods as their own, and as a consequence lower their womanhood." A Boulder County woman complained that it "has brought out a bold element in the lower classes which is, many times, offensively aggressive."

EFFECT ON WOMEN OF COLORADO

TABLE XXXV

Question — What has been the effect of equal suffrage on the intelligence and public spirit of women?

	Good Men	Good Women	None Men	None Women	Bad Men	Bad Women	No definite answer Men	No definite answer Women
I. Favorable to Equal Suffrage								
A. State officials	23	41	6	4	1		2	4
B. Political workers—state	29	90	1	7	1		5	7
C. Other citizens—state	175	71	22	4	7		38	20
D. Delegates—Denver	13	135	2	5			4	19
E. Prominent citizens—Denver	9	14	2					1
Total	249	351	33	20	9		49	51
Per cent	73.2	83.2	9.7	4.7	2.7		14.4	12.1
II. Unfavorable to Equal Suffrage								
A. State officials		1	11	2	1			1
B. Political workers—state	3	8	14	7	2		6	1
C. Other citizens—state	14	1	59	8	12	1	35	9
D. Delegates—Denver	1	18	12	14	6	6	3	12
E. Prominent citizens—Denver	1	1	2					
Total	19	29	98	31	21	7	44	23
Per cent	10.4	32.2	53.9	34.5	11.5	7.7	24.2	25.6
III. Indifferent to Equal Suffrage								
A. State officials	6	1	3	1			4	3
B. Political workers—state		9	4	1			3	6
C. Other citizens—state	14	12	20	3	2		27	9
D. Delegates—Denver	2	15	2	2		1	3	10
E. Prominent citizens—Denver	3		1					
Total	25	37	30	7	2	1	37	28
Per cent	26.6	50.6	31.9	9.6	2.1	1.4	39.4	38.4
Grand total	293	417	161	58	32	8	130	102
Grand per cent	47.6	71.3	26.1	9.9	5.2	1.4	21.1	17.4

EQUAL SUFFRAGE

A number of persons mentioned, in this connection, the woman's-club movement. Thus, a Denver woman remarked: "Equal suffrage has been so mixed up with the woman's-club movement that it is hard to distinguish between their work, but the two together have had a very broadening effect upon Colorado women." Several asserted that the clubs are a more important factor than equal suffrage. A prominent Denver man, for instance, whose opinion is worthy of consideration, said: "The advent of woman's suffrage and the modern movement for organization of women's clubs occurring at the same time in Colorado prevents a wise answer to this question. My own opinion is that the movement for organization of women's clubs is largely responsible for the advancement made in women as to public spirit and increase of public influence and the advance in the knowledge and intelligence of women generally. I do not believe the right of suffrage has contributed in any marked degree to this end, but the discussion of political questions which might have otherwise occurred, and which has occurred in states where equal suffrage is not enacted, composes an important part of the work of women's clubs. My opinion is that the national movement for women's clubs has been equally as efficient and responsible for the improvement of the public spirit of women in states where equal suffrage does not exist as it has been where it does exist, and it has not been attended by some of the complications which equal suffrage permits."

The majority of persons who answered the blank,

however, seem to have agreed with the county chairman who said: "The effect has been to broaden women intellectually by creating a desire and ambition to study public questions and to familiarize themselves with government affairs." One Teller County woman thought that it has created among women a desire "to become posted so as to converse intelligently with their husbands"; and another thought that it has encouraged them "to fit themselves for positions that will bring them a living salary." A Boulder County woman remarked: "I do not know of anything that could do more, for it has given them a hope without which neither sex accomplishes very much. Few seek to cultivate their minds along lines in which they cannot hope to take a part." Another view was that equal suffrage has brought to the service of the public the intelligence and public spirit of brilliant women and of women of leisure who would otherwise have frittered away their time and energy in comparatively trivial interests.

A number of persons said that "the average woman voter is more intelligent and better informed than the average male voter." For example, a Pueblo man said, "She studies, more than men, books relating to political economy and ethics." The statement has frequently been made that, during the first eight months after the equal-suffrage victory, one firm in Denver sold a larger number of books on political economy than it had sold in twenty years before. A Denver woman delegate, with more wisdom than grammar, said that equal suffrage has had a good effect on the intelligence and public spirit of women because "if you have an education and don't keep on repairing of it all the time it gets stale."

A prominent Denver woman called this good effect "the one great result of equal suffrage," and another said: "I know of no women anywhere equal as a whole to the women of Colorado in civic intelligence and devotion." A third Denver woman stated: "It has been of more benefit to women than they have been to politics, so far, in broadening their minds and inducing public spirit."

7. Effect on the Home and the Children

The answers to the general question as to the effect of equal suffrage on the home and the children are summarized in Table XXXVI. Of all the persons who answered any of the questions on the blank, 39.9 per cent. of the men and 32.5 per cent. of the women thought it has had no influence. But there were decided differences of opinion between the men and the women who believed that it has had an appreciable effect one way or the other. The largest proportion of women, indeed, 33.7 per cent. of all, thought that the effect has been good, but only 15.6 per cent. of the men gave this answer. On the other hand, 21 per cent. of the men as against 8.5 per cent. of the women asserted that the influence has been bad. Even of those who believed in equal suffrage, 7.1 per cent. of the men and 3.1 per cent. of the women said that its effect on the home and the children has been

EFFECT ON WOMEN OF COLORADO

TABLE XXXVI

Question—What has been the effect of equal suffrage on the home and the children?

	Good		None		Bad		No definite answer	
	Men	Women	Men	Women	Men	Women	Men	Women
I. Favorable to Equal Suffrage								
A. State officials	10	15	10	22	6	3	6	9
B. Political workers—state	8	60	18	34	6	2	4	8
C. Other citizens—state	68	39	104	23	11	4	59	29
D. Delegates—Denver	3	63	8	57		4	8	35
E. Prominent citizens—Denver	3	9	4	4	1		3	2
Total	92	186	144	140	24	13	80	83
Per cent	27.1	44.1	42.3	33.1	7.1	3.1	23.5	19.7
II. Unfavorable to Equal Suffrage								
A. State officials			9	2	3			2
B. Political workers—state	1	1	7	10	13	3	4	2
C. Other citizens—state	1		51	2	48	8	20	9
D. Delegates—Denver		4	3	13	18	15	1	18
E. Prominent citizens—Denver				1	3			
Total	2	5	70	28	85	26	25	31
Per cent	1.1	5.6	38.4	31.1	46.7	28.9	13.8	34.4
III. Indifferent to Equal Suffrage								
A. State officials	1		5		4		3	5
B. Political workers—state		2	6	4		2	1	8
C. Other citizens—state	1	3	15	10	14	2	33	9
D. Delegates—Denver		1	2	8	2	7	3	12
E. Prominent citizens—Denver			4					
Total	2	6	32	22	20	11	40	34
Per cent	2.1	8.2	34	30.1	21.3	15.1	42.6	46.6
Grand total	96	197	246	190	129	50	145	148
Grand per cent	15.6	33.7	39.9	32.5	21	8.5	23.5	25.3

EQUAL SUFFRAGE

bad.[1] In nearly every case, however, the complaint was merely against the "political woman," and not against the ordinary voter.

Since the complaints of equal suffrage on this score were nearly all directed against the women who are active in politics, it would be well to consider, before taking up in detail the reasons advanced for opinions on the subject, some of the facts gathered with reference to these women, whether they were married or single, the number and ages of their children, and their occupations. Taking into consideration only women who have done active political work, it is found that 66.1 per cent. of them were married, 18.9 per cent. widowed, and 13.8 per cent. single. It has already been seen[2] that of all the women in Colorado over twenty years of age in 1900, 70.6 per cent. were married, 12.4 per cent. widowed, and 16.5 per cent. single. Evidently the widows, and to a lesser extent the single, furnished more than their proportion of political workers.

Table XXXVII shows also that the proportion of single women was very much greater among the office-holders and candidates than among the women who did party work, though in every case the married women were in the majority. Of all the public officers and candidates, 31.1 per cent. were single, but of the "political workers" only 9 per cent. were single. There was a

---

[1] Of the 129 men and 50 women who answered "bad," 85 men and 26 women did not believe in equal suffrage. But out of the 96 men and 197 women who answered "good," 92 men and 186 women favored equal suffrage. There was doubtless some bias in the answers to this question, due to belief or non-belief in the general proposition. [2] Chap. iii, section 4.

EFFECT ON WOMEN OF COLORADO

TABLE XXXVII

Question—Please state whether you are married or single, and, if married, how many children you have and their ages

	Public officers and candidates[1]			Political workers				Totals	Per cent.
	County superint'd'ts	Other officers	Per cent.	State	Denver	Per cent.
Single	20	13	31.1	13	21	9.0	67	13.8
Married	26	22	45.3	97	176	71.8	321	66.1
Widowed				24	43	17.6	92	18.9
Divorced				1	1	0.5	2	0.4
Not stated	12	13	23.6	1	3	1.1	4	0.8
NUMBER OF CHILDREN
No children	12	5	23.0	17	31	14.0	65	15.5
One child	9	9	24.3	31	45	22.0	94	22.4
Two children	6	6	16.2	31	49	23.2	92	22.0
Three children	5	7	16.2	20	34	15.6	66	15.8
More than three children	4	3	9.5	14	37	14.8	58	13.8
Not stated	3	5	10.8	8	28	10.4	44	10.5
AGE OF CHILDREN[2]
Under fourteen	14	7	36.8	31	70	34.1	122	34.6
Fourteen to twenty-one	4	5	15.8	27	40	22.6	76	21.5
Over twenty-one	2	12	24.6	31	47	26.4	92	26.1
Not stated	7	6	22.8	15	35	16.9	63	17.8

[1] These are also "political workers," but are separately classified here in order to show the status of women in office, or who desire office, in distinction from that of women who merely do party work.
[2] The figures represent the number of married, widowed, and divorced women who have one, two, or three children, etc. If a woman had one child under fourteen and others from fourteen to twenty-one, she was counted as having children under fourteen and not in the other classes. Also if she had one child between fourteen and twenty-one and others over twenty-one, she was counted in the class "fourteen to twenty-one." This method would tend to increase the figures in the lower classes at the expense of the upper.

247

much larger proportion of widows, too, among the public officers and candidates, 23.6 per cent. as compared with 17.6 per cent. of the "political workers." More than half of all the officers and candidates were either single or widowed—*i.e.*, may be presumed to have been obliged to support themselves. But of those who did merely party work, 71.8 per cent. were married women. Many of these, of course, received no pay for their work, and, with the others, the money earned was supplementary to some other source of income, either from the husband or from more or less irregular work of their own.

As for the children, nearly half of the married women and widows had either one or two children, 22.4 per cent. having one child, and 22 per cent. having two children. However, 15.8 per cent. had three children and 13.8 per cent. more than three children, while 15.5 per cent. had no children. The figures for the public officers and candidates and for the political workers differ widely. Of the former, 23 per cent. had no children and 24.3 per cent. had only one child, while of the latter 22 per cent. had one child, and 23.2 per cent. had two children. A far larger proportion of political workers than of public officers and candidates, 14.8 per cent. as against 9.5 per cent., had more than three children. The women who held public offices, then, had decidedly fewer children than the women who did party work.

The ages of the children of these two classes of women did not differ so widely, the proportion who had children under fourteen being the largest in both cases, 34.6 per cent. of the whole. Many of these women also had older children, but they were counted in the lowest class to which any of their children belonged in order to show how many had young children, regardless of older sons and daughters. This method would naturally increase the numbers in the lower classifications. But it is significant that 26.1 per cent. of the married women and the widows had only grown sons and daughters over twenty-one

EFFECT ON WOMEN OF COLORADO

years of age. This proportion is nearly as high for the public officers and candidates as for the political workers. In 17.8 per cent. of the cases the ages of the children were not stated, but next to this the smallest proportion of women, 21.5 per cent., were found to have children from fourteen to twenty-one years of age.

Taking the public officers and candidates and the political workers together, 63 did not state the facts in regard to their children, 65 had no children, 67 were single, 76 had children from fourteen to twenty-one, 92 had only children over twenty-one, and 122 had children under fourteen. The large proportion under "not stated" makes it impossible to draw any very definite conclusion, but it certainly appears that women with young children were doing a considerable amount of political work, both as office-holders and as party workers.

In order to obtain additional information in regard to the children of widows and women engaged in gainful occupations, the figures for them were separately classified. It was found that of 79 widows included in "county superintendents" and "political workers," 7 had no children, 20 had one child, 19 two children, 13 three, 10 more than three, and 10 did not state the number of their children. Of the 12 county superintendents who were widows, 3 had no children, 2 one child, 1 two children, 3 three children, 2 more than three, and 1 did not state the number. But of all the widows who had children, by far the largest number, 31 out of 72, had only grown sons and daughters over twenty-one years of age. Only 11 had children under fourteen, and 12 children from fourteen to twenty-one, but 18 did not state ages. Of the 9 widows who were county superintendents and had children, 3 did not give the ages, 4 had children under fourteen, and 2 only children over twenty-one.

Of the 67 widows, exclusive of the county superintendents, however, only 25 stated that they were engaged in a gainful occupation. Of 73 women, indeed, who named some definite gainful occupation, 25 were widowed, 28 married, and 20 single. Of the 53 married and widowed, 6 had no children, 12 one child, 17 two children, 5 three, 6 more than three, and 7 did not state the number. Twelve had children under fourteen years of age, 11 children from fourteen to twenty-one, 12 children over twenty-one, and 12 did not state ages.

The support of children is doubtless a strong motive with widows for political work, but even stronger with married women who, for one reason or another, are obliged to enter some gainful employment. Their work is usually irregular, like that of a dressmaker, and the additional income derived from a few days' political work at a high rate of pay is most helpful. In a considerable number of cases, too, in which the woman is not actually obliged to support herself and her children, the money earned is, nevertheless, a very welcome supplement to the meagre income received by the head of the family. There is, then, a strong economic motive for political service, and if, occasionally, young children are neglected for a few days while the mother is out canvassing a precinct or attending a convention, this is in a measure compensated for by the additional comforts which she is able to furnish them with the money earned. Moreover, the objection sometimes offered to the work of married women, that it lowers the wages of men, does not hold here, because political work is irregular, is scattered through a mixed industrial population, and is done probably as often by the wives of small tradesmen as by the wives of wage-earners.

As regards pay for political work, two interesting

points of view appeared. A Pueblo man who did not believe in equal suffrage said: "Home and children are neglected while 'mamma' attends political meetings and hoofs it around the ward in the interest of some candidate in the hope of getting a political job after election. This is what she calls 'patriotism.'" On the other hand, a Denver man, who did not state definitely whether or not he believed in equal suffrage, answered: "Very little effect. It has enabled a lot of deserving women with children, and in some cases with husbands unable to support themselves, to gain a livelihood. I know of a number of women who, by the efficiency of their work, have gained for themselves good positions. Without woman suffrage these positions would have been filled by friends of men workers. One of the great arguments, to my notion, in favor of equal suffrage is that it enables a large number of deserving women to gain money by hard work and also enables the deserving woman to obtain for herself political positions." One of the women county superintendents said: "It enables me by my salary to give to my child the opportunities which I craved for her, and which otherwise she could never have had."

The figures in regard to the occupations of women who have done active political work may be compared with those in Table XVIII, which gives the occupations of women voters. Practically half, 49 per cent., were housewives, and 21.5 per cent. were in professional service, most of the latter being teachers or county superintendents of schools. Of the remainder, 10.1 per cent. had to be classified as "miscellaneous and indefinite," so that only about 20 per cent. were in the other occupational divisions.

Of these, 1.4 per cent. were in agricultural pursuits, 5.1 per cent. in domestic and personal service, 7.8 per cent. in trade and transportation, and 5.1 per cent. in manufacturing and mechanical pursuits. But, as in the case of women voters, little of value can be derived from a study of these occupation statistics.

Other figures which might be expected to throw light upon the effect of equal suffrage upon the home and the children relate to the number of divorces and the proportion of young children to women of child-bearing age. The divorce question is of course, a difficult one to treat satisfactorily, because of differences between states in the laws on this subject. The women of Colorado, however, have had the full franchise since 1894, and it therefore seems fairly reasonable to compare the number of divorces in cities of nearly the same population. Appendix J gives the number of divorces granted in Denver and Pueblo and in the five cities ranging next above and the five cities ranging next below each in population in 1902–1903. It appears that Denver had more divorces than any of the other ten cities except Indianapolis, Kansas City, and Los Angeles, but the number in Pueblo was less than that in any of the other ten cities with which it was compared except La Crosse, Wisconsin; Newport, Kentucky; and New Britain, Connecticut. These results, however, are not by any means decisive.

These figures, moreover, do not tell the whole story. Of all males and females fifteen years of age and over living in Colorado in 1900, 0.6 per cent. of the males and 0.8 per cent. of the females were divorced. In the entire Western Division the same proportion of males, 0.6 per cent., and a slightly higher proportion of females, 0.9 per cent., were divorced. These percentages are all higher than for the whole United States, which are 0.3 per cent. for males and 0.5 per cent. for females; but the laws of Colorado allow easier divorce than those of most of the Eastern states. The proportion of divorced men was, however, lower in Colorado than in Maine, New Hampshire, New Mexico, Arizona, Nevada, Idaho, Washington, and Oregon, and the same as in Vermont, Indiana, Montana, and California. The proportion of divorced women was lower than in New Hampshire, Montana, New Mexico, Arizona, Utah, Nevada, Washington, Oregon, and California, and the same as in Indiana and Idaho.[1]

The facts here presented are not particularly favorable to Colorado, but, considering the divorce laws of the state, they are not sufficient to prove an increase due to equal suffrage. Senator Patterson, who has had wide experience as a lawyer in Colorado both before and since the passage of the equal-suffrage amendment, stated in 1902 that he had never heard of a case in which political differences had been alleged as a cause of divorce. The probability is that the enfranchisement of women has had no appreciable effect.

It is not probable, either, that equal suffrage has had any effect upon the birth-rate. Table XXXVIII, however, is given as an exhibit in connection with this question. The number of children under five years of age to one thousand women of child-bearing age decreased in Colorado between 1890 and 1900 from 464 to 416, a decrease of 48 as against a decrease of 11 for the entire United States. The decrease is greater, indeed, in Colorado than in any of the seventeen states named except Nebraska, Idaho, Washington, and Oregon, all of which had a larger number of children than Colorado. This, however, is a natural phenomenon of frontier communities which are in the process of becoming industrial, and it is impossible to isolate the influence of such a factor as equal suffrage from others of far greater importance.

Returning to the testimony concerning the influence of equal suffrage on the home and the children

[1] *United States Census*, 1900, vol. ii, Population, part ii, p. lxxxiv.

EQUAL SUFFRAGE

TABLE XXXVIII

NUMBER OF CHILDREN UNDER 5 YEARS OF AGE TO 1000 FEMALES 15 TO 49 YEARS OF AGE, 1890 AND 1900 [1]

States	1900	1890	Decrease	Increase
Continental United States	474	485	11	
North Atlantic Division	390	373		17
Massachusetts	347	310		37
New York	370	357		13
Pennsylvania	443	441		2
South Atlantic Division	560	557		3
Georgia	603	608	5	
North Central Division	457	495	38	
Ohio	393	418	25	
Illinois	437	482	45	
Minnesota	556	583	27	
Nebraska	526	598	72	
Kansas	482	545		37
South Central Division	596	612	16	
Tennessee	550	571	21	
Western Division	439	473	34	
Idaho	644	702	58	
Wyoming	585	592	7	
Utah	649	689	40	
Washington	469	536	67	
Oregon	425	494	69	
California	340	378	38	
Colorado	416	464	48	

[1] Derived from part of table in *Census Bulletin* 22, Proportion of Children in the United States, p. 13. The decrease shown from 1890 to 1900 is probably, owing to a change in the form of the age question, less in all divisions and states than here shown. It will be observed that in the seventeen states selected for comparison all four of the equal-suffrage states are included.

given in answer to this question on the blanks, those who expressed the opinion that it has had a bad effect usually gave as a reason that it has caused neglect. A Denver woman, for instance, who did not believe in equal suffrage, expressed the time-worn sentiment, "It takes the wife and mother from her home more or less, and what is home without a mother?" A Pueblo man thought that it has "made many mothers and wives dissatisfied with home-

EFFECT ON WOMEN OF COLORADO

making and the rearing of children." A Denver man who did not believe in equal suffrage asserted: "The homes have been disrupted and the children left homeless and motherless." A number of persons, however, who said that the effect is bad for the homes and children of the women who are actively engaged in politics, added that it is good for those of the women who merely vote.

Of those persons who thought that equal suffrage has had no effect on the home and the children, a few acknowledged that in some cases women have neglected both, but said, with a prominent Denver woman, that "the woman who would neglect her home for politics would do so for some other reason." Another prominent Denver woman answered: "I don't think it has made the slightest difference. The mother trundles her baby past the voting-place, leaves it in some convenient place while she puts her slip of paper in the box, and then goes on to the market or store. I never yet saw a mother neglect her children for politics." A Weld County man thought that "social obligations interfere with women's home duties a hundred times where suffrage does once." A number of others agreed substantially with this opinion. One of the county superintendents said: "I see no change in the care of homes and children. Women are found here occasionally who neglect their homes and children for society, card-playing, clubs, church, and busybodying, and once in a great while one who neglects her home for politics. She, however, is invariably one who used to neglect it for some of the previously mentioned reasons before she had the right to participate in political affairs." Another county superintendent suggested: "It does not take a woman out of her home as long to go to the polls as it does to go to church. She is thrown into closer contact with men at the post-office than at the polls."

The reasons given for the belief that equal suffrage has had a good effect on the home and the children may be divided into three classes. First, were those which cited the legal measures for the protection of women and children passed since women were enfranchised. These measures have already been considered in Chapter VI. Second, were those which asserted that by increasing the mother's knowledge of public affairs, broadening her ideals, and increasing her influence over her children, equal suffrage has made the home more pleasant and has caused the children to be better trained. One prominent Denver woman said: "Children have two chances to absorb ideas of good citizenship instead of one," and another added: "Children learn to think of their mothers as responsible citizens." This latter idea was confirmed by others, as, for instance, by a woman who has been prominent in state politics, who said: "My own opinion is that it will help to create more respect for the mother in the home, she being equal to the father, which the children are not slow to realize, and we all know that mothers generally stand for all that is good for children. I also notice children share the mother's political faith when it is different from the father's." Another prominent Denver woman answered: "I think it has a good effect, as the mothers consider public questions and discuss them freely before and with their children, thus educating them to give thought to many important subjects that in the past were never considered part of their training." There was a great deal of testimony to the effect that political questions are discussed more in the home than they were before women voted. One woman remarked that the "mother will be patient and answer questions concerning politics which the father will put off."

The third reason assigned for the belief that equal suffrage is a benefit to the home was that it has made men and women more companionable to one another. Thus, a Boulder County woman thought that equal suffrage has brought "happiness and contentment, because father and mother are equal in thought and understanding, and are able to converse about outside matters which become the interest of all." A La Plata County woman suggested that it has led to "home discussion instead of going out to talk politics on the part of the men," and a La Plata County man said that equal suffrage produces "a higher standard of knowledge of public affairs in the home, and has a tendency to make the home the unit rather than the individual when the tendency is to double the power of the home vote. The home in this country always produces the best citizenship. The single person, as a rule, is not likely to be interested in good government, like the parent, husband, or wife." A Denver woman testified that "it brings husbands and wives nearer to each other. Their interests are more closely related, and wives who are able to converse intelligently with their husbands upon political questions are more companionable."

8. Conclusion

The effect of equal suffrage upon the women themselves, their outlook upon life, and their relationship to the home, is, in the opinion of many, the crux of the problem. Its effect upon party politics has been slight. But the reason is to be found primarily in the character of the present political machinery. To fully perform, under the existing system, the duties of an enfranchised citizen requires not only an inflexible moral code, but the public spirit, the self-immolation, and the unselfish devotion of a martyr. Politics in Colorado are at least as corrupt as in other states, and the woman of ideals who goes into political life for reform soon finds, not merely that she is working in the mire, but that she is *personâ non gratâ* with the habitual denizens of the mire and with those persons who profit by its existence. Sometimes she becomes unutterably disgusted and ceases her political activity; sometimes her grit rouses antagonism, and she is more or less politely shoved out by experts at the business; and sometimes she stays and is taught "the tricks of the trade." The last case illustrates the one direct evil of equal suffrage, but, fortunately, it is of rare occurrence, and affects only women of weak moral fibre.

Over the majority of women, indeed, it is already evident that equal suffrage has exercised a good influence, and one which inevitably reacts, to a certain

EFFECT ON WOMEN OF COLORADO

extent, upon political life. It has tended, for instance, to cultivate intelligent public spirit among the women of Colorado. Many have not been aroused; many have become discouraged and lost interest after the failure of their early efforts; comparatively few have taken an active part in political life; but thousands vote, and to every one of these thousands the ballot means a little broadening in the outlook, a little glimpse of wider interests than pots and kettles, trivial scandal, and bridge whist.

As for the loss in womanly characteristics sometimes alleged to have resulted, it is difficult to find any evidence to show that voting affects this side of a woman's character any more than purchasing a garden-hose. Families usually go to the polls together, old and young, men and women. In Pueblo, in 1906, one woman one hundred and two years old cast her first ballot. Many mothers have cast their first ballots with sons just arrived of age. Women at the polls meet, not rough and unfamiliar persons, but their own neighbors and friends. In political conventions they often exchange receipts for cooking egg-plant and choice information about the baby, the servant, and the dressmaker, just as they would at any other gathering.

There are, it is true, a thousand and one psychological points in which women differ more or less decidedly from men, and their enfranchisement has probably tended to slightly modify some of these points of difference in some women. Social divisions, for instance, sometimes impede women's political work. They are not usually as democratic as men, primarily because they do not have as much occasion in their daily lives to associate with other classes than their own. But to assert that equal suffrage is capable of destroying real womanliness is to assert that the characteristics which make women women and men men are only skin deep. As for man's chivalry, one woman remarked rather pathetically that she never knew what real chivalry meant until she could vote, and there are doubtless many others who have had the same experience. The fundamental emotional characteristics of men and women, whether good or bad, are far too deeply rooted to be subverted by the franchise privilege.

Equal suffrage has brought, then, practically no loss and some decided gain, the latter mainly evident in the effect of the possession of the ballot upon the women of Colorado. It has enlarged their interests, quickened their civic consciousness, and developed in many cases ability of a high order which has been of service to the city, the county, and the state. Closely allied to this wider outlook and richer opportunity, and also distinctly visible as at least a tendency, is the development of the spirit of comradeship between the sexes. It is still too early to measure adequately these factors, and perhaps it will never be possible to determine exactly how much equal suffrage has contributed. But the Colorado experiment certainly indicates that equal suffrage is a step in the direction of a better citizenship, a more effective use of the ability of women as an integral part of the race, and a closer understanding and comradeship between men and women

APPENDIXES

APPENDIX A

TEXT OF EQUAL-SUFFRAGE BILL AND EQUAL-SUFFRAGE PROCLAMATION

I—The text of the equal-suffrage law is as follows:[1]

"Section 1. That every female person shall be entitled to vote at all elections in the same manner in all respects as male persons are, or shall be entitled to vote by the constitution and laws of this state, and the same qualification as to age, citizenship and time of residence in the state, county, city, ward and precinct and all other qualifications required by law to entitle male persons to vote shall be required to entitle female persons to vote."

II—The following is the equal-suffrage proclamation:[2]

"PROCLAMATION BY THE GOVERNOR OF THE STATE OF COLORADO

"*Whereas*, The Ninth General Assembly of the State of Colorado passed an act, approved April 7, 1893, entitled 'An Act to submit to the qualified electors of the state the question of extending the right of suffrage to

---

[1] Mills, *Annotated Statutes*, vol. iii, *Revised Supplement*, p. 405.
[2] *Legislative Manual*, 1903, State of Colorado, p. 237.

women of lawful age, and otherwise qualified, according to the provisions of article vii, section 2, of the Constitution of Colorado'; and,

"*Whereas*, The said question, as provided in section 2 of said act, was submitted to the qualified voters of the state of Colorado at the general election held on Tuesday, November 7, 1893; and,

"*Whereas*, After canvass of the official returns of said election by the state canvassing board, it appeared that of the votes cast,

"35,798 votes were cast for 'Equal Suffrage Approved' and 29,451 votes were cast for 'Equal Suffrage Not Approved,' and that the majority for 'Equal Suffrage Approved' was 6,347 votes.

"Now, therefore, I, Davis H. Waite, Governor of Colorado, do hereby proclaim, as provided in section 5 of said act, that every female person, a resident of Colorado, shall be entitled to vote at all elections in the same manner in all respects as male persons, and subject to the same qualifications.

"'*God and Liberty.*'

"Done at Denver, December 2, 1893.

"Davis H. Waite,
"Governor of Colorado.

(Seal)
"Nelson O. McClees,
        "Secretary of State."

APPENDIXES

APPENDIX B

DOCUMENTS, WOMAN'S REPUBLICAN LEAGUE OF COLORADO, 1900

I—THE WOMAN'S REPUBLICAN LEAGUE OF COLORADO

Headquarters: 334 Brown Palace Hotel

Officers	Executive Committee
NETTIE E. CASPAR, President	MRS. FRED BUTLER
MINERVA C. WELCH, Vice-President	MRS. LOUISE LAVELLE
ELLEN G. VAN KLEECK, Vice-President	MRS. A. J. PEAVEY
MARY A. THORN, Secretary	MRS. G. L. SCOTT
	MRS. W. S. WARD
	MRS. G. C. YOUNG

The co-operation of every woman who desires good government for our city and county is necessary to secure the election of the Republican ticket in this county in November next. Too large a percentage of the Republican women have neglected to vote at the elections since 1894, when the franchise was a novelty and a large number of women voted and doubtless contributed largely to the success of the party. As this is a Presidential election, greater interest will be manifested by all parties, and good, loyal women cannot afford to neglect their responsibility at the coming election. To this end the members of the Republican League desire to meet the ladies of District .... on October ...., ..., at their headquarters—Room 334 Brown Palace.

NETTIE E. CASPAR,
President.

MARY A. THORN,
Secretary.

EQUAL SUFFRAGE

II—THE WOMAN'S REPUBLICAN LEAGUE OF COLORADO

Officers

Mrs. S. M. Caspar, President
Mrs. A. L. Welch, Vice-President
Miss Mary A. Thorn, Secretary

Vice-Presidents
Mrs. W. N. W. Blayney
Mrs. C. B. Kountze
Mrs. R. H. McMann
Mrs. W. P. G. Hayward
Mrs. J. A. Cooper
Mrs. C. A. Eldredge,
   Colorado Springs
Mrs. M. J. Noble, Pueblo
Mrs. H. N. Lee, Cripple Creek
Mrs. Jesse Gale, Greeley
Mrs. Dr. Dawson, Canon City

Executive Committee
Mrs. Fred Butler
Mrs. Louise Lavelle
Mrs. A. F. Peavey
Mrs. George L. Scott
Mrs. William Shaw Ward
Mrs. Frank C. Young
Mrs. Henry Van Kleeck

334 Brown Palace Hotel,
Denver, Colorado.

ARE YOU REGISTERED?

The Registration-books will be closed October 21.

A scheme is in progress by our opponents to put the names of unregistered women on the registration-books. On election day an effort will be made to have these names claimed and voted by women acting under coercion or bribery. By failing to register and vote you are helping fraud and dishonesty, for you *may* be represented at the polls by the worst and lowest types of womanhood.

There is also a plan to vote "repeaters" on the names of women who are late in going to the polls. If you do not vote early you may find yourself deprived of the right of suffrage. Will you express your own opinions at the polls or shall they be expressed for you by the unspeakable element of your sex?

The opportunity of the bad lies in the indifference of the good. Will you give them this opportunity by your indifference?

This campaign is one of supreme importance. It involves questions of law and order in conflict with violence,

APPENDIXES

destruction, and misrule. The issue is no longer an economic, but a *moral* one. It is an issue that affects the home as well as the State and the Nation. The Republican nominees are pledged to home rule for our city. We feel that the entire Republican ticket is one we can heartily endorse.

Do you not think every earnest woman should feel her individual responsibility in settling these questions?

Your city, your state, and your country need your influence and your vote. Will you withhold them at this critical time?

By Order of the Executive Committee.

III—THE WOMAN'S REPUBLICAN LEAGUE OF COLORADO

Officers
Mrs. S. M. Caspar, President
Mrs. A. L. Welch, Vice-President
Miss Mary A. Thorn, Secretary

Vice-Presidents
Mrs. W. N. W. Blayney
Mrs. C. B. Kountze
Mrs. R. H. McMann
Mrs. W. P. G. Hayward
Mrs. J. A. Cooper
Mrs. C. A. Eldredge, Colorado Springs
Mrs. M. J. Noble, Pueblo
Mrs. Annie B. Brand, Cripple Creek
Mrs. Jesse S. Gale, Greeley
Mrs. Carrie P. Dawson, Cañon City
Mrs. J. P. Kelly, Golden
Mrs. K. K. Roberts, Montrose
Mrs. R. S. Braddock, Silver Cliff
Mrs. E. W. Clark, Akron
Mrs. I. B. Cowie, Boulder
Mrs. G. C. Fernsel, La Junta
Mrs. Gordon Kimball, Ouray

Executive Committee
Mrs. Fred Butler
Mrs. Louise Lavelle
Mrs. A. J. Peavey
Mrs. George L. Scott
Mrs. William Shaw Ward
Mrs. Frank C. Young
Mrs. Henry Van Kleeck

334 Brown Palace Hotel,
Denver, Colorado, *September* 1, 1900.

Will you, as a member of the Woman's Republican League, help the Committee Women in getting out careless or indifferent voters on Election Day?

EQUAL SUFFRAGE

This will be the most important work of the campaign.

Registration is useless unless everybody who has registered also votes.

If you can give two or three hours of your time on November 6th, you may do much toward the result of a fine Republican majority. You owe this to the State.

If you cannot use the enclosed badge, please do not allow it to be used by some indifferent person.

We desire to remind you of the change in the style of the ballot. Instead of making a cross opposite an emblem, you must write the name of the party in a blank space on the ticket. If you write "REPUBLICAN" in that space you will make no mistake.

APPENDIXES

APPENDIX C

Vote and Registration in Pueblo County[1]
Fourteen Typical Precincts in Pueblo County, 1904

Precinct	Registration, per cent. Men	Registration, per cent. Women	Vote, per cent. Men	Vote, per cent. Women
4	54.41	45.58	56.32	43.67
23	54.07	45.92	55.84	44.15
13	60.93	39.06	60.56	39.43
28	60.47	39.52	60.33	39.66
27	72.47	27.52	72.42	27.57
20	61.92	38.07	62.88	37.11
11	65.44	34.56	69.74	30.25
8	64.48	35.51	66.81	33.18
39	67.67	32.32	69.35	30.64
36	62.33	37.66	59.23	40.76
41	73.80	26.19	75	25
34	68.18	31.81	72.22	27.77
31	65.51	34.48	67.56	32.43
30	58.41	41.58	67.92	32.07

Eight Typical Precincts in City of Pueblo, 1905

Precinct	Registration, per cent. Men	Registration, per cent. Women	Vote, per cent. Men	Vote, per cent. Women
4	53	49.99	58.81	46.18
23	54.40	45.59	53.88	46.11
13	56.67	43.32	58.88	41.11
28	59.96	40.03	63.36	36.63
27	71.64	28.35	70.73	29.26
20	62.64	27.35	62.03	37.96
11	64.78	35.21	66.92	33.07
8	59.28	40.74	56.78	43.21

[1] Part of tables given by Mr. Lawrence Lewis in article on "How Woman Suffrage Works in Colorado," in *The Outlook*, January 27, 1906.

Precinct 4—Best residence.
Precinct 23—Second best residence.
Precinct 13—In part best residence, in part skilled artisans and railroad men.
Precinct 28—Artisans, small tradesmen, mechanics, laborers—skilled and unskilled—clerks, a few superintendents, foremen, engineers, professional men.
Precinct 27—Mechanics, skilled and common laborers at steel works.
Precinct 20—Slavs and Italians, steel workers and smelter laborers.
Precinct 11—Cheap lodging-houses, saloons. "Tough." A few small manufacturers, alien laborers.
Precinct 8—Some aliens and respectable people, but generally disreputable. Brothels and lowest saloons. Female rooming-houses.
Precinct 39—Beulah—small village in agricultural region.
Precinct 36—Rye—small village in agricultural and stock region.
Precinct 41—Agricultural and horticultural region.
Precinct 34—Stanley's Ranch—cattle-raising community.
Precinct 31—Ranching community, some agriculture, mostly cattle.
Precinct 30—Ranching community.

APPENDIX D

TABLES SHOWING TENANCY, NATURALIZATION AND CONJUGAL CONDITION OF DENVER PERSONS REGISTERED, IN 1906 BY WARDS

I—OWNERSHIP AND TENANCY OF PERSONS REGISTERED IN DENVER AT NOVEMBER, 1906, ELECTION, BY WARDS[1]

Ward	Owner Women Number	Owner Women Per ct.	Owner Men Number	Owner Men Per ct.	Tenant Women Number	Tenant Women Per ct.	Tenant Men Number	Tenant Men Per ct.	Lodger Women Number	Lodger Women Per ct.	Lodger Men Number	Lodger Men Per ct.	Not given Women Numb'r	Not given Women Per ct.	Not given Men Numb'r	Not given Men Per ct.
1	110	16.9	133	13.1	500	77	612	60.6	25	3.9	266	26.3	14	2.5	...	...
2	69	9	68	4.7	447	58.2	532	36.6	232	30.2	853	58.7	20	2.6	..[3]	...
3	34	4.6	38	2.3	407	55.2	390	23.8	293	39.9	1,210	73.9	2	0.3	..[3]	...
4	107	9.6	155	9.3	761	68.5	876	52.5	206	18.5	537	32.3	38	3.4	..[3]	...
5	215	22	258	18.9	699	71.9	899	66	61	6.1	207	15.1	..[3]	..[3]	56	5.9
6	842	46.5	982	40.7	812	44.9	1,050	43.4	112	6.2	335	13.8	43	2.4	50	2.1
7	471	40.3	548	32.4	581	49.7	764	45.2	9	0.8	146	8.6	107[4]	9.2[4]	234[4]	13.8[4]
8	885	39.3	1,022	39.3	1,111	49.3	1,276	49	233	10.3	245	9.4	25	1.1	59	2.3
9	467	16.3	452	14.6	1,649	57.6	1,587	51.1	679	23.7	983	31.7	70	2.4	80	2.6
10	928	29.6	990	29.5	1,478	61	1,633	48.6	480	8.7	575	17.1	174	0.7	163	4.8
11	457	29.7	504	27.5	941	61	1,124	54.8	135	8.7	344	16.6	10	0.6	20	0.9
12	838	38.2	909	35.4	1,095	50	1,193	46.5	170	8.7	246	9.6	88[4]	4[4]	217[4]	8.5[4]
13	888	55	1,003	51.9	569	35.4	720	37.3	134	8.3	189	9.8	20	1.3	19	1
14	454	45	488	43.4	342	33.9	377	33.6	124	12.3	146	13	389[5]	8.8[5]	112[5]	10[5]
15	895	47.6	1,021	45.8	794	42.3	939	42.1	182	9.7	271	12.1	7	0.4	..[3]	...
16	753	50.8	841	43.7	513	34.6	739	38.4	75	5	195	10.2	142[6]	9.6[6]	148[6]	7.7[6]
Total[2]	8,413	34.6	9,472	30.7	12,699	52.4	14,711	47.5	3,150	13	6,748	21.8				

[1] For descriptions of wards, see remarks on Table XIV., pp. 108-109
[2] The percentages for totals are obtained upon the basis of owners, tenants, and lodgers, omitting those under "not given."
[3] In this ward the figures, for some unknown reason, show a slight surplus of owners, tenants, and lodgers over the total registration.
[4] Precinct 7 not given.   [5] Precinct 11 not given.   [6] Precinct 3 not given.

APPENDIXES

II.—NATURALIZED CITIZENS REGISTERED IN DENVER AT NOVEMBER, 1906, ELECTION, BY WARDS[1]

Ward	Germans Women	Per cent.	Germans Men	Per cent.	Swedes Women	Per cent.	Swedes Men	Per cent.	Italians Women	Per cent.	Italians Men	Per cent.	Slavs Women	Per cent.	Slavs Men	Per cent.	Miscellaneous Women	Per cent.	Miscellaneous Men	Per cent.	Total naturalized Women	Per cent.	Total naturalized Men	Per cent.
1	63	31.8	135	68.2	6	30	14	70	6	37.5	10	62.5	17	40.5	25	59.5	53	25	159	75	145	29.7	343	70.3
2	30	29.1	73	70.9	6	27.3	16	72.7	3	20	12	80	3	27.3	8	72.7	46	24.3	123	75.7	88	27.5	232	72.5
3	9	14.8	52	85.2	6	15.8	32	84.2	2	33.3	4	66.7	5	29.4	12	70.6	40	24.5	124	75.5	62	21.7	224	78.3
4	37	29.6	88	70.4	8	25.8	23	74.2			4	88.2	16	27.1	43	72.9	47	28.1	120	71.9	112	27	303	73
5	39	25.5	114	74.5	19	33.9	37	66.1	4	11.8	29	88.2	12	30.8	27	69.2	78	36.3	137	63.7	148	31.6	320	68.4
6	141	45.1	172	54.9	111	30.8	149	69.2	114	37.4	191	62.6	81	42.6	109	57.4	217	42.6	295	57.4	664	42	916	58
7	69	38.8	109	61.2	95	32.8	195	67.2			5	100	8	42.1	11	57.9	145	39.8	219	60.2	313	36.6	542	63.4
8	72	37.1	122	62.9	41	32.8	84	67.2	2	33.3	4	66.7	15	88.2	2	11.8	140	38.8	221	61.2	259	36.3	455	63.7
9	55	33.1	111	66.9	21	46.7	24	53.3	1	33.3	2	66.7	5	16.1	26	83.9	141	42.9	188	57.1	225	40.2	335	59.8
10	59	33.2	119	66.8	30	46.9	34	53.1	1	25	3	75	6	43.8	9	56.2	134	39.6	204	60.4	229	38	373	62
11	98	40.3	145	59.7	46	32.6	95	67.4			3	100	13	33.3	78	66.7	136	39.7	207	60.3	331	38.5	528	61.5
12	43	31.9	92	68.1	33	35.1	61	64.9	1	25	3	75	5	27.8	13	72.2	127	43.2	167	56.8	208	38.4	334	61.6
13	30	31.3	66	68.7	31	33.7	61	66.3			1	100	4	30.8	9	69.2	106	46.9	120	53.1	171	40.1	256	59.9
14	23	36.3	37	63.7	22	40.7	32	59.3					2	25	6	75	54	31.7	113	68.3	101	34.8	189	65.2
15	33	33.7	65	66.3	26	35.1	48	64.9	1	25	3	75	5	29.4	12	70.6	99	39	155	61	164	36.7	283	63.3
16	60	37.3	101	62.7	25	32.9	51	67.1	1	25	3	75	320	42.5	433	57.5	122	45.5	146	54.5	528	41.8	734	58.2
Total	861	34.9	1601	65.1	526	35.6	956	64.4	136	33.2	274	66.8	540	39.4	838	60.6	1685	38.4	2698	61.6	3748	37.1	6367	62.9

[1] For descriptions of wards, see remarks on Table XIV., pp. 108–109

III—CONJUGAL CONDITION OF WOMEN REGISTERED IN DENVER AT NOVEMBER, 1906, ELECTION, BY WARDS [1]

Ward	Single Number	Single Per ct.	Married Number	Married Per ct.	Widowed Number	Widowed Per ct.	Not given Numb'r	Not given Per ct.
1	54	8.3	426	65.7	48	7.4	121	18.6
2	221	28.8	429	55.8	99	12.9	19	2.5
3	221	30.1	451	61.3	54	7.3	10	1.3
4	280	25.2	738	66.4	60	5.4	34	3
5	116	12	741	75.1	110	12.3	6	0.6
6	159	8.8	1,527	84.4	102	5.6	21	1.2
7	115	9.8	999	85.5	47	4.1	7	0.6
8	508	22.5	1,564	69.4	125	5.6	57	2.5
9	877	30.6	1,677	57.9	273	9.7	38	1.8
10	754	24.6	2,062	67.4	219	7.2	25	0.8
11	238	15.4	1,173	76.1	79	5.1	53	3.4
12	480	21.9	1,532	69.9	146	6.7	33	1.5
13	232	14.4	1,270	78.9	101	6.2	8	0.5
14	185	18.4	758	75.1	64	6.3	2	0.2
15	281	14.9	1,395	74.3	126	6.7	76	4.1
16	136	9.2	1,241	83.7	70	4.7	36	2.4
Total	4,857	19.3	17,983	71.6	1,723	6.9	546	2.2

[1] For descriptions of wards, see remarks on Table XIV., pp. 108–109

APPENDIXES

APPENDIX E

PROPORTION OF TEACHERS TO PERSONS OF SCHOOL AGE IN SEVENTEEN STATES AND THE UNITED STATES

NUMBER OF TEACHERS TO 10,000 PERSONS 5 TO 24 YEARS OF AGE[1]

States and Divisions	1900	1890	1900 In cities having at least 25,000 inhabitants	1900 In smaller cities or country districts
Continental United States	140	127	146	138
North Atlantic Division	162	147	137	184
Massachusetts	188	164	167	218
New York	164	151	134	215
Pennsylvania	137	120	126	143
South Atlantic Division	93	79	155	86
Georgia	80	61	142	75
North Central Division	174	161	150	181
Ohio	176	166	144	188
Illinois	160	144	138	173
Minnesota	181	172	191	178
Nebraska	206	170	205	206
Kansas	182	165	141	184
South Central Division	83	74	133	79
Tennessee	82	77	130	76
Western Division	181	146	213	171
Idaho	138	101	...	138
Wyoming	142	104	...	142
Utah	136	84	199	122
Washington	189	124	230	174
Oregon	215	177	206	217
California	212	176	203	217
Colorado	181	142	246	154

[1] Consolidation of parts of two tables in *Census Bulletin* 23, Census Statistics of Teachers, pp. 17, 18. The seventeen states given separately are selected for comparative purposes. It will be observed that all four of the equal-suffrage states are given.

APPENDIX F.

WOMEN IN OFFICE

I—WOMEN IN COUNTY OFFICES

Office	County	Year
County Clerk	Boulder	1896
" "	"	1898
" "	Kiowa	1900
" "	Logan	1896
" "	"	1898
" "	"	1900
" "	"	1902
" "	"	1904
" "	"	1905
" "	"	1907
" "	San Juan	1898
" "	Sedgwick	1905
" "	"	1907
" "	Weld	1898
County Treasurer	Gunnison	1907
" "	San Juan	1900
Coroner	Archuleta	1898
"	Cheyenne	1896
"	"	1898
Clerk District Court	Ouray	1907
" " "	Prowers	1900
Clerk County Court	Arapahoe	1898
" " "	"	1900
" " "	Boulder	1902
" " "	"	1904
" " "	"	1905
" " "	"	1907
" " "	Lake	1904
" " "	Logan	1905

APPENDIXES

II—WOMEN IN CITY OFFICES

Office	City or Town	Population, 1906[1]	Year
Clerk and Recorder	Aguilar	1200	One year[3]
" " "	Altman	200	1902–1907
" " "	Aspen	5000	1907
" " "	Burlington	300	May, 1898–Oct., 1898
" " "	Carbondale	300	Eight years[3]
" " "	Colfax	....	1894, '95, '96, '97
" " "	Creede	250	1905
" " "	"	250	1907
" " "	Crested Butte	1600	1903–1907
" " "	Delta	2000	1896–1900
" " "	"	2000	1906–1907
" " "	Durango	6000	1894–1896
" " "	Florence	5000	1900
" " "	"	5000	1903
" " "	"	5000	1907
" " "	Goldfield	1000	1900–1901
" " "	"	1000	1907–1909
" " "	Grand Junction	7500	1896–1908
" " "	Green Mountain Falls	100	1905–1907
" " "	Highlands	....	1896
" " "	Hotchkiss	1000	1898–1899
" " "	Las Animas	1800	1904–1905
" " "	" "	1800	1907
" " "	La Junta	5500	1891–1894
" " "	La Veta	450	1895–1898
" " "	Littleton	1500	Two clerks for short periods[3]
" " "	Manitou	1400	1893–1906
" " "	Montclair	....	1899
" " "	Montrose	....	1897
" " "	"	....	1901–1907
" " "	Silverton	3000	Two years[3]
" " "	"	3000	1906–1907
" " "	St. Elmo	100	Two years[3]
Treasurer.........	Alma	400	1907
"	Altman	200	1900–1902
"	"	200	1904–1908
"	Aspen	5000	1907–1909
"	Barnum	....	1894, '95, '96
"	Bellevue	100	1902–1907
"	Berkeley	....	1902
"	Bonanza	141	Three years[3]
"	Colorado City[2]	6000	One year[3]
"	" "	6000	1905–1907
"	" "	6000	1907–1909

[1] According to State Directory, 1906.
[2] Incomplete list for this city.
[3] Date not given.

273

EQUAL SUFFRAGE

II—WOMEN IN CITY OFFICES—CONTINUED

Office	City or Town	Population 1906[1]	Year
Treasurer	Colfax	....	1894, '95, '96, '97
"	Creede	250	1907
"	Fairplay	320	1907
"	Goldfield	1000	1900–1901
"	Greeley	6500	1894–1896
"	"	6500	1897–1899
"	"	6500	1899–1903
"	"	6500	1903
"	Hotchkiss	1000	1905–1908
"	Highlands	....	1894, '95, '96
"	Idaho Springs	3500	Same woman for seven years[2]
"	" "	3500	1907–1909
"	Lamar	2500	1896–1902
"	Marble	150	Five years[2]
"	Montezuma	100	One year[2]
"	New Castle	450	1898–1900
"	" "	450	1901
"	" "	450	1907
"	Paonia	1200	Four years[2]
"	"	1200	1907–1909
"	Rico	500	1907
"	Saw Pit	150	Three years[2]
"	Silverton	3000	Two years[2]
"	Sterling	2000	One year[2]
"	Victor	9000	Four years[2]
"	"	9000	1907–1909
Trustee	Burlington	300	Two women, 1898-1902
"	"	300	Two women, 1902-1904
"	"	300	One woman, 1903-1904
"	Green Mountain Falls	100	Two women 1903
"	Montezuma	100	One woman one year[2]
"	St. Elmo	100	Two women, 2 yrs. each[2]
Common Council	Bellevue	100	One woman, 1904-1905
" "	"	100	Two women, 1905-1906

[1] According to State Directory, 1906.
[2] Date not given.

APPENDIX G

TEACHERS IN COLORADO BY COUNTIES, SEX, AND SALARIES IN 1906[1]

Counties	Graded Schools Teachers Male	Graded Schools Teachers Female	Graded Schools Salaries Male	Graded Schools Salaries Female	Rural Schools Teachers Male	Rural Schools Teachers Female	Rural Schools Salaries Male	Rural Schools Salaries Female
Adams	2	13	$90.00	$60.00	4	34	$52.50	$56.80
Arapahoe	6	21	72.50	60.73	2	18	55.00	47.34
Archuleta	1	6	85.00	61.41	1	7	60.33	54.38
Baca					6	7	45.00	42.85
Bent	1	9	75.00	63.50	2	18	50.00	46.00
Boulder	15	98	99.97	65.97	4	61	64.40	47.75
Chaffee	8	26	88.04	63.46	1	26	72.50	51.32
Cheyenne	1	2	75.00	50.00		8		48.90
Clear Creek	6	31	117.50	67.00		5		51.00
Conejos	8	18	72.62	49.50	12	13	48.44	48.27
Costilla	2	4	70.00	59.16	15	15	49.57	43.20
Custer	2	3	80.00	50.00	3	16	55.00	41.56
Delta	5	31	101.00	63.00	14	18	56.00	53.00
Denver	110	689	107.41	66.31				
Dolores		2		87.50	1	2	60.00	50.00
Douglas	1	3	100.00	66.66	1	33	47.00	47.00
Eagle	3	9	83.33	67.50	1	18	70.00	57.65
Elbert	1	3	65.00	55.75	2	49	55.00	37.98
El Paso	21	154	102.80	65.60	8	50	57.00	47.00
Fremont	21	70	96.45	65.31	3	28	56.66	51.81
Garfield	8	24	89.58	72.33	6	27	68.00	52.00
Gilpin	5	20	112.75	69.80		11		50.43
Grand	2	6	62.50	39.50		7		40.00
Gunnison	5	13	94.00	64.00	1	32	60.00	54.00
Hinsdale	2	3	89.00	65.00		4		51.25
Huerfano	7	22	77.71	58.03	10	24	59.75	49.00
Jefferson	9	29	85.36	61.25	5	50	85.00	48.57
Kiowa					2	11	52.50	49.29
Kit Carson	3	5	58.33	47.50	7	28	40.00	37.09
Lake	7	36	93.45	61.73		14		75.20
La Plata	4	28	82.50	58.40	5	23	62.00	57.00
Larimer	11	65	105.91	63.59	8	58	62.38	48.45
Las Animas	19	77	73.50	56.30	26	24	51.00	47.00
Lincoln	1	3	75.00	62.50	2	18	55.00	46.00
Logan	3	8	100.00	55.83	4	31	52.14	39.72
Mesa	9	52	107.00	67.00	11	39	63.00	51.00
Mineral	2	4	100.00	71.25		1		45.00
Montezuma	4	8	79.22	56.50	4	12	63.75	51.66
Montrose	3	20	98.53	64.72	6	22	57.50	54.96
Morgan	7	19	96.52	66.46	3	19	61.66	51.55
Otero	14	60	85.00	56.00	4	19	55.00	50.00
Ouray	4	9	75.00	76.11	3	14	68.00	62.12
Park	3	3	98.33	61.66	4	18	51.25	47.66
Phillips	1	4	90.00	50.00	1	28	40.00	38.24
Pitkin	8	22	101.47	72.84	1	13	60.00	58.84
Prowers	5	23	107.50	56.00	7	21	51.00	45.00
Pueblo	17	189	131.00	72.00	7	55	71.00	52.00
Rio Blanco	2	4	67.50	62.50	3	7	63.33	54.00
Rio Grande	7	15	87.66	59.33	4	20	57.40	47.82
Routt	5	11	88.75	64.75	3	35	52.50	45.85
Saguache	2	4	90.00	55.00	5	23	60.00	52.77
San Juan	1	7	150.00	80.00		4		65.00
San Miguel	3	9	123.50	73.25	1	14	65.00	63.91
Sedgwick	1	4	90.00	56.25	1	20	35.00	38.60
Summit	2	4	104.50	67.50	1	9	67.50	49.03
Teller	8	92	101.04	63.48	2	15	75.00	55.50
Washington	1	3	80.00	50.00	1	45	50.00	35.00
Weld	16	95	94.47	62.71	18	61	62.22	53.61
Yuma	2	8	75.00	50.00	3	65	40.50	37.20
Totals	427	2200	$90.24	$62.10	249	1367	$57.46	$40.57

[1] From the *Sixteenth Report of the State Superintendent of Public Instruction*.

APPENDIX H

WAGES OF MEN AND WOMEN IN MANUFACTURING INDUSTRIES IN DENVER AND PUEBLO, 1905

I—WAGES OF MEN AND WOMEN IN MANUFACTURING INDUSTRIES IN DENVER, 1905[1]

Industry	Men, 16 years and over			Women, 16 years and over			Per cent. men's of women's wages
	Average number	Wages	Average wage[2]	Average number	Wages	Average wage[2]	
All industries....................	8,476	$6,283,448	$741	1,048	$392,300	$374	198.1
Awnings, tents, and sails........	17	13,531	796	40	17,621	441	180.5
Boxes, cigar.....................	8	4,474	559	12	4,690	391	143
Bread and other bakery products.	296	189,919	642	140	58,136	415	154.7
Brooms and brushes..............	15	12,074	805	3	1,200	400	201.3
Butter..........................	47	33,005	704	16	4,796	300	234.7
Carpets, rag....................	9	3,780	420	3	1,000	333	126.4
Cars and general shop construction, etc.	1,268	952,821	751	3	1,591	530	141.7
Clothing, men's.................	21	15,080	718	218	66,432	305	235.4
Clothing, women's...............	..	1,530	..	45	23,990	378	202.4
Confectionery...................	101	58,686	581	82	23,990	293	198.3
Electrical machinery, apparatus, and supplies	45	34,574	768	41	17,500	427	179.9
Flavoring extracts...............	41	34,460	840	10	3,432	343	244.9
Food preparations...............	25	13,194	528	4	1,300	325	162.5
Furniture.......................	155	136,437	880	1	600	600	146.6
Mattresses and spring beds......	38	19,060	502	18	7,249	403	124.6
Optical goods...................	20	15,500	775	8	3,860	483	160.5
Patent medicines and compounds..	19	12,253	645	1	110	110	586.4
Photographic materials..........	0	5,330	..	4	1,404	351	168.7
Pickles, preserves, and sauces...	48	35,972	749	55	21,048	383	195.6
Pottery, terra cotta, and fire clay products.	333	203,665	612	2	624	312	196.1
Printing and publishing, book and job..	548	402,216	734	114	42,123	369	198.9
Printing and publishing, newspapers and periodicals	442	372,190	842	18	14,159	787	107
Soap...........................	21	13,807	660	6	1,940	323	204.3
Tobacco, cigars, and cigarettes..	282	198,833	705	76	33,154	436	161.7
All other industries.............	1,908	1,397,851	733	128	47,351	370	198.1

[1] Only those industries in which women are employed are given separately, though the total for men is for *all* industries. This table is derived from *Census Bulletin* 37, Census of Manufactures, 1905, Colorado, Idaho, Nevada, and Utah, pp. 18–19.
[2] This means an average yearly *rate* of wages and not average earnings.

APPENDIXES

APPENDIX H—*Continued.*

II—WAGES OF MEN AND WOMEN IN MANUFACTURING INDUSTRIES IN PUEBLO, 1905[1]

Industry	Men, 16 years and over			Women, 16 years and over			Per cent. men's of women's wages
	Average number	Wages	Average wage[3]	Average number	Wages	Average Wages[3]	
All industries	863	$647,581	$739	75	$22,540	$301	245.5
Bread and other bakery products	35	27,920	798	5	1,600	320	249.4
Printing and publishing, book and job	40	33,500	838	6	2,100	350	239.6
Printing and publishing, newspapers and periodicals	68	63,945	940	3	1,365	455	206.6
Tobacco, cigars, and cigarettes	23	15,388	669	2	700	350	191.1
All other industries	123	78,393	637	59	16,775	284	224.3

III—WAGES OF MEN AND WOMEN IN MANUFACTURING INDUSTRIES IN OTHER COLORADO CITIES, 1905[2]

Municipality	Men, 16 years and over			Women, 16 years and over			Per cent. men's of women's wages
	Average number	Wages	Average wage[3]	Average number	Wages	Average Wages[3]	
Colorado Springs	327	$253,983	$777	51	$19,422	$381	203.9
Cripple Creek	47	42,897	913	...	...	...	...
Leadville	829	707,200	853	7	2,544	363	235

[1] Only those industries in which women are employed are given separately, though the total for men is for *all* industries. This table is derived from *Census Bulletin 37*, Census of Manufactures, 1905, Colorado, Idaho, Nevada, and Utah, pp. 18–19.
[2] This table is derived from *Census Bulletin 37*, Census of Manufactures, 1905, Colorado, Idaho, Nevada, and Utah, pp. 20–21.
[3] This means an average yearly *rate* of wages, and not average earnings.

APPENDIX I

POPULATION AND NUMBER OF RETAIL LIQUOR SALOONS IN DENVER AND PUEBLO, AND IN THE FIVE CITIES RANGING NEXT ABOVE AND THE FIVE CITIES RANGING NEXT BELOW EACH IN POPULATION, 1903.[1]

City	Population	Number of retail liquor saloons	City	Population	Number of retail liquor saloons
Indianapolis, Ind.	197,555	624	Sacramento, Cal.	30,152	182
Providence, R. I.	186,742	495	La Crosse, Wis.	30,038	147
Kansas City, Mo.	173,064	No license	Oshkosh, Wis.	29,919	126
St. Paul, Minn.	172,038	356	Newport, Ky.	29,315	97
Rochester, N. Y.	170,798	510	Williamsport, Pa.	29,246	49
Denver, Colo.	147,111	410	Pueblo, Colo.	29,237	130
Toledo, Ohio	145,901	876	Council Bluffs, Iowa	29,171	49
Alleghany, Pa.	138,064	233	New Britain, Conn.	28,506	57
Columbus, Ohio	135,487	610	Kalamazoo, Mich.	28,438	50
Worcester, Mass.	128,552	91	Everett, Mass.	28,317	No license
Los Angeles, Cal.	116,420	200	Cedar Rapids, Iowa	27,948	55

[1] From tables in *Census Bulletin* 20, Statistics of Cities Having a Population of Over 25,000, 1902 and 1903, pp. 65, 67, 74–76.

APPENDIX J

NUMBER OF DIVORCES GRANTED IN DENVER AND PUEBLO, THE FIVE CITIES RANGING NEXT ABOVE AND THE FIVE CITIES RANGING NEXT BELOW EACH IN POPULATION, 1903 [1]

Cities		Cities	
Indianapolis, Ind.[2]	427	Sacramento, Cal.[2]	100
Providence, R. I.	236	La Crosse, Wis.[2]	30
Kansas City, Mo.[2]	545	Oshkosh, Wis.[2]	68
St. Paul, Minn.[2]	155	Newport, Ky.[2]	33
Rochester, N. Y.	47	Williamsport, Pa.[2]	45
Denver, Colo.[2]	406	Pueblo, Colo.[2]	42
Toledo, Ohio[2]	321[3]	Council Bluffs, Iowa[2]	72
Alleghany, Pa.		New Britain, Conn.	15
Columbus, Ohio[2]	289	Kalamazoo, Mich.	105
Worcester, Mass.	82	Everett, Mass.[2]	301
Los Angeles, Cal.[2]	476	Cedar Rapids, Iowa[2]	109

[1] From table in *Census Bulletin* 20, Statistics of Cities Having a Population of Over 25,000, 1902 and 1903, p. 134.
[2] Data are for county.
[3] Included in Pittsburg.

EQUAL SUFFRAGE

APPENDIX K

EQUAL SUFFRAGE TESTIMONIALS

I. In January, 1899, the Colorado State Legislature passed, by a vote of 45 to 3 in the House and 30 to 1 in the Senate, the following resolution:[1]

"WHEREAS, Equal suffrage has been in operation in Colorado for five years, during which time women have exercised the privilege as generally as men, with the result that better candidates have been selected for office, methods of election have been purified, the character of legislation improved, civic intelligence increased, and womanhood developed to greater usefulness by political responsibility; therefore,

"*Resolved*, by the House of Representatives, the Senate concurring, That in view of these results the enfranchisement of women in every State and Territory of the American Union is hereby recommended as a measure tending to the advancement of a higher and better social order.

"That an authenticated copy of these resolutions be forwarded by the Governor of the State to the Legislature of every State and Territory, and the press be requested to call public attention to them."

II. In 1898, in answer to the continued misrepresentations of the Eastern press, the friends of woman suffrage issued the following:

"We, citizens of the State of Colorado, desire, as lovers of truth and justice, to give our testimony to the value

---

[1] *Laws Passed at the Twelfth Session of the General Assembly of the State of Colorado*, Denver, 1899, p. 439. House Joint Resolution No. 10.

APPENDIXES

of equal suffrage. We believe that the greatest good of the home, the state, and the nation is advanced through the operation of equal suffrage. The evils predicted have not come to pass. The benefits claimed for it have been secured or are in progress of development. A very large proportion of Colorado women have conscientiously accepted their responsibility as citizens. In 1894 more than half the total vote for governor was cast by women. Between 85 and 90 per cent. of the women of the state voted at that time. The exact vote of the last election has not yet been estimated, but there is reason to believe that the proportional vote of women was as large as in previous years. The vote of good women, like that of good men, is involved in the evils resulting from the abuse of our present political system; but the vote of women is noticeably more conscientious than that of men, and will be an important factor in bringing about a better order.

"This was signed by the governor, three ex-governors, both senators, both members of Congress and ex-senators, the chief-justice and two associate justices of the supreme court, three judges of the court of appeals, four judges of the district court, the secretary of state, the state treasurer, state auditor, attorney-general, the mayor of Denver, the president of the State University, the president of Colorado College, the representative of the General Federation of Women's Clubs, the vice-regent of the Mount Vernon Association, and the presidents of thirteen women's clubs." [1]

III. "The most noteworthy result is the improved character of the candidates, as one of the most important points to be considered is whether they can get the votes of women. The addition of a large

[1] Susan B. Anthony and Ida Husted Harper, *History of Woman Suffrage*, pp. 1085–1086.

number of independent and conscientious voters to the electorate; the wider outlook given to woman herself through the exercise of civic rights; and the higher degree of comradeship made possible by the removal of political inequality between man and woman; these are the greatest benefits which equal suffrage has brought to Colorado."[1]

[1] Susan B. Anthony and Ida Husted Harper, *History of Woman Suffrage*, p. 534.

THE END

DATE DUE